Meredith Levy Diana Goodey

Messages

Teacher's Book

3

CAMBRIDGE
UNIVERSITY PRESS

CAMBRIDGE UNIVERSITY PRESS
Cambridge, New York, Melbourne, Madrid, Cape Town, Singapore, São Paulo, Delhi

Cambridge University Press
The Edinburgh Building, Cambridge CB2 8RU, UK

www.cambridge.org
Information on this title: www.cambridge.org/9780521614351

© Cambridge University Press 2006

This publication is in copyright. Subject to statutory exception
and to the provisions of relevant collective licensing agreements,
no reproduction of any part may take place without the written
permission of Cambridge University Press.

First published 2006
3rd printing 2008

Printed in the United Kingdom at the University Press, Cambridge

A catalogue record for this publication is available from the British Library

ISBN 978-0-521-61435-1 Teacher's Book
ISBN 978-0-521-61433-7 Student's Book
ISBN 978-0-521-61434-4 Workbook with Audio CD
ISBN 978-0-521-61436-8 Teacher's Resource Pack
ISBN 978-0-521-61437-5 Class Cassettes
ISBN 978-0-521-61438-2 Class Audio CDs

Contents

Map of the Student's Book	4
Introduction	6

Teacher's notes and keys

Module 1 Present and past
1 Connections	10
2 Past events	18
Module 1 Review	25

Module 2 Descriptions
3 People	28
4 Places	36
Module 2 Review	42

Module 3 The future
5 Goals	45
6 Choices	52
Module 3 Review	58

Module 4 Your world
7 Achievements	60
8 Experiences	68
Module 4 Review	75

Module 5 The way it's done
9 Getting it right	78
10 Where is it made?	85
Module 5 Review	92

Module 6 The way we live
11 Talking	95
12 New beginnings	101
Module 6 Review	108

Games	110
Workbook key and tapescripts	111
Acknowledgements	120

		Grammar and Expressions	Vocabulary and Pronunciation	Listening and Reading skills	Communicative tasks
Module 1 Present and past	**Unit 1** Connections	• Questions and answers • Present continuous and present simple • *Expressions*: greetings and introductions	• Countries and nationalities • Language • Using numbers • *Pronunciation*: weak forms /ə/	• Listen to a song • Read a magazine article about the English language • Understand the main idea of an article • *Life and culture*: What a mixture!	• Ask questions when you meet new people • Talk about yourself and your friends • Describe someone you know • Write a report about your class
	Unit 2 Past events	• Past simple • Past continuous and past simple • *Expressions*: giving and accepting an apology	• Verbs describing actions • Adventure • Link words • *Pronunciation*: intonation in questions	• Listen to a story about a lucky discovery • Listen and complete a form • Read a short adventure story • Guess meaning from context • *Life and culture*: Journeys and explorers	• Write and act a conversation about events in the past • Interview a friend about a discovery • Write a short story
	Review	*Grammar check* *Study skills*: Your coursebook *Progress check* *Coursework*: Home life			
Module 2 Descriptions	**Unit 3** People	• Comparatives and superlatives • (not) as … as • *Expressions*: asking for a description	• Adjectives describing personality • The Internet • Opposites: un- + adjective • *Pronunciation*: stress in words	• Listen to a personality test • Read a Web page • Use pronouns and possessive adjectives • *Life and culture*: The British	• Write a description using comparatives and superlatives • Describe people's personality • Write a Web page about yourself
	Unit 4 Places	• Suggestions • Expressions of quantity: too much/many, (not) enough, a lot of • *Expressions*: responding to suggestions	• Places • School • Uses of *get* • *Pronunciation*: /k/ /p/ /t/	• Listen to someone talking about a place • Read an article about a Japanese student's day • Scan a text for information • *Life and culture*: Australia	• Plan a day out with friends • Describe a place you know, and things you like and don't like there • Write about a typical day
	Review	*Grammar check* *Study skills*: Thinking about learning *Progress check* *Coursework*: Getting around			
Module 3 The future	**Unit 5** Goals	• Present continuous used for the future • The future with *going to* • The future with *will* and *going to* • *Expressions*: shopping	• Sports clothes • Competitive sport • Adjective/verb + preposition: *good at/worry about* • *Pronunciation*: /aɪ/ /ʊ/ /æ/	• Listen to a talk about a cycling trip • Read an interview with a young athlete • Skim a text for the general idea • *Life and culture*: The history of the Olympics	• Talk about future plans • Talk about the future and make offers • Make a conversation in a shop • Interview a friend and then write about him/her
	Unit 6 Choices	• First conditional • The future with *will* and *might* • will/won't + probably • *Expressions*: polite requests	• At the table • Artificial intelligence • Compound nouns: *coffee maker* • *Pronunciation*: /e/ /eɪ/ /ʌ/	• Listen to a song • Read an article about artificial intelligence • Identify the topic • *Life and culture*: Journey into space	• Make a conversation in a restaurant • Describe things that aren't certain and things that are probable in the future • Write about future plans • Make predictions about life in the future
	Review	*Grammar check* *Study skills*: Making a vocabulary notebook *Progress check* *Coursework*: Shopping in London			

4 Map of the Student's Book

	Grammar and Expressions	Vocabulary and Pronunciation	Listening and Reading skills	Communicative tasks
Module 4 Your world				
Unit 7 Achievements	• Present perfect • Present perfect and past simple • The infinitive of purpose • *Expressions*: I think so. / I don't think so.	• Using a machine • The environment • *Pronunciation*: /ɪ/ /ɒ/ /əʊ/	• Listen to a radio advert • Read a newsletter about a campaign • Understand the main idea of a text • *Life and culture*: Saving Gwrych Castle	• Talk about things you've done this week • Write and act an advert • Make a conversation about using a machine • Write a letter about a campaign
Unit 8 Experiences	• Present perfect + *ever* and *never* + *just* + *for* and *since* • *Expressions*: time expressions with *for* and *since*	• Outdoor activities • Music • Prepositions of time • *Pronunciation*: Stress in words	• Listen to a student describing important people in his life • Read a biography of a rock band • Guess meaning from context • *Life and culture*: A poem: What has happened to Lulu?	• Describe your experiences • Talk about present situations and how long they have continued • Write a description of a person you know • Write a biography
Review	*Grammar check* *Study skills*: Learning to listen *Progress check* *Coursework*: Useful information			
Module 5 The way it's done				
Unit 9 Getting it right	• *have to*, *don't have to*, *mustn't* • *should*, *shouldn't* • *Expressions*: thanking people and responding to thanks	• Illnesses and injuries • Customs • Adverbs • *Pronunciation*: /s/ /ʃ/	• Listen to two friends following instructions • Do a quiz about customs around the world • Identify the topic • *Life and culture*: Mardi Gras	• Describe rules at your school and your ideal school • Talk about problems and give advice • Write about customs in your country
Unit 10 Where is it made?	• Present simple passive • Past simple passive • *Expressions*: expressing a reaction	• Materials • Animated films • Parts of speech • *Pronunciation*: weak forms /wəz/ /wə/	• Listen and identify mistakes • Listen to a song • Read about animated films • Use pronouns and possessive adjectives • *Life and culture*: Living in an international world	• Describe where things are made or produced • Write a general knowledge quiz to do with the class • Describe a film you know well
Review	*Grammar check* *Study skills*: Speaking *Progress check* *Coursework*: Mini phrase book			
Module 6 The way we live				
Unit 11 Talking	• Reported speech • *Say* and *tell* • Question tags • *Expressions*: asking for clarification	• Relationships • On the phone • Verbs that describe speaking • Punctuation marks • *Pronunciation*: intonation in question tags	• Listen to an argument • Read a story from the Internet about a telephone conversation • Skim a text for the general idea • *Life and culture*: Central Park	• Interview people about teenage life and report what they said • Check information about a friend • Write a conversation using the correct punctuation
Unit 12 New beginnings	• *used to* • Second conditional • *Expressions*: saying goodbye	• Words from American English • Synonyms • *Pronunciation*: /θ/ /ð/	• Listen to a song • Read some extracts from an encyclopaedia • Scan a text for information • *Life and culture*: Living in the past	• Describe your past and changes in your life • Talk about imaginary situations • Write an essay about your country
Review	*Grammar check* *Study skills*: Checking your work *Progress check* *Coursework*: Entertainment			

• **Grammar index**   • **Communicative functions index**   • **Wordlist**   • **Phonetic symbols**   • **Verb forms and irregular verbs**   • **Songs**

Map of the Student's Book

Introduction

Welcome to *Messages*, a lower-secondary course providing **80–90 hours of classwork**. *Messages* is designed to meet the needs of you and your students by making both learning and teaching **simple and effective**. It has a **clearly structured** progression in both grammar and vocabulary, and a wealth of opportunities for students to practise the language they are learning.

We hope that students will find *Messages* an enjoyable, engaging course, with its clear signposting of aims, **interesting and motivating themes**, and a wide range of **rich resources**, while teachers will find it offers **practical, easy-to-use material** that can be adapted to **mixed-ability classes**. *Messages* 3 is designed for students who have studied English for two years at secondary level, and includes revision of many basic structures.

Course components

Student's Book
- Six modules of two units each
- Module opening pages
- Extra exercises page with KET-style activities
- Extra readings on Life and Culture
- Review sections at the end of every module, containing grammar 'work it out' tasks and consolidation exercises, vocabulary summaries, study skills and a progress check
- Coursework
- Reference section that contains:
  - Grammar index
  - Communicative functions index
  - Wordlist
  - Phonetic symbols
  - Verb forms and irregular verbs
  - Song lyrics

Workbook
- Full range of exercises, including more KET-style activities
- Extension activities for stronger learners
- Learning diary
- Comprehensive grammar notes
- CD with Workbook audio and animated tour of the Infoquests

Teacher's Book
- Step-by-step, easy-to-follow instructions
- Student's Book answers
- Background information on texts
- Guidelines for how and when to include supplementary material
- Ideas for language games in the classroom
- Tapescript for the Student's Book audio
- Workbook answer key

Teacher's Resource Pack
- Photocopiable activities:
  - Entry test
  - Communicative activities
  - Grammar worksheets
  - Module tests
  - Final test
- Pattern drills
- Teaching notes and answers

Audio CDs/Cassettes
- Student's Book audio
- Pattern drills
- Tests audio

Web material
- Infoquests at www.cambridge.org/elt/messages/infoquest
- Downloadable worksheets and Teacher's guides for Infoquests at www.cambridge.org/elt/messages/teacherquest
- Downloadable grammar worksheets for weaker learners at www.cambridge.org/elt/messages

About *Messages* 3

A sense of purpose and achievement

In *Messages*, there are three levels at which students focus on what they can do in English:
- The units are divided into three steps. The step begins with a description of the target language and the communicative task(s) (**Use what you know**) which students will be able to do, using that language. Each step takes students through a series of related activities, which lead them quickly from 'input' to meaningful, communicative 'output'. Short, carefully prepared and guided tasks ensure that even weaker students can enjoy a sense of success.
- At the end of each module, students complete one part of a portfolio of information entitled 'My guidebook'. This is a continuous **Coursework** project, based on different aspects of the overall theme of the book (see below) and on the language of the preceding units. Language is recycled and revised in the modules themselves and in the reviews, tests and additional material.
- There is **an overall purpose to each year's work**. Each book has its own theme, exemplified in the six Coursework tasks. In Book 3, the theme is visiting an English-speaking country. By the end of the year, students should be able to describe their own social environment, interact successfully with English-speaking visitors, and feel prepared to interact with English speakers if they are travelling abroad.

Authentic and meaningful language learning

As in *Messages* 1 and 2, the language is controlled but is as natural and realistic as possible, presented and practised in authentic contexts. Students will continue to learn about their English-speaking counterparts, and about the world around them.

Active, responsible learners

In the units, students engage actively with the material and use a range of cognitive skills such as guessing, deducing, comparing, matching and sequencing. Students are asked to discover sentence patterns and grammar rules for themselves, to make their own exercises and to 'test a friend'. There are frequent opportunities for students to talk about themselves and their interests.

In the reviews, a series of exercises and tasks help learners to monitor what they can do. In **How's it going?** they make their own assessment of their grasp of the language points covered. This is reinforced when they complete the **Learning diary** in the Workbook.

Using *Messages* 3

Module openers

These two pages allow teachers to 'set the scene' for their students and help to motivate them by creating interest and by showing them what they will be able to do by the end of the module.

The pages contain a selection of visuals from the coming units, a list of what students will study in the module and what they will be able to do at the end of it, and a brief matching exercise.

You may need to translate some of the language points for weaker classes, but encourage all classes to say as much as they can about the pictures before they do the matching exercise.

With stronger classes, you may want to ask students to identify which language point each of the sentences relates to, or to supply similar sentences.

Presentation

In Steps 1 and 2 of each unit, there is a wide variety of presentation texts and dialogues. They each present the new grammar point in a context which illustrates its concept and meaning, as well as providing plenty of natural examples of it.

In some cases, students listen first with their books closed (or the text covered). This will enable them to focus on the sounds of the language without being distracted – and sometimes confused – by its written equivalent.

Ask plenty of comprehension questions, and get students to repeat the key sentences. They should listen to/read the conversation/text at least twice during this phase of the lesson.

Share your ideas

The presentation is often preceded by this preparatory discussion, which reactivates and revises known language and sets the scene for the students, so that they can anticipate what they are about to hear or read.

Key grammar

Key grammar activities follow on from the presentations and focus on the language within them. Give students a few moments to look at the grammar box and reflect before they discuss and complete the examples and explanations orally. They can then copy the completed sentences into their notebooks. In some cases, students translate the examples and compare them with the mother tongue equivalent.

Practice

The controlled practice exercises which always follow Key grammar sections can be done orally with the whole class, and then individually in writing.

Students are then often asked to make their own 'exercise' and **Test a friend**. Look at the example in the book with the whole class first, adding further examples on the board if necessary. This is an excellent opportunity for students to focus actively on the new grammar and test their understanding. It also gives you a chance to monitor and deal with any difficulties they may have before you move on.

For additional oral practice, there is a set of **pattern drills** in the Teacher's Resource Pack, with the corresponding audio on the Class CDs/Cassettes. Recommendations for when to use the pattern drills are made in the unit notes of the Teacher's Books, and the audio components contain the recordings in the corresponding position. We suggest you play the complete drill through at least once, before pausing for the students to respond each time. You may prefer to do the drills yourself, without the recorded version.

Key vocabulary

These are often matching activities, but with more emphasis now on using words in context. Some of the lexical groups recycle items which students should know, as well as introducing new words. Students can work alone or in pairs, and use their dictionaries for words they don't know.

The core vocabulary of each unit is practised further in the Workbook. Encourage students to start their own vocabulary notebooks and to record new vocabulary in them.

Key expressions

In each unit, students learn a set of practical, functional expressions that they can use in everyday situations (for example, for apologising, making polite requests, expressing thanks). These expressions are first encountered in the presentation dialogues, and students practise them through pairwork. There is further practice of the expressions in the Workbook.

Key pronunciation

Messages 3 further develops basic areas, such as stress in multi-syllable words and weak forms. It also focuses on features such as vowel sounds and intonation in sentences. The pronunciation activities are always linked to the language of the unit.

Use what you know

The **Use what you know** tasks at the end of each step enable students to use what they have learnt for an authentic, communicative purpose. Many of these tasks can be prepared in writing and then done orally, or vice versa. Students are always given examples to follow, and you will find a model answer where applicable in the notes that follow in this Teacher's Book.

Introduction 7

Speaking

Students are encouraged to repeat key vocabulary/expressions and the key sentences of each presentation. In addition, new language is practised in meaningful contexts that involve an element of creativity on the part of the learner, with an emphasis on moving from accuracy to fluency. Students ask questions, share opinions, talk about themselves, their country and the environment around them.

Speaking can also be encouraged by giving students the chance to act out rough or reduced versions of some of the presentation dialogues, and also to engage in **role plays**. The aim here should be to reproduce the situation rather than the original conversation word for word. Stronger students can work in groups and write a slightly different conversation.

Writing

Writing is involved in many of the **Use what you know** activities, where students write sentences, paragraphs or short dialogues. In *Messages* 3, a more extended writing task comes at the end of Step 3 in each unit. Here students are asked to write a variety of text types (for example, a report, a short story, a letter, a biography). To help them to organise their work and choose appropriate language, a step-by-step **Writing guide** is provided, with practical advice and examples that they can use or adapt. These writing tasks can be prepared in class and done for **homework**.

For longer writing tasks, encourage students to first write a rough draft, then read through and check their work before writing a final version. They could also check each other's work.

Listening

Messages 3 provides plenty of practice of this skill. Students listen to presentation and reading texts, and in each unit there is a specific listening task, covering a variety of text types, for example, a conversation, an interview, a radio advertisement.

Four authentic **songs** are included for listening comprehension. The words are given on page 144 of the Student's Book.

The listening texts may include language which is slightly beyond the students' productive level. However, they are not expected to understand or reproduce everything they have heard. You should focus on the key sentences only. Remember that learners may need to listen more than twice during these activities.

Reading

Step 3 of each unit of *Messages* 3 opens with a reading text connected with the unit theme, with a 'warm-up' **Share your ideas** exercise. Most of the texts are recorded, but students are asked to read the text themselves before listening and reading as a second step.

Tasks provide practice in specific **reading skills** (for example, identifying the topic, skimming, scanning, guessing meaning from context), and there are also questions to check comprehension. A **Word work** section highlights certain word patterns or grammatical forms, based on language used in the text.

Additional reading practice is provided through an extra reading text with each unit, dealing with **Life and culture** in the English-speaking world.

Consolidation and testing

At the end of each unit, there is a page of extra exercises on the language of the unit, providing practice of **KET-style tasks**.

At the end of every module, preceding work is pulled together in the **Review**. For each language point, students work through a simple analysis of the grammar and complete one or two tasks showing how they can use the language.

In the **Coursework** there is a model each time, based on the character Ana, for you to study with the whole class. Individual coursework can then be done at home over a period of a couple of weeks or so. At the end of the year, the student's coursework comprises a 'mini guidebook' for English-speaking visitors to their country, based on a clear model.

In addition, the Review section includes work on **study skills** to help students become more independent and effective learners, and a chance for students to assess their own progress.

Further consolidation of the language in the modules can be achieved through the **communicative activities** and **grammar worksheets** from the Teacher's Resource Pack, which should be done at the end of each unit when all the work has been covered, and through the accompanying **Infoquests** on the web (see below).

Students' progress can be more formally tested through the use of the **photocopiable module tests** in the Teacher's Resource Pack, which examine grammar, vocabulary, reading, writing, listening and speaking, often through KET-style activities. The audio for the listening element of the tests can be found on the class CDs/cassettes.

Workbook

Workbook activities should, in the main, be done for homework, though they can be prepared in class with weaker students if necessary, and you can also give stronger students the **Extension exercises** if they finish earlier than their classmates. Make sure you have covered the relevant part of the step before students begin the corresponding Workbook exercises. **Sentences for translation** are introduced for the first time in Step 3.

At the end of the unit, students complete their **Learning diary**. The **Workbook answer key** can be found on pages 111–120 of the Teacher's Book.

Infoquests

Each module of the course is accompanied by an Infoquest, in which students are encouraged to find information on **specially designed websites** and to work co-operatively. The websites are housed at http://www.cambridge.org/elt/messages/infoquest and are designed to reinforce the language of each module, and should therefore be done at the end of the module.

Free **accompanying worksheets** and clear **Teacher's guides** can be found at http://www.cambridge.org/elt/messages/teacherquest. You will need to complete a simple form to register and then get access to these items, and will need to log in with your user name and password each time you want to use them.

Classroom management

Creating an 'English' atmosphere

Use every opportunity to bring 'the real world' into the classroom: maps, posters, magazines etc. Encourage students to look for examples of English 'text' outside the classroom: words from pop songs, instructions for a machine, English food packaging in a supermarket etc.

Use classroom instructions in English from the beginning, and get students to address you in English as much as possible.

Making good progress

A wide variety of task types ensures regular changes of pace and activity, with frequent opportunities for students to work at their own level. Work at a lively pace and have the courage to move on even though students may not have learnt everything in a lesson perfectly. Some of the activities include a time limit, to encourage students to work quickly and to introduce a 'game' element.

Dealing with classes of mixed ability

There are a large number of personalised and open-ended activities which allow students to respond in different ways, depending on their ability. The rubric **do at least ...** also enables students to work at their own level. Other activities (**If you have time**, **Try this!** and the **Extension** exercises in the Workbook) can also be used by pupils who finish early.

Try to make sure you involve all the students. For example, ask weaker students to suggest single words to describe a photo, while stronger students might think of a question to ask about it. When you ask a question, give everyone the chance to think of the answer before calling on individuals to do so. When doing individual repetition, ask stronger students first, but be careful not to make this too obvious by always varying the order, and who you call on.

Use the different skills of the students in as many ways as you can. The student who hates speaking may enjoy writing vocabulary on the board, while another student may be good at drawing, or making posters.

Try to build an atmosphere in which students communicate with you and with each other in a respectful, courteous and good-humoured manner. Never underestimate the importance of praise and encouragement: *That's great! Well done! Good!*

Explaining new words

New vocabulary which arises other than in the Key vocabulary section can be explained using visual aids such as your own set of flash cards, pictures on the blackboard, mime, contextualised examples or, if necessary, translation. Encourage students to guess the meaning of new words as well as using their dictionaries.

Controlled oral repetition

Key vocabulary and expressions and key sentences in presentations can be reinforced through choral and individual repetition. This helps students 'get their tongues round' the sounds of the new language.

When asking a question, give everyone time to think of the answer before asking an individual student by name. When two or three individuals have responded, finish by getting the whole class to repeat.

Get students to ask as well as answer questions. Questions and answers can be drilled by dividing the class in two and getting the groups to take it in turns to ask and answer, before moving on to drilling with two individual students.

When drilling words or sentences, you can beat the stress of words and sentences with your hand to show where the main stress is — exaggerate slightly if necessary. You can also use your hand to show whether the sentence goes up or down at the end.

With long sentences, use 'back-chaining':
... half past ten.
... to bed at half past ten.
I usually go to bed at half past ten.

Pairwork

Getting students to work in pairs will greatly increase the amount of English spoken in the classroom, even if some students may use the mother tongue. Walk round and listen whilst students are speaking. Vary the pairings so that students do not always work with the same partner. Always give examples of what you want students to do and check that they understand the activity clearly.

Group work

Some of the activities in *Messages* 3 can be done in groups if you wish. Ensure first that everyone is clear about what they are doing, then monitor their work and don't let the activity drag on for too long. Use mixed-ability groups and appoint a group leader.

Correcting oral mistakes

When correcting students, be sensitive and realistic about what you can expect at their level. Give them an opportunity to correct their own or each others' mistakes whenever possible.

Focus on fluency rather than on accuracy when students are engaging in communicative activities such as pairwork and talking about themselves. You can note down any important and recurring errors and go over them with the whole class at the end of the lesson.

Try to focus on content as well as on accuracy, and respond accordingly if something is interesting.

Correcting written work

Make your corrections clear by indicating the type of error, for example, vocabulary, grammar, spelling etc. Comment positively on content where applicable, e.g. *This is very interesting, Carlos*. Again, bear in mind the student's level and the focus of the activity, as you may not want to correct every mistake.

Enjoy it

We hope that the material in *Messages* 3 will motivate the students and facilitate their learning, and that the way the material has been structured will make your job as straightforward and effective as possible. Most of all, we hope it proves a rewarding experience for you and your students.

Module 1

Present and past

See page 7 of the Introduction for ideas on how to use the Module opening pages.

Answers
1 c   2 d   3 b   4 a

1 Connections

STEP 1

Revision: Questions and answers
Expressions: Greetings and introductions
Communicative tasks:
  Asking questions when you meet new people
  Greeting and introducing people

1 Share your ideas

- Look at the photo with the class and establish that the park is in London.
- Ask students to say what they can see in the photo. If necessary, prompt them with questions, for example, *Is the girl British? Where do you think she's from? How's she feeling? Why do you think she's unhappy?* (Preteach *homesick*.) *What do you think she's saying? What's the boy saying?* Encourage students to suggest a range of possible answers, but don't confirm or correct them at this stage.

Example answers
Perhaps she's from Spain/Italy/South America.
The boy is (probably) British.
The girl is unhappy. (Perhaps she doesn't feel well. / Perhaps she's homesick.)
The boy is asking why she's unhappy.

2 Reading and speaking
Where do you come from?

BACKGROUND

Mexico City (Ciudad de México) is the capital of Mexico. With a population of over 20 million, it is one of the biggest cities in the world.

Veracruz is a busy port on the Gulf of Mexico, 430 km east of Mexico City. It has a warm tropical climate and is well known for its music, food and lively café life.

a
- Look at the questions with the class. Check comprehension by asking students to suggest answers for each question.

- Students predict which questions the boy in the photo is asking. Don't confirm or correct their answers yet.

b
- If possible, use a map to show the location of Ana's city, Veracruz.
- Students read Ana's answers and complete the conversation with the correct questions. They can do this individually, in pairs, or with the whole class working together.
- 🔊 Play the recording. Students listen and check their answers.
- Check understanding of *What's the matter?*
- Focus on Jay's last speech. Check that students understand the meaning of *Pleased to meet you*. Explain that *Do you fancy ...?* means 'Do you want ...?' but is only used in very informal conversation.
- 🔊 Play the recording again. Pause after the questions and ask students to repeat them.

Tapescript/Answers
JAY: ^a Are you all right?
ANA: No, I'm not.
JAY: ^b What's the matter?
ANA: I'm homesick.
JAY: ^c Where do you come from?
ANA: I come from Mexico.
JAY: ^d Do you live in Mexico City?
ANA: No, I don't. I live in Veracruz.
JAY: ^e What are you doing in England?
ANA: I'm studying English. I'm staying with a family here.
JAY: ^f What do you think of London?
ANA: I like it, but I sometimes feel a bit homesick.
JAY: ^g Have you got any friends here?
ANA: No, I haven't.
JAY: ^h What's your name?
ANA: Ana.
JAY: Pleased to meet you, Ana. I'm Jay, Jay Sayer. Er ... do you fancy an ice cream?

c
- In pairs, students practise the conversation.
- Invite one or two pairs to perform their conversation for the class.

Unit 1

> **OPTION**
>
> Some pairs may prefer simply to read the conversation aloud from their books. However, students will get more useful practice if you can persuade them to put the book aside and produce their own version of the conversation, working partly from memory and partly by improvisation. To help them, you could write some cues on the board, for example:
>
> | | |
> |---|---|
> | All right? | Homesick. |
> | Where? | Mexico. Veracruz. |
> | England? | Studying English. Staying with English family. |
> | Friends? | No. |
> | Name? | – Ana. – Jay. |

3 Grammar revision *Questions and answers*

- Look at the two examples with the class. Emphasise the connection between the question and the short answer: *Is Ana ...? Yes, she is. Does she ...? No she doesn't.*
- Students complete the questions.
- Remind students of the formation of present simple questions with *be*. Contrast this with the use of *do/does* for other verbs.
- Revise the use of the present continuous to talk about actions that are happening at the present time. (Note that the difference between the present simple and the present continuous is revised in Step 2.)

Answers
Is
Are
Do
Does
Has
Have
does
is

4 Practice

a
- Look at the example. Make it clear that *old friends* means 'people whose friendship started a long time ago'.
- Students write the questions.

Answers
2 Where are they?
3 Is Jay Mexican?
4 Has Ana got any English friends?
5 Is she homesick?
6 Where does she come from?
7 What's Ana studying?
8 Does Jay live in Veracruz?

b
- In pairs, students ask and answer the questions.
- Choose students to ask and answer across the class. When they give the answers, you could ask them for further information, for example:
  2 *Is the park in London? (Yes, it is.)*
     Is it raining? (No, it isn't.)
  3 *Where's he from? (England.)*

Answers
2 They're in a park/in London.
3 No, he isn't.
4 No, she hasn't.
5 Yes, she is.
6 Mexico/Veracruz.
7 English.
8 No, he doesn't.

5 Key expressions *Greetings and introductions*

> **BACKGROUND**
>
> In Britain it is normal, but not necessary, for adults to shake hands when they are introduced or when they meet in formal situations. However, young people don't usually shake hands when they meet.
>
> Adults commonly address and introduce one another using first names. The titles *Mr, Mrs, Ms* and *Miss* are very formal, used especially in business or professional relationships. Young people may be expected to use these titles for older people (especially for teachers), but it's increasingly common for them to use first names when addressing neighbours, family friends or their own friends' parents. The more formal greeting *How do you do?* is now used less and less.

a
- Focus on the pictures and ask about the relationships between the people: *Does (he) know (her)? Are they friends?* Establish that the first picture shows a formal conversation between two school teachers and a parent.
- Students read the conversations and complete them with one word for each gap.
- 📻 Play the recording. Students listen and check their answers, then practise the conversations in pairs.

Tapescript/Answers
1 A: This is Mrs Jones, the head teacher.
   B: How do you do, Mrs Jones?
   C: How do you do?
2 A: Hi, Jenny. How are you today?
   B: I'm fine, thanks.
3 A: This is my friend Tom.
   B: Nice to meet you, Tom.

Connections

b
- Read through the information in the Remember! box. Point out that we use the expression *How do you do?* following a formal introduction, and that we reply to this by repeating the question. Make sure that students recognise the difference between *How do you do?* and *How are you?*
- Point out that we use *This is* (not *He is* or *She is*) to introduce someone.
- Students match the expressions with the explanations.
- Discuss the translations with the class.

Answers 1 b 2 c 3 a

6 Key pronunciation *Weak forms* /ə/

- 🔊 Play the recording while students read and listen.
- 🔊 Play the recording again and ask the class to repeat. Start with choral repetition and then ask individuals to repeat. Give special attention to the unstressed /ə/. Check the falling intonation that is usual at the end of *Wh-* questions.
- You could continue this exercise by asking students to practise the conversations from 5a in pairs.

7 Writing and speaking *Meeting people*

- Choose two students to read out the example conversation.
- Elicit the answer to David's last question (*I'm from/I come from ...*). Invite students to suggest how the conversation could continue, for example:
  B: I'm from England.
  A: Do you live in London?
  B: No, I don't. I live in Manchester.
- In pairs, students write their own version of the conversation. They can choose other names and they should continue the conversation as in the example above.
- Ask pairs to practise their conversation.

OPTION

You could give students some other situations:

Karen Johnson is 15. She's introducing her father to her friend Suzanne Barry.

Tony Brown and Diana Thomas work together in a bank. They're greeting each other in the morning.

Mr Harris is introducing his son Robert to Mrs Carol Palmer who works at his office.

Discuss with the class what language the people should use and how they should address each other. Ask pairs to make conversations for these situations and to practise them together.

STEP 2

Grammar: Present continuous and present simple
Vocabulary: Countries and nationalities
Communicative tasks:
  Describing nationality and where a person comes from
  Talking about yourself and your friends

1 Key vocabulary *Countries and nationalities*

a
- Explain that the list contains both countries and nationalities.
- Look at the example. Elicit sentences to demonstrate the difference between *Poland* and *Polish*. For example, *I come from Poland. I'm Polish.*
- Students find the matching pairs of words in the list and write them under the two headings. Some words will be new, but students should be able to guess the answers by observing patterns in the formation of nationalities that they know.
- 🔊 Play the recording. Students listen and check their answers.
- Point out the common endings for nationalities: *-(i)an*, *-ish* and *-ese*. Draw attention to the exceptions in the list: *French* and *Greek*.
- Note that although *the USA* (the United States of America) is the official name of the country, it is very commonly known as *America*.
- 🔊 Play the recording again. Students listen and repeat. Give special attention to the change of stress in *Italy – Italian*, *Canada – Canadian* and *Japan – Japanese*.

Tapescript/Answers

Country	Nationality
Poland	Polish
Australia	Australian
Italy	Italian
France	French
Argentina	Argentinian
Britain	British
Greece	Greek
the USA	American
Canada	Canadian
Mexico	Mexican
Spain	Spanish
Japan	Japanese

b
- Set the time limit and ask students to add to their lists. They can work individually, in pairs or in small groups.
- Ask different students for their answers and write them on the board. Answers could include: *Brazil – Brazilian, China – Chinese, Germany – German, India – Indian, Ireland – Irish, Russia – Russian*. Add any others that have a special relevance for the students.
- Practise the pronunciation of the words on the board.

c
- Read out the example. Remind students of the third person *-s* ending for verbs in the present simple (*I come – he comes*).

12 Unit 1

- Give students a few moments to consider what they want to say about themselves or their favourite star. Then invite different students to say their sentences to the class.
- Read through the information about the use of capital letters in the Remember! box.

2 Presentation *What are they doing?*

> **BACKGROUND**
> *Chilaquiles* are made from left-over *tortillas* (Mexican pancakes made from corn flour). The *tortillas* are cut up and cooked with layers of cheese, spicy sauce and a range of other ingredients. *Chilaquiles* may be eaten at any time, not only for breakfast.

a
- Focus on the photo and make sure students identify Ana from Step 1.
- Ask them who the other people in the photo might be. (*The family that Ana is staying with in London.*)
- Ask them to suggest one or two questions that they could ask about the photo, for example, *Who's the person on the right?* Encourage students to use the present continuous in some of their questions: *What's Ana doing?* Elicit answers. If the information is not known at this stage, remind students of the expressions *I think ...* , *I'm not sure* and *I don't know.*
- In pairs, students ask and answer questions about the photo.

b
- 📷 Read the introduction. Ask the question, then play the recording. With books closed, students listen for the answer to the question.
- Ask them to identify the two adults on the right of the photo. (*Mr and Mrs Grant.*) Ask students who the boy in the background might be. (*He's their son, Charlie.*)

> **Answer** She's thinking about her sister in Veracruz.

c
- 📷 Read out the six questions. Then play the recording again while students listen and read.
- Help with any new vocabulary, for example, *a piece of toast* and the Spanish word *chilaquiles*. In reference to the sentence *The Grants are talking about the weather again*, you may want to explain that the weather is a common topic of conversation in England, probably because the English weather is so unpredictable.
- Give students a few moments to look for the answers to the questions in the text. Then choose different students to ask and answer across the class. Encourage them to answer in full sentences.
- As students give their answers, you could follow up with further questions, for example:
  - *What do you usually have for breakfast?*
  - *Do you sometimes have a hot chocolate?*
  - *What's Ana's sister's name?* (*Clara.*)
  - *How's Ana feeling?* (*Sad, homesick.*)

- Contrast the two present tenses in questions 1 and 2 and in questions 3 and 4. Ask students to explain the difference, in their own language if necessary. Make sure they recognise that in 1 and 4 the questions are asking about things that happen normally or all the time, while in 2 and 3 they are asking about this particular morning.

> **Answers**
> 1 She usually has *chilaquiles* and a hot chocolate.
> 2 She's having a cup of coffee and a piece of toast.
> 3 No, she isn't.
> 4 Yes, she does.
> 5 They're talking about the weather.
> 6 She's looking at the rain and she's thinking about her sister.

3 Key grammar
Present continuous and present simple

a
- Read out the two examples and elicit the full form of *Ana's* (*Ana is*).
- Students complete the explanations.
- You could substitute other subjects and elicit the correct verb forms, for example, with *sitting in the kitchen*:
  - *Mr and Mrs Grant ... are sitting in the kitchen.*
  - *I ... am sitting in the kitchen.*
- Elicit negative sentences with different subjects, for example:
  - *I'm not having breakfast.*
  - *Ana isn't eating chilaquiles.*
  - *The Grants aren't thinking about Veracruz.*
  - *Ana doesn't usually have toast for breakfast.*
  - *The Grants don't eat Mexican food.*
- Remind students that adverbs of frequency (*usually, always* etc.) often go with the present simple. These adverbs go after the verb *be*, but before all other verbs.

> **Answers** continuous, simple

b
- Students look for other examples in the text.

> **Answers**
> *Present continuous*
> She's having a cup of coffee ...
> It's raining outside ...
> ... the Grants are talking ...
> But Ana isn't listening ...
> She's looking at the rain ...
> ... she's thinking about her sister ...
>
> *Present simple*
> Ana usually starts the day ...
> She always has breakfast ...
> ... they talk about their plans for the day.

Connections 13

4 Practice

a
- Students complete the sentences. They can do this orally and/or in writing. Tell them to look carefully at the time expressions to help them choose the right tense.

Answers
2 isn't talking   3 doesn't like   4 has   5 live
6 's raining   7 's getting up, 's going   8 sends

b
- Look at the examples. Elicit one or two more examples for each tense.
- Set the time limit. Students write as many sentences as they can. Ask them to use both tenses.
- Invite different students to read out some of their sentences.
- Note that there is further work on comprehension and practice of the present simple and the present continuous in the Module 1 Review at the end of Unit 2.
- 🔊 Pattern drill: TRP page 11 (Unit 1, Step 2, drills 1 and 2)

Try this!
Answer: There are six days.
(The only missing day is *Friday*.)

5 Listening and speaking *Song*

a
- 🔊 Ask students to close their books. Play the song. The first time through, let students simply listen and get a sense of the rhythm and melody of the song.
- 🔊 Play the song again. Students listen for the word *jeans*. Tell them to keep score using their fingers or by making a note each time they hear the word.
- Explain or elicit the meaning of *pull on*. In this song, it means the same as 'put on'.

Answer 20 times

b
- Look at the pictures and ask students to say what each one shows.
- 🔊 Play the song again. Students write down the picture numbers as they hear the words in the song.
- Ask students to turn to the song words on page 144 of their books to check their answers. Explain that *my tank* refers to the fuel tank on the singer's motorbike. You could also explain that *Put a tiger in your tank* was the advertising slogan for a brand of petrol.
- Ask students to give the full form of *'cause* (*because*) and the usual grammatical form for *I got* (*I've got*). Explain that *I got* is common in casual speech, particularly in American English.
- 🔊 Play the song again and encourage the class to sing along.

Answers 1, 3, 4, 5, 7, 8, 9

6 Speaking *Who is it?*

- Look at the example. Emphasise the contrast between the present continuous (he's wearing a black sweater today – he doesn't always wear it) and the present simple (it's generally true that he plays a lot of volleyball – but he isn't doing it now).
- Demonstrate the activity. Choose a member of the class and make a brief description using both present tenses. Invite the class to guess the person: *Is it …?*
- In pairs, students take it in turns to describe and guess. Warn them not to look at the person they're describing, or they will immediately give the game away!
- You can invite some students to give their description to the class and ask the others to guess who the person is.

OPTION
If you want to practise question forms in the two present tenses, you could adapt Exercise 6 to a version of 'Twenty questions' (see Games, page 110 in the Teacher's Book). In this case, the number of questions should be reduced from 20 to five. Students work out who the person is by asking *yes/no* questions such as *Is he wearing blue jeans? Does he support Juventus?* etc. The game can be played either by the whole class or in groups of four or five.

Reading skills: Understanding the main idea
Word work: Numbers
Communicative task: Writing a report about the class

STEP 3

OPTION
Before the lesson, you could ask students to keep a record of English words, phrases or sentences that they see/hear in their life outside the classroom. They should make a note of where each example occurred. This information can feed into the discussion in Exercise 1 and may provide ideas for questions in Exercise 4.

1 Share your ideas *Learning English*

- Ask the question and brainstorm ideas with the class. Use this discussion to introduce or revise key words in the reading text (for example: *communicate, foreign language, travel abroad, business*) and write them on the board.

2 Reading

a
- Ask students to read the text themselves. Tell them not to stop if they come to new words or difficult sentences, but to skim over them. Explain that the aim here is to get a <u>general</u> sense of the ideas in the text, not to pick up every detail.
- Students pick out any of the ideas on the board that are mentioned in the text. Ask them to identify the paragraph where each of these ideas occurs.

b Comprehension check
- 🔊 Play the recording of the text while students follow in their books. At the end of each paragraph, pause the recording to check comprehension and elicit or explain the meaning of new words (for example, *home page*, *connect*).
- Ask the class why Tara, Sandro and Mohammed speak English. Make sure that students are clear about the difference between *first language*, *second language* and *foreign language*.
- Pick out the numbers mentioned in the text, write them on the board and ask students to say them aloud. Remind them that the English for the % sign is *per cent*.
- Students complete the matching task. They can do this individually or in pairs.

> **Answers**
> 1 c 2 f 3 a 4 e 5 b 6 g 7 d

c Reading skills
Understanding the main idea

1
- Ask students to choose the topic. Make sure they recognise that, although lots of countries are mentioned in the text, the main focus is not on countries or culture but on the English language.

> **Answer** b language

2
- Students choose the main idea. Ask them to say why the other two are not accurate. (a: Spanish and the languages of India are in the text, but there are no other languages in it. c: The text is not about English people, but about people who speak English.)
- Tell the class that the beginning (and sometimes the ending) of an informative text like this one often sets out the main idea. The title and opening paragraph establish what the text will be about and the closing paragraph sometimes restates this idea.

> **Answer**
> b English as an international language.

3 Word work *Numbers*

a
- Remind students of the numbers they met in the text. Then they work individually to match the written numbers with the figures.

> **Answers**
> 1 b 2 e 3 g 4 h 5 a 6 d 7 f 8 c

b
- Students write the numbers as figures.

> **Answers**
> 2 ¾ 3 5½ 4 9.2 5 ¼ 6 60%
> 7 1,000,000 8 18%

c
- Look at the example. Point out the way we break the number up into sections when we say and write it. Remind students of the use of *and* after hundreds.
- Draw attention to the reminder about hyphens in the Remember! box.
- Give another example. Say a large number for the class to write down. If students are having difficulty with these numbers, write up some more on the board and work through them with the class before starting the pairwork.
- Students write down numbers to read out to their partner. Pairs then check their answers together.

> **OPTION**
> You could make this activity into a team competition (see 'Team quiz' in Games, page 110 in the Teacher's Book). Teams think of four numbers and write them down in words and figures. In turn, teams read out their numbers for the others to write in figures. To check the answers, a member of each team comes to the front and writes their team's figures on the board.

4 Speaking and writing *About my class*

- Ask students to read the example questions and to consider their answers to them. While they are doing this, write the questions on the board.
- Elicit other questions about using English, for example:
  – *Do you know any songs in English?*
  – *Do you sometimes look at English websites?*
  – *Do other members of your family speak English?*
  – *Are you interested in travelling to an English-speaking country?*
  – *Do you like learning English?*
  – *Is English easy to learn?*

  Write the questions on the board. Leave space after each question to write the responses.
- Students talk with their neighbours, asking and answering questions.

Connections

- Ask the class to decide which questions they want to use for a class survey. Rub the others off the board.
- Invite two students to come to the front to conduct the survey. One student asks the questions and the other helps to count up the answers as class members raise their hands. Write the answers next to the questions on the board yourself, making sure to record the number of students clearly for each reply.
- Ask students – especially those who are good at maths – to express the results as percentages and fractions. Write these on the board next to the number of students.
- Read through the Writing guide with the class. Use the examples to show that a report presents factual information in a very clear form, and that the style is formal.
- Students follow the Writing guide to write their own report, using the information on the board.

> **Example answer**
> Use of English in Class 4B   8th September
> We asked four questions about using English. These are our results.
> Eighty-five per cent of the students in the class think English is useful.
> Two thirds of the class enjoy learning English.
> Ninety-five per cent of the students know songs in English.
> Fourteen people sometimes look at websites in English.

Extra exercises

The Extra exercises can be used as consolidation at the end of the unit. The teaching notes explain how they can be exploited in class, but they can also be given as homework, depending on time available.

1
- Students look at the three alternatives and choose the right answer.

> **Answers** 1 a 2 b 3 c 4 b 5 c

2
- Remind students to look at the time expressions to help them choose the right tense.
- As you check the answers, you could elicit sentences with the alternative verb forms.

> **Answers**
> 1 gets   2 isn't writing   3 speak   4 Are you staying
> 5 's raining   6 feel

3
- Explain to students that they have to think of questions for the answers, and that there could be several different questions. Make sure they realise that each answer is independent.
- Do the question for 2 with the class as an example. Point out that the reply doesn't start with *Yes* or *No*, so the question needs a question word at the beginning. You may want to go through the whole exercise and ask students to say which question words are needed to produce the replies.

> **Example answers**
> 2 Where do you live? / Where is the cinema?
> 3 Do you speak English?
> 4 Does your brother/your friend/Jay live in a house?
> 5 How many people in the world speak English?
> 6 Why do you like [*Friends*]?
> 7 What's the matter?
> 8 Is Ana happy?

4
- Point out to students that they make questions again here, but that the questions and answers form a complete conversation, so they can use the answers before and after the questions to help them.

> **Answers**
> 2 Are you studying?
> 3 Who are you playing with?
> 4 Where does he live?
> 5 Do you play this game every day? / Do you often play this game?
> 6 Who's winning?

5
- Students match the sentence parts. They then put the sentences together to form three more two-line conversations.

> **Answers**
> 2 h   Hi, Steve. How are you?
> 5 f   I'm fine, thanks.
> 3 g   This is my best friend, Ben.
> 8 d   Nice to meet you, Ben.
> 4 a   Are you all right?
> 7 c   No, I've got a cold.

6
- Students write the nationalities and the countries. Remind them to start both words with a capital letter.

> **Answers**
> 2 Italian Italy   3 Canadian Canada
> 4 Argentinian Argentina   5 Spanish Spain
> 6 British Britain   7 Greek Greece
> 8 American the USA   9 French France
> 10 Japanese Japan

7
- Ask students to work on the translations in pairs or small groups, and then discuss with the whole class.

Extra reading

Life and culture What a mixture!

> **BACKGROUND**
>
> The **Celts** /kelts/, who may have come originally from Eastern Europe, were once widespread throughout Europe. After losing battles against the Roman Empire and Germanic tribes, they survived mainly in Britain, Ireland and northern France.
>
> The first **Roman** expedition into Celtic Britain was led by Julius Caesar in 55BC and a full-scale invasion followed in AD43. Britain was part of the Roman Empire until the early 5th century.
>
> When the Romans left, Britain was gradually occupied by the **Anglo-Saxons**, a collection of Germanic tribes who invaded and settled over the next two centuries. The Celts were driven to the edges of Britain, where Celtic languages still survive as Gaelic (spoken in Ireland and Scotland), Welsh (Wales) and Cornish (Cornwall).
>
> In the 9th to 11th centuries, the **Vikings** from Scandinavia set up colonies in much of Europe and the North Atlantic. They raided and made settlements in the north and east of Britain and in Ireland, and in 1013 they conquered the whole of England. (See also the Extra reading text in Unit 2.)
>
> In the early 10th century the Vikings were already settled in Normandy, adopting the French language and culture. It was their descendants, the **Normans** (the word comes from 'Norsemen'), who invaded Britain in 1066. French became the main language until the 14th century.

Lead in

- Brainstorm to gather as many English words as possible which have become part of the students' language. Write them up on the board as students suggest them. You can group them under headings, for example, *Food, Technology, Sport, Music, Other things*.

- You could ask students for their opinions about the spread of English. Do English words make their language richer? Or are there too many English words in their language?

Task

- Before students read, write on the board some of the names of countries, population groups, nationalities and languages in the text: *Latin, Anglo-Saxon, Scandinavian, British Isles, Celts, Romans, Vikings, Normandy*. Ask students to translate and say a little about the ones they recognise. Give a brief explanation of any that are unfamiliar.

- Give students time to read the text themselves.

- Read the text aloud and help with new vocabulary (for example, *gods, law, parliament, inhabitants, settlers, invaded, defeated, battle, ruled, official*). There is quite a load of historical information here – move along fairly briskly, without making the students feel that they have to learn or remember all the details. The main thing is for them to become aware of the mixture of influences that have created the English language.

- Look at the map with the class. Ask students to identify the invaders who are represented by the arrows.

- Read out the sentences or choose students to do so. Point out that for some sentences the answer is ? (= we don't know if the sentence is true or false because the text doesn't tell us).

- Students look back at the text to find the answers. They could do this individually or in pairs.

> **Answers**
> 1 T
> 2 F It's very difficult.
> 3 T
> 4 F She writes a French expression to show her agreement to a new law.
> 5 T
> 6 T
> 7 ?
> 8 T

Connections

2 Past events

STEP 1

Grammar: Past simple
Expressions: Apologies
Communicative tasks:
 Talking about events in the past
 Making and responding to apologies

1 Share your ideas

- Ask students to look at the photo. Ask them who is in it and where they might be. Explain that the pictures in Exercise 1 tell a story about Jay and Ana.
- Look at the pictures with the class. Ask them to describe the actions in each picture, using the past simple. Make sure they remember the key words *flat*, *tube* and *cinema* and, if necessary, remind them of the irregular past forms *went*, *left* and *got (on/off)*.
- You may want to tell the class that the cinemas are in *Leicester Square*. Help with the pronunciation /ˈlestə ˈskweə/ and explain that this is a big cinema and entertainment area in central London.

Example answers
Picture 2 Jay left his flat at five to seven.
Picture 3 Ana left her flat.
Picture 4 Jay caught/got a bus.
Picture 5 Ana caught/got the tube/a train.
Picture 7 Ana waited outside the cinema.
Picture 8 Ana left the cinema.

2 Presentation *Did you forget?*

a ▪ Read the introduction. Ask the question, then play the recording. With books closed, students listen for the answer to the question.

Answer No, he isn't.

b ▪ Play the recording again while students listen and read.
- Explain or elicit the meaning of key expressions in the conversation, for example, *Hang on a minute!*, *That's funny*, *It's my fault*, *It doesn't matter*. Note that in this context, Jay uses the word *funny* to mean 'strange' rather than 'comical'.
- Focus on the past simple verbs. Ask students to pick out irregular forms and to say them in the infinitive form. Remind them of the use of *did/didn't* in negatives, questions and short answers.
- Drill some of the past simple sentences in the conversation.

- Read through the questions with the class. Students answer either orally or in writing.
- For question 5, explain that although Ana uses the verb *came*, they will need to use *went* in the answer. Explain briefly that *come* means to move towards the place where the speaker is – Ana uses *came home* because she's at home when she's having this conversation with Jay.

Answers
1 At seven o'clock.
2 By/On the tube. / She caught/got the tube.
3 Outside the Empire cinema.
4 No, she didn't.
5 She went home.

c ▪ Give students a few moments to find the answers about Jay from the pictures. In question 4, they should substitute *Ana* for *Jay*.
- In pairs, students ask and answer.

Answers
1 What time did Jay leave his flat? – At five to seven.
2 How did he get to the cinema? – By/On the bus. / He caught/got the bus.
3 Where did he wait? – Outside the Odeon cinema.
4 Did he see Ana? – No, he didn't.
5 What did he do after that? – He rang/called/phoned Ana on his mobile.

OPTION
You can ask pairs to practise the conversation, if possible by improvising their own version without reading from the book. To help them with this, you could write up some cues on the board, as suggested in Unit 1 (page 11 in the Teacher's Book).
Alternatively, you may choose not to organise pair practice here, as the speaking activity in Exercise 7 is also based on this conversation.

3 Key grammar *Past simple*

- Remind students of the regular past form (for example, *wait – waited*). Ask them to give some examples of irregular past forms.
- Students complete the examples.
- For the first pair of sentences, which uses the verb *be*, substitute other subjects to elicit *were* and *weren't*.
- Remind students that the form of other simple past verbs remains the same for all subjects.

Unit 2

Answers
wasn't
didn't
went
didn't
Did

4 Practice

BACKGROUND

Trafalgar Square /trəˈfælgə ˈskweə/, with its four lions and the statue of Nelson on a pillar in the centre, is one of London's best-known landmarks. **The National Gallery** occupies the north side of the square. It houses one of the world's greatest collections of western European paintings.

Piccadilly Circus is a junction of five major London roads, quite close to Trafalgar Square. There is a winged statue of Eros over a fountain at the centre.

a
- Give students a few moments to read through the sentences quickly on their own.
- Tell the class that the nine sentences make up a story about Ana, but are in the wrong order. Look at the example and establish that this is the first sentence in the story, but explain that they don't need to put the sentences in order yet.
- Check that they understand what a *record shop* is (sentence a) and elicit or explain the meaning of *get off* (sentence e) and *gallery* (sentence i).
- Students supply the past simple form of the verbs. They can do this orally and/or in writing. You can ask them to check written answers by consulting the list of irregular verbs on page 143 of the Student's Book.
- As you check the answers, practise the pronunciation of the past simple forms. Give special attention to the irregular verbs *caught* /kɔːt/ and *bought* /bɔːt/. For the *-ed* ending in regular verbs, make sure students recognise that the usual pronunciation is /d/ or /t/. However, in verbs which already end with a /d/ or /t/ sound (for example, *decide, want*), the *-ed* ending is pronounced as a separate syllable /ɪd/.
- Ask the class to find the second sentence (i).
- Students could work in pairs to complete the exercise. Tell them to look carefully for repeated words (for example, *bus, record shop*) or word associations (for example, *record shop – bought a CD*) to help them decide on the most logical order.

Answers
2 i decided, wanted   3 b caught, sat
4 e got off, didn't get off   5 h was
6 a looked, saw   7 d went   8 f listened, bought
9 c didn't see, had

b
- Choose a student to read out the example question, and a second student to answer it (*At Piccadilly Circus*).
- As a further example, ask a different question (for example, *What did she buy in the record shop?*) and elicit the answer. (*A CD for her sister.*)
- Students write their own questions about the story. If they have any difficulties with this, you can help by supplying some question openings, for example, *Did she ...? When did she ...? What did ...? Where ...? How ...? Why ...?* Walk round the class, checking the question forms and giving help where necessary.
- In pairs, students take it in turns to ask and answer.
- Invite different students to ask one of their questions for the class to answer.
- Pattern drill: TRP page 11 (Unit 2, Step 1, drill 1)

OPTION

As an extension to 4b, you could introduce a more difficult guessing game. Prepare four or five general knowledge questions about the past and write down both the questions and the answers. The answers must be full sentences. Here are some examples, but these may need to be adapted to events that are more familiar to your students:

1 (When did Princess Diana die?)
   She died in 1997.
2 (What was Mozart's first name?)
   His first name was Wolfgang.
3 (Where did the Beatles come from?)
   They came from Liverpool, in England.

Read out each answer. Working in pairs or small groups, students have two minutes in which to write down what they think the question is. At the end, check with the whole class. Note that there may be more than one correct question for some of your answers.

5 Key pronunciation *Intonation in questions*

- Ask students to read the questions quickly.
- Play the recording through while students listen. Use hand movements to emphasise the rising or falling intonation at the end of each question.
- Play the recording again. Pause at the end of each question and ask students to repeat, first all together and then individually.
- Write this incomplete explanation on the board:
  In Wh- questions, the intonation goes ..... . (down)
  In yes/no questions, the intonation goes ..... . (up)

Past events

- 🔊 Play the recording again and ask students to complete the explanation.

  (Note that intonation varies, depending on the meaning or emphasis intended, so there are many exceptions to the statements given here. It is normally true that in *Wh-* questions the intonation falls. However, *yes/no* questions may fall also. If we are expecting a certain answer – either *yes* or *no* – when we ask the question, we tend to use falling, not rising, intonation. For example:

  Did you go to the cinema? ↗ (= I don't know if you went there or not.)

  Did you go to the cinema? ↘ (= I think you probably did.)

  However, this explanation is not necessary for students at this stage. It's enough if they can hear and produce the intonation in the given examples.)

- 🔊 Pattern drill: TRP page 11 (Unit 2, Step 1, drill 2)

> **Try this!**
> **Answers:** looked, went, waited, came, arrived, caught, disappeared, bought

6 Key expressions *Apologies*

a
- Look at the pictures with the class. For each one, ask *What's the problem?* and make sure that the situation is clear.
- Students put the sentences in order. Don't confirm or correct their answers yet.

b
- 🔊 Play the recording. Students listen and check.
- 🔊 Play the recording again. Pause at the end of the apologies and the responses. Check comprehension by asking students to translate the expressions into their own language.
- You could tell them that the expression *Don't worry about it* may be shortened to *Don't worry*.
- Ask students to repeat the expressions, giving special attention to the intonation.
- In pairs, students practise the two conversations.

Tapescript/Answers

1 – Am I in your seat?
  – Yes, you are.
  – Oh! I'm sorry.
  – That's all right. Don't worry about it.

2 – At last! It's quarter past eight. Why are you so late?
  – I'm sorry. It isn't my fault. The bus was late.
  – Oh, I see. Well, it doesn't matter. We've got five minutes.
  – Come on, then. Let's get our tickets.

7 Writing and speaking *The wrong place*

- Explain the task and ask students to look at the questions. Elicit some suggestions for a meeting place and for reasons why the meeting doesn't take place as planned.

- In pairs, students discuss the questions and write their conversation together. Ask them to include an apology and a suitable response.
- Pairs practise their conversation. Encourage them to put their written 'script' aside if they can.
- Invite some pairs to perform their conversation.

STEP 2

> **Grammar:** Past continuous and past simple
> **Vocabulary:** Verbs describing actions
> **Communicative tasks:** Describing events in the past

1 Key vocabulary *Verbs describing actions*

- Read out the verbs and then set the time limit for the matching task. Some of the verbs should be familiar. For new verbs, ask students to guess the meaning and to use a dictionary to check if they have time.
- 🔊 Play the recording. Students listen and check their answers.
- Teach or revise the past simple form of the irregular verbs (*fell, hit, flew, sank*).
- 🔊 Play the recording again and ask students to repeat.

Tapescript/Answers

1 jump 2 sail 3 fly 4 fall
5 land 6 crash 7 sink 8 hit

2 Presentation *What were they doing?*

> **BACKGROUND**
>
> The *Titanic* was the most luxurious passenger ship of its day and was considered to be 'unsinkable'. However, on its maiden (first) voyage from Southampton to New York in 1912, it hit an iceberg in the Atlantic on 14th April and sank, causing the deaths of over 1,500 passengers and crew. There were 705 survivors.
>
> **Sir Isaac Newton** (1642–1727) was an important English scientist and mathematician. Among many other scientific achievements, he was the first to discover the law of gravity. The story is that his theory took shape when he observed an apple falling from a tree. (This has developed into the popular story that the apple fell on his head, but there seems to be no truth in this.)
>
> **Amelia Earhart** (1898–1937) was an American pilot in the days of early aeroplanes. She became the first woman to fly across the Atlantic in 1928. She was attempting a round-the-world flight when her plane went down over the Pacific in 1937.
>
> **Christopher Columbus** (1451–1506) was an explorer from Genoa in Italy. On a voyage sponsored by Ferdinand and Isabella of Castile, he set out in 1492 to reach India by sailing westward. Instead, he discovered the Bahamas and so opened up the way to the European settlement of America.

Unit 2

> **Archimedes** (c. 287–212 BC), a Greek mathematician from Syracuse, was one of the most famous scientists of the ancient world. There is a story that he leapt from his bath and ran naked through the streets crying 'Eureka!' ('I have found it!') when he worked out the principle of fluid displacement.

a
- Look at the example with the class and point out that the two jigsaw pieces are joined by *when*. Use the picture to teach the word *iceberg*.
- Students join the other jigsaw pairs then match the sentences with the pictures.
- 🔊 Play the recording. Students listen and check their answers.
- Ask them for any other information they can give about the events shown in the pictures.

Tapescript/Answers

1 d The *Titanic* was a famous ship. It was sailing to New York when it hit an iceberg and sank.
2 b Isaac Newton was a scientist. He was sitting under a tree when an apple fell on his head.
3 a Amelia Earhart was one of the first women pilots. She was flying to Australia when her plane crashed and she disappeared.
4 e Columbus was an explorer. He was trying to find India when he landed in the Bahamas.
5 c Archimedes was a Greek inventor. He was having a bath when he jumped up and shouted 'Eureka!'

Answers
1 Picture C   2 Picture A   3 Picture B
4 Picture D   5 Picture E

b
- Focus on the second sentence in each jigsaw pair. Draw attention to the difference in form between the past simple and the past continuous.
- Drill the past continuous verbs.
- Read out the questions. Check that students remember the meaning of *hurt* and tell them that the past simple form is also *hurt*.
- Give students a few moments to consider their answers to the questions. Then choose different students to ask and answer across the class. Encourage them to answer in full sentences.

Answers
1 It was going to New York.
2 Because it hit an iceberg.
3 No, he wasn't.
4 No, he didn't.
5 She disappeared when she was flying to Australia.
6 No, he didn't.
7 He was having a bath.

OPTION

Include a substitution drill to give practice with different forms and subjects. For example, using sentence 1:

It was sailing to New York.
they   (They were sailing to New York.)
I   (I was sailing to New York.)
not   (I wasn't sailing to New York.)
travel   (I wasn't travelling to New York.)
you   (You weren't travelling to New York.)
question?   (Were you travelling to New York?)
he   (Was he travelling to New York?)

3 Key grammar
Past continuous and past simple

- Read through the examples and ask students to complete the explanations.
- Emphasise that a past simple action happened and finished at a certain time. A past continuous action provides a 'background' for this action. It started some time beforehand and was continuing to happen when the past simple action took place.
- Note that in some cases, the past continuous action stopped when the past simple action interrupted it (for example, *She was flying to Australia when her plane crashed*). In other cases, the past continuous action continued after the past simple action happened (as in the third example). This is shown in the time line.

Answers
simple
continuous
past continuous, past simple

4 Practice

a
- Students supply the correct verb forms. They can do this orally and/or in writing.
- Check the spelling of *sitting*. Remind students that when a verb ends in one vowel + one consonant, we double the final consonant before adding *-ing*.

Answers
2 was having, rang, was
3 was waiting, saw, was wearing
4 met, were sitting, was crying, started

- 🔊 Pattern drill: TRP page 12 (Unit 2, Step 2)

b
- Choose two students to read out the example question and answer.
- In pairs, students take it in turns to ask the question and to answer with their own information.

Past events   **21**

- Ask some students to report back to the class on what their partner told them.
- Note that there is further work on comprehension and practice of the past simple and past continuous in the Module 1 Review at the end of Unit 2.

5 Listening A lucky discovery

a
- Look at the exercise title and make sure that students understand the meaning of (*make a*) *discovery*.
- Look at the picture and tell students that the boy's name is Mark Taylor. Ask: *Who's he talking to? (A reporter.) What's he talking about?* Introduce some of the key words from the listening (for example, *coins, dig, gold*).
- 🔊 Read out the two questions and then play the recording. Students listen for answers to the questions.

Answers
1 He was in the park.
2 He was walking with his dog.

Tapescript

REPORTER: Here I am in the park in the quiet town of Swaffam, and with me is Mark Taylor, a local teenager. So, Mark, you recently made a fascinating discovery.
MARK: Yes, I did.
REPORTER: Tell the listeners what happened.
MARK: Yes, well, er … I was walking with my dog, here in the park, when he started digging in the ground. I looked and saw something small on the ground where he was digging.
REPORTER: Oh yes …
MARK: When I picked it up, I could see that it was gold.
REPORTER: Gold! How exciting!
MARK: Yes. It was a coin. A gold coin!
REPORTER: Wow! Then what did you do?
MARK: Well, I looked again, really carefully, and I found lots more! There were eight. I took them home and showed my parents. We took them to the police station and they telephoned the local museum. Then someone from the museum came and looked at the coins. And, well, they're Roman coins – two thousand years old.
REPORTER: Roman coins! That's incredible!
MARK: Yes. The museum gave me eight hundred pounds for them. So I bought a new computer this morning.
REPORTER: That's great. A lucky discovery. Well, from Mark Taylor and me, Trisha Johnson, it's goodbye from Swaffam and back to the studio.

b
- 🔊 Play the recording again. Pause after Mark's three main speeches to check comprehension. Ask, for example: *How did Mark find the coins? (His dog was digging in the ground.) How many coins did he find? (Eight.) How old were they? (2,000 years old.)*

- Students complete the sentences. They could work in pairs, or they could write answers individually and then discuss them with a partner.
- 🔊 Play the recording again so that students can check their answers. Then check with the whole class.

Answers
1 the park   2 his parents   3 the police station
4 the museum   5 £800   6 computer

c
- Look at the form with the class. Make sure that students understand that this is a record kept by Swaffam Museum. Explain the meaning of *item* and *location*.
- Students copy out the form and complete it with the correct information.

Answers
Name: Mark Taylor
Item(s) found: Eight Roman coins
Location: The park in Swaffam
Price: £800

6 Writing and speaking Discoveries

- Ask students to suggest a few other exciting discoveries. Try to get a range of different ideas, for example:
  – an ancient statue
  – an important painting
  – a letter that a famous person wrote
- Choose one of the students' suggestions, read out the questions and elicit some possible answers.
- Ask students to think of their own discovery and write answers to the questions.
- In pairs, students ask each other the questions. Encourage them to reply without reading from their written answers.
- If possible, they can broaden the dialogue to make it more like a real interview.

Example answers
I was in my bedroom. I was looking at a music book from the market. I found an old letter inside the book. It was a letter from Elvis Presley! I sold it on the Internet. I got £1,200. I used the money to buy a new TV and DVD player.

Reading skills: Guessing meaning from context
Word work: Link words
Communicative task: Writing a short story

STEP 3

1 Share your ideas Stories

- Read out the six story types and elicit or explain the meanings.

Unit 2

- Ask the question, inviting a range of replies. Ask students to give examples of stories that they know for each category. These could be novels, short stories (for example, in magazines), plays, comics or film stories.

2 Reading

BACKGROUND

Brian Robeson is a fictional character who appears in several novels for young teenagers by the American writer Gary Paulsen.

a
- Look at the picture and ask students to predict what type of story this will be (*adventure story*).
- Ask them to say what they can see in the picture and use it to revise known words (for example, *plane, lake, forest, trees, survive*). However, don't introduce any of the new vocabulary at this stage.
- Read out the question and ask students to read the text through quickly to find the answer. Tell them not to stop and worry over new words when they come to them. They should just try to get a general idea of what happened. Explain that it will be easier to understand the details when they know what the story is about.

Answer Yes, it has.

b **Reading skills** *Guessing meaning from context*
1
- Tell students they are going to look at some new vocabulary before they read the story again.
- Direct them to the end of paragraph 1 where the expression *heart attack* appears. Draw attention to the words *suddenly* and *died*. Ask students to guess what *had a heart attack* means and to give a translation in their language.
- Do the same with the other four words, emphasising these connections:
  shaking – terrified
  exhausted – swam to the beach, fell asleep
  branches – from the trees
  surface – came, of the lake
  Point out that it's often possible to work out the meaning of new words by looking at the words around them.

2
- Ask students to study the context and look at the picture to guess the meaning of the words. They could discuss this in pairs.
- As you check the answers, ask students to identify clues in the text that helped them to work out the meanings.
- Say all the new words in 2b and ask students to repeat them. Note the pronunciation of *hatchet* /ˈhætʃɪt/, *spear* /spɪə/ and *bow* /bəʊ/.

c **Comprehension check**
- Play the recording of the story, pausing after each paragraph to ask the relevant questions from the list. For question 7, explain that *reappear* means 'appear again'.
- You could add other questions to help with comprehension, for example:

Paragraph 1
– What was the pilot doing when he died? (He was flying the plane.)

Paragraph 2
– Who became the pilot? (Brian.)
– Did it crash? (No.) Did it sink? (Yes.)

Paragraph 3
– Did anyone help Brian? (No.)

Paragraph 5
– What was the noise? (Another plane.)
– What was this plane doing there? (Looking for Brian.)

- Draw attention to the irregular past simple verbs and make sure that students recognise them. Refer to the Remember! box for revision of *could*.

Answers
1 To Canada to see his father.
2 On the lake.
3 Yes, he could.
4 He remembered a TV programme about how to survive in the wild.
5 In a shelter of grass and branches.
6 Fruit, fish, rabbits and birds.
7 Because the storm moved it to the surface of the lake.
8 Some food, a knife and a radio.
9 No, he didn't.
10 He was fishing.

3 Word work *Link words*

a
- Explain that the words in the box are important for making links between one event and another in a story. They help the reader to understand when things took place, and whether the events are similar or different.

b
- Students read the sentences themselves and choose the best word to complete them.

Answers
1 b 2 b 3 a 4 b 5 a 6 c 7 c 8 b

4 Writing *A short story*

- Read out the instruction for the writing task. Explain that the story can be about something that really happened or about an imaginary event.
- Read through the Writing guide with the class. Using the examples for paragraph 1, invite students to suggest a situation, and write up brief notes on the board.

Past events

- Then brainstorm to gather as many ideas as possible for the 'problem' in paragraph 2. Write up all the ideas in note form on the board as students suggest them. It doesn't matter if some of these aren't very suitable for a story – the aim is to get the students thinking.
- Select one of the problems and ask students to develop the idea. What happened, exactly?
- Finally, ask for some suggestions about the ending. What happened to solve the problem?
- Now direct students to the questions and ask them to plan their own story. They should think of their answers to the questions and make notes.
- Students follow the Writing guide to write their story, using the notes they have made.
- In pairs, students read their stories aloud.

Example answer

Last summer I went to Siberia with my friend Boris. We were travelling on the train from Moscow when, suddenly, the train stopped. We were in the middle of a forest and all the passengers got off the train. There was a huge bear on the line! Everyone waited and I took some photos of the bear. After about half an hour it stood up and walked into the forest, and then we all got on the train again.

Extra exercises

1
- Students complete the sentences.
- You could choose pairs of students to read out the completed conversations.

Answers
1 sorry 2 right 3 matter 4 fault 5 worry

2
- Ask students to read the paragraph. You can ask them to cover the alternatives below and to predict what the missing words will be as they read. They then look at the alternatives and choose the correct answers.

Answers 1 a 2 b 3 a 4 b 5 c 6 b

3
- Students choose the correct replies.

Answers 2 b 3 c 4 b 5 a

4
- Student choose the correct verbs.

Answers 1 a 2 c 3 a 4 b 5 b

5
- Do the first sentence with the class as an example. Point out that the rain started some time beforehand and was continuing when (and probably after) the speaker got up.

- Students complete the sentences with the correct form of the verbs.

Answers
1 was raining, got up   2 phoned, were having, called
3 had, was flying   4 was waiting, saw
5 was walking, hit   6 met, was running

6
- Ask students to work on the translations in pairs or small groups, and then discuss with the whole class.

Extra reading

Life and culture Journeys and explorers

Lead in

- Introduce the word *explorer*. Ask the questions about explorers that students know and elicit some very basic information about each one.
- If students haven't already mentioned them, write the names of the explorers from the text on the board: Marco Polo, Vikings, Magellan, Amundsen, Scott, Vespucci. Ask: *Where did they come from? What did they do?* Make notes on the board of any facts (or even just vague ideas) that students may have about these people.

Task

- Look at the map and pictures with the class. Ask students to check the information on the board and to say a bit more about the explorers based on the map.
- Give students time to read the texts themselves.
- Read the texts aloud and help with new vocabulary (for example, *silk, spices, return, expedition, voyage, leader*).
- You could add further questions to test comprehension.
- Read out the questions in the Student's Book. Tell students to look carefully at the question words to make sure they select the right information.
- Students answer the questions. They could work on this individually or in pairs.

Answers
1 It started in China and ended in Europe. [*Note that the two places could be in the reverse order.*]
2 They used camels.
3 In 1295.
4 The Vikings.
5 Scandinavia.
6 It comes from Vespucci's first name, Amerigo.
7 It went around the world.
8 On 14th December, 1911.
9 33 days later.
10 Ferdinand Magellan and Robert Scott.

24 Unit 2

Module 1 Review

Grammar check

1 Present simple and present continuous

Work it out for yourself

A
- Students choose the correct sentence for picture A. Ask them to say why the alternative isn't correct. (*Because Mario isn't speaking at the moment.*)

Answer 2

B
- Students choose the correct sentences for picture B. Make it clear that there is more than one correct sentence.
- Ask students why question 2 is wrong. (*We know Mario is Italian from his passport, so we can assume he speaks Italian.*)

Answer 1, 3 and 4

C
- Students match the examples with the explanations.

Answers
1 c   2 a   3 b

1.1
- Look at the example and question 1. Make sure students recognise that this question is asking about something happening now. Contrast this with question 2, which is asking about what always or normally happens.
- Students match the other questions and answers.

Answers
2 a   3 a   4 b   5 b   6 a
7 b   8 a   9 a   10 b

1.2
- Ask students to read through the text first. They then complete it with the correct form of the verbs.
- When checking the answers, make sure that students have used the -s ending for the third person singular form of present simple verbs.

Answers
2 lives   3 speaks   4 doesn't speak   5 's staying
6 's raining   7 're spending   8 'm watching
9 isn't watching   10 doesn't like   11 prefer

2 Past simple and past continuous

Work it out for yourself

A
- Students match the sentences with explanations a and b. Make sure they see that the cooking started earlier and was still continuing at 7.15.
- Students choose the correct sentence for the picture (1 or 2).

Answers
1 b   2 a
Sentence 2 describes the picture.

B
- Students choose the correct sentence for this picture. Make it clear that the cooking was the background activity that started before the face appeared.

Answer 2

C
- Ask students to match the explanations with the past simple and past continuous sentences.

Answers 1 b   2 a

2.1
- Students complete the sentences with the verbs in the past continuous.

Answers
2 were sailing
3 weren't listening
4 wasn't working
5 was talking
6 wasn't wearing

2.2
- Students make questions using the past continuous.
- Then they think of an answer to each question, and ask and answer in pairs across the class.

Answers
2 What were they doing?
3 Who was she phoning?
4 Why were you using my computer?

2.3
- First ask students to match the sentence parts. They then write the complete sentences, using the correct verb forms. They could work on this individually or in pairs.

> **Answers**
> 2 a I was doing the shopping this morning when I met Gemma in the street.
> 3 b I didn't go into the living room because my parents were arguing.
> 4 d I shouted at my brother because he was wearing my new T-shirt.
> 5 c The passengers were getting ready for bed when the *Titanic* hit the iceberg.

Study skills 1 *Your coursebook*

- This exercise is to make students aware of the content of the Student's Book and the way it is structured, so that they can use it efficiently on their own. Having worked through two units, students should be familiar enough with the book to do this exercise easily.
- Draw students' attention to the map of the book (pages 2–3), which gives an overview of the content of the course. Also point out the summary at the beginning of each step in a unit, which explains what students will be learning in the step that follows.
- Emphasise the importance of going over the Student's Book material when they have finished working on it.
- Remind students of the wordlist and the list of irregular verbs at the back of the book.
- Read through the questions and set the time limit. Students could work in pairs or small groups to find the information.
- Discuss the answers with the class. As you talk about question 3, draw attention to the reading text and the guidance given for reading and writing in Step 3 of each unit. For question 4, point out that each unit includes new language work under the same 'Key' headings. For question 7, ask students to find out when the Coursework activities appear and invite them to look through them.

> **Answers**
> 1 [Student's own answer.]
> 2 Three.
> 3 No, it isn't.
> 4 Key grammar, Key vocabulary, Key expressions, Key pronunciation.
> 5 Practice, What about you?, Test a friend, Use what you know.
> 6 In London.
> 7 My guidebook (a guide for visitors to my country).
> 8 Use a dictionary, look at the Wordlist and find where the word first comes in the book, look at the Vocabulary list to find other words from the same topic, ask your teacher.

How's it going?

Your rating

- Students look back at the exercises in the Grammar check and make their own assessment of how well they understand and remember the different language points.

Vocabulary

- Ask students to choose two of the vocabulary sets from the Vocabulary list and give them a few moments to look at them.
- Invite different students to come to the board and write the words they remember. Ask the rest of the class to check the accuracy of these words in the Vocabulary list and to supply others that belong to the topic.

Test a friend

- Look at the example questions and elicit the correct answers.
- Students refer back to the texts in Units 1 and 2 and write several questions to test their partner. They then ask and answer in pairs.

> **Answers**
> Ana is Mexican.
> Mark Taylor found some Roman coins.

Correcting mistakes

- The sentences listed here contain some common errors. Ask students to rewrite them correctly.
- Some sentences contain more than one error. Make sure students are aware of this and that they identify both errors in sentences 4 and 5.
- Emphasise the importance of going back over their work to check for errors when they finish a piece of writing.

> **Answers**
> 2 At the moment it's raining outside.
> 3 Last night I went to a restaurant.
> 4 What time did Jay leave his flat?
> 5 I was having a bath when my friend rang me.

Your Workbook

- Students should complete the Learning diary when they come to the end of each unit.

Module 1 Review

Coursework 1

My guidebook

Home life

BACKGROUND

Hampstead Heath, just four miles from the city centre, is the largest green space in London. It has 791 acres of grassy heathland, meadows, wooded areas, ponds and lakes. People use the heath for walking, running, swimming, picnicking, playing sports and flying kites. Children's activities, funfairs and concerts are also held there.

- Start by asking students to have a quick look at all six Coursework projects, pointing out that they will do one at the end of every two units. Explain that a guidebook gives useful help and information to people who are visiting a place, especially if they're going there for the first time. The pages of the guidebook that students produce will make an interesting collection of material about their environment and culture, and will serve as a guidebook for students from English-speaking countries who may visit their country.
- These Coursework guidebook pages can be written and illustrated by hand or designed on screen. They should be kept in a special Coursework portfolio. Here are some ideas on the ways they could be used:
  - Handwritten pages can be photocopied or scanned into a computer to be reproduced and given out to all members of the class.
  - The pages can be designed on screen and sent electronically to members of another English class, or to students in a school in an English-speaking country, if this can be arranged, or to individual students' pen friends/e-friends.
  - They can form a booklet, with pages stapled and a cover designed by the student.
  - They can be designed as posters and displayed in the classroom.
  - They can form the basis for a presentation to the class.

  You may prefer to make a decision about the form the projects will take, or you could discuss it with students and allow them to decide.
- Elicit all the information that students can remember about Ana from Units 1 and 2. You can prompt them with questions, for example:
  - *What nationality is she? (Mexican.)*
  - *What part of Mexico is she from? (She's from Veracruz.)*
  - *What's she doing in England? (She's studying English at a language school.)*
  - *Is she staying on her own? (No, she's staying with an English family.)*
  - *What's the name of the family? (Grant.)*
- Ask students to say what they can see in the photos on Ana's first guidebook page. Use these to revise key words and to introduce new ones (for example, *rush hour* and *shelf/shelves*).
- Give students time to read through the text on their own.
- You can ask some questions to check comprehension, for example:
  - *What's Mr Grant's/Mrs Grant's first name? What's their son's name? (Tim, Penny, Charlie.)*
  - *Do they all have the same thing for breakfast? (No.)*
  - *Do nearly all English people have coffee at breakfast time? (No – a lot of people prefer tea.)*
  - *How do Tim and Penny get to work? (By/On the tube.)*
  - *What time do the Grants have dinner? (At about half past seven.)*
  - *What are some examples of 'housework'? (Cleaning, tidying, washing the floor, doing the dishes.)*
  - *Who does the shopping? (Tim.) Where? (At the supermarket.)*
- Point out the use of the present simple in Ana's text, to describe habits and normal routines. Ask students to describe some similarities and differences between their own normal routines and those in the Grants' household.
- Ask them to think about the way Ana's page is organised. Can they identify a topic for each paragraph? (Example answers: *paragraph 1: introduction, 2: weekday mornings, 3: getting to work/school, 4: evenings, 5: weekends, 6: interests.*) Ask them to use some of these topics to organise their own text. They should write at least four paragraphs and illustrate them as they wish.
- Set a time limit, allowing one to two weeks for work on the project. If students want to spend longer on this work, you could negotiate an extension of time. Some work may be done in class and some at home.
- Ask students to check their text before they write a final version and design their page. Tell them to use Ana's page as a model and remind them to look back at Units 1 and 2 if they need help with language.

Module 1 Review 27

Module 2

Descriptions

See page 7 of the Introduction for ideas on how to use the Module opening pages.

Answers
1 c   2 e   3 b   4 d   5 a

3 People

STEP 1

Grammar: Comparatives and superlatives
Communicative tasks:
    Giving descriptions and making comparisons

1 Share your ideas

- Brainstorm with the class to gather as many adjectives as possible to describe appearance in a couple of minutes. Write them up quickly on the board. If students suggest other adjectives (for example, describing feelings or personality types), you could put these in a separate box in one corner of the board.
- Focus on the picture. Ask: *What are the people doing?* (*They're waiting for the bus.*) Read through the example description and ask students to find the person in the picture.
- Ask them to describe each of the other people in the bus queue.
- Draw attention to the Remember! box to remind students about the form and position of adjectives.

2 Presentation *Everyone's shorter than me!*

a
- When handling this text, make sure that any students who are unusually tall (or 'different' in some other way) are not made to feel uncomfortable. Encourage the class to engage sympathetically with the difficulties that Megan describes. Emphasise her positive attitude and the advantages of her extra height.
- Look at the photo with the class. Ask students to describe the girl briefly and to say what she's doing.
- Read out the questions and ask students to predict the answers from the photo.
- Play the recording. Students listen and read.

Answers
She's taller than her friends. No, she doesn't like it (but there are some advantages).

b
- Play the recording again or read the text aloud, pausing to help with new vocabulary (for example, *secondary school, stared, mates, advantages, earn*). Ask students to guess the meaning from the context wherever possible, and practise the pronunciation. Explain that *mate*, meaning 'friend', is an informal word.
- Focus on the comparative and superlative adjectives (for example, *shorter, tallest, more helpful*). Draw special attention to the irregular forms *better/best* and *worse* and elicit the normal adjectives for these (*good* and *bad*).
- Note that in comparative sentences, the comparison between two things may be implied rather than directly stated. For example: *People were friendlier at primary school* (than at secondary school). *Shoes are even worse* (than clothes). *Tall people often get better jobs* (than short people).
- Drill some sentences with comparatives and superlatives, for example:
  – My friends are shorter than me.
  – They're more expensive.
  – They get better jobs.
  – I'm the tallest person in my family.
  – I'm the best player in the school.
  – The most difficult thing is …
- Ask students to match the sentence parts. They could work on this in pairs.
- When checking sentences 7 and 8, draw attention to the Remember! box on page 29. Point out that we don't use *than* with *different* and *the same* (in British English: *different than* is acceptable in American English).

Answers
1 g   2 d   3 h   4 e   5 b   6 c   7 a   8 f

3 Key grammar
Comparatives and superlatives

- Ask students to complete the examples, looking back at the text if necessary. Then discuss the translations with the class.
- Go through the rest of the table. For the regular forms, help students to count the syllables in the adjectives in the first column (*tall, easy* etc.).

28   Unit 3

- You may want to mention that, as well as those ending in -y, some other two-syllable adjectives take -er/-est endings. For example, *simple – simpler/simplest*, *clever – cleverer/cleverest*.
- Point out the change of -y to -i in the spelling of *easier/easiest*.

> **Answers**
> than
> more
> the
> most

4 Practice

a
- Look at the examples. Remind students that they need to use *the* with superlative forms.
- Tell students that they need to decide whether to use comparative or superlative adjectives.

> **Answers**
> 3 more expensive than   4 the cheapest
> 5 the most popular   6 the fastest
> 7 better than   8 more exciting than   9 more careful

> **Try this!**
> Answer: There are nine adjectives: *tall, kind, friendly, short, old, black, optimistic, crazy, young*.

b
- Look at the examples and elicit another example sentence for each adjective, for example: *Sara is more positive than Becky. Jenny is the oldest.*
- Ask students to suggest other adjectives that they can use for the information in the table (*young, tall, short, negative*).
- Note that while students can make sentences using *the most* (*the most positive/negative*), they should be discouraged from trying to say the opposite (*the least positive/negative*) as they don't have this language yet.
- Set the time limit. Students can work individually or in pairs. There are a lot of possible answers here.

> **Example answers**
> Jenny is older than Sara.
> Shereen is younger than Jenny.
> Tessa is the youngest.
> Sara is taller than Becky.
> Shereen is the tallest.
> Becky is shorter than Jenny.
> Tessa is the shortest.
> Jenny is more negative than Sara.
> Becky is the most negative.

c
- Choose a pair of students to read out the example question and answer.
- Students think of their own questions. In pairs they take it in turns to ask a question and to reply by checking in the table.
- 🔊 Pattern drill: TRP page 12 (Unit 3, Step 1)

d
- Look at the example with the class. Elicit some other adjectives that can be used, as well as those for age and appearance, to describe a friend (for example, *funny, interesting, intelligent, friendly, popular, kind, quiet, honest*). You could write these on the board for students to refer to. (Note that adjectives describing personality are covered in more depth in Step 2.)
- Students describe one of their friends in two or three sentences. They could write down their answer and then read it out to the class.
- Note that there is further work on comprehension and practice of the comparative and superlative in the Module 2 Review at the end of Unit 4.

5 Writing and speaking *Can you guess?*

- Read through the instruction and the example. Point out that the aim is for students to help their partner to guess the thing/animal without saying its name. Show how the speaker in the example compares the bus with similar things (a bike, a train and a car), so that the other person can get a general idea of what it is.
- Give students some practice. Choose something from a different category and write it on the board. Ask the class to suggest suitable sentences using comparatives and superlatives. For example, you could choose *Rome*, and sentences could include:
  – It's bigger than Milan.
  – It's hotter than London.
  – It's older than New York.
  – It's the largest city in Italy.
  – It's one of the most famous cities in the world.
- Give students an example using a person, too. You could use a person in the class or a famous person, for example:
  – She's one of the best runners in the world.
  – She's the most famous athlete from [country].
- Students work on their own to think of a topic and write a description. Walk round the class, giving help where necessary.
- In pairs, students take it in turns to read and guess. If they can't guess the answer, tell them to ask questions and encourage their partner to add some more clues.
- You could ask some students to read their description for the whole class to guess.

> **Example answer**
> It's bigger and fiercer than a cat, but it's smaller than a lion. It's the fastest animal in the world. It begins with 'c'.
> Answer: A cheetah.

People 29

> **OPTION**
> You can make this activity into a team game. In this case, write the topics yourself on small pieces of paper and hand them out. Topics could include: a mobile phone, a washing machine, a horse, an elephant, a blue whale, London, Antarctica, and the names of some well-known celebrities. Students write a description as in Exercise 5, without showing anyone else. Then divide the class into two teams. In turn, students read out their description and the rest of their team has a time limit of one minute to guess the answer.

> **OPTION**
> For further practice, you could ask students to name characters in films, TV shows or books who fit each of the adjectives.

STEP 2

Grammar: *(not) as ... as*
Vocabulary: Adjectives describing personality
Expressions: Asking for a description
Communicative tasks:
  Describing differences and similarities
  Asking for and giving descriptions

1 Key vocabulary
Adjectives describing personality

a
- Read out the list of adjectives and then the sentences. Some words should be familiar (for example, *adventurous, clever, lazy*) but most of them will probably be new. Ask students to guess what they can from English words they know or from similar words in their language and to use a dictionary to check if they have time.
- Set the time limit for the matching task. Students could work on this in pairs.
- 🔊 Play the recording. Students listen and check their answers.
- As you go through the answers, you could ask students to explain how they worked out the meanings.

Tapescript/Answers
1 independent   6 clever
2 moody   7 generous
3 adventurous   8 shy
4 hard-working   9 easy-going
5 lazy   10 confident

b
- Look at the example and draw attention to the *-ing* form of the verb after *(don't) like*.
- Students make sentences about themselves. They could write these down and then say them to a partner. (If you like, you could ask students to write these on a piece of paper and hand them in. You then read them out and the class has to guess which student wrote each one.)

2 Key pronunciation *Stress in words*

- To prepare for this exercise, you may want to read out the adjectives in Exercise 1 and ask students to say how many syllables are in each one.
- Look at the example with the class. Say the adjective slowly and beat time with your hand to emphasise the stress.
- Go through the other six patterns, using nonsense syllables to make the sounds, for example, *da DUM da da*.
- Encourage students to say the words quietly to themselves in order to match them with the stress patterns.
- 🔊 Play the recording. Students listen and check their answers.
- 🔊 Play the recording again and ask students to repeat.

Tapescript/Answers
1 easy-going
2 adventurous
3 independent
4 hard-working
5 confident, generous
6 clever, lazy, moody
7 shy

3 Presentation *What are they like?*

a
- Remind students of the question *What's he like?* Make sure students understand that it asks for a description of the person and has no connection with the verb *like*.
- Read out the introduction to the conversation. Ask students to say anything they remember about Ana's family, for example: *They're Mexican. They're from Veracruz. She's got a sister called Clara.*
- Look at the photo with the class and ask students to guess who the people are.
- 🔊 Play the recording while students listen and read.

Answers
1 Carlos (Clara's boyfriend)
2 Clara (Ana's sister)
3 Emilia (Ana's best friend)

b
- 🔊 Play the recording again. Pause to elicit the meaning of new vocabulary (for example, *annoy, good-looking*). Explain that *Anyway* is often used in conversation when we want to move on from one subject to another.
- Focus on the second half of the conversation. Point out the question *What does he look like?* Use Ana's answers about Julio to emphasise the difference between *What's he like?* and *What does he look like?* Ask students to translate the sentences with *as ... as* and *the same*.

30 Unit 3

- Drill some sentences containing the target language, for example:
  - *What's your brother like?*
  - *What does he look like?*
  - *Does he look like you?*
  - *It isn't as curly as mine.*
  - *Is he as good-looking as you?*
  - *We've got the same colour eyes.*
- Students read the sentences and look back at the text to decide if they're true or false. You may want to do the first sentence with the class as an example.
- As you check the answers, you can follow up with some further questions, for example:
  1 *How old is Clara?* (21.)
  2 *How old is Jay?* (17.) *Why does he say he's 18 at first?* (Because he doesn't want to seem a lot younger than Ana.)
  3 *Look at the photo. What does Emilia look like?* (She's got long black hair. She looks friendly.)
  4 *What's his name?* (Julio.)
  5 *Look at the photo. What does Carlos look like?* (He's got short black hair. He's quite good-looking.)

OPTION
You can ask pairs to practise the conversation, if possible by improvising their own version without reading from the book but referring to the photo. To help them with this, you could write up some cues on the board, as suggested in Unit 1 (page 11 in the Teacher's Book). You may want to invite one or two pairs to perform their conversation for the class.

Answers
1 False. She's younger than Clara. / Clara is older than Ana.
2 True.
3 True.
4 True.
5 False. He's quite shy.
6 False. He's really easy-going.
7 False. He's very lazy.
8 True.
9 True.

4 Key grammar (not) as ... as

- Students complete the examples. Make sure they understand that *His hair isn't as curly as mine* = 'My hair is curlier than his'. Give another example: *My brother's only ten but he's as tall as me* = 'He's the same height as me.'

Answers as, as

5 Practice

a
- Elicit the questions. Pay attention to the intonation, with the unstressed /ə/ sound for *as*.
- In pairs, students ask and answer. (Note that students can also use *as ... as* in their answers, for example: *I don't think tennis is as exciting as football*.)

Answers
2 Is tennis as exciting as football?
  I think tennis is more exciting than football / football is more exciting than tennis.
3 Is flying as dangerous as travelling by car?
  I think flying is more dangerous than travelling by car / travelling by car is more dangerous than flying.
4 Are cats as intelligent as dogs?
  I think cats are more intelligent than dogs / dogs are more intelligent than cats.
5 Are boys as moody as girls?
  I think boys are moodier than girls / girls are moodier than boys.

b
- Look at the example with the class. You could ask students to suggest other possible adjectives for this sentence (for example, *cold, busy, expensive*).
- You may want to give another example yourself, such as *Violins aren't as ... as electric guitars*. Write it on the board and elicit a range of adjectives to fit in the gap (*big, heavy, loud, popular, powerful*).
- Students write their own gapped sentence.
- In pairs, they complete each other's sentences.
- Pattern drill: TRP page 12 (Unit 3, Step 2)

6 Key expressions *Asking for a description*

- Students match the questions with the answers.
- Play the recording. Students listen and check.
- Ask students to translate the questions into their language.
- Ask: *Who does Jay look like?* (His father.) Contrast this with *What does he look like?* and remind students that the second question asks for a description of Jay's appearance.
- Write or dictate these four questions:
  - *What does Ana look like?*
  - *What does your best friend look like?*
  - *What's your bedroom like?*
  - *What's the weather like today?*
- Students ask and answer the questions in pairs.

Tapescript/Answers
1 c Does Jay look like his father? Yes, he does. They've both got the same nose and eyes.
2 a What does Jay look like? He's quite tall, with light brown hair.
3 b What's Jay like? He's an independent person and he's very generous.

People

7 Listening and speaking Personality test

a
- Explain the meaning of the word *shape*.
- Focus on the five pictures and read out the names of the shapes. Ask students to repeat.
- Students decide individually which shape is their favourite. Don't let them take this too seriously – the 'personality test' is really just for fun and certainly shouldn't be taken as serious scientific research.

b
- Explain that Jay is interviewing his friends for a 'test' which tells people what kind of personality they have.
- 🔊 Play the first conversation, between Jay and Martin. Pause to make sure that everyone heard Martin's choice of the triangle.
- 🔊 Ask students to write the other four names in a list. Then play the rest of the recording. Students listen and write down the shape that each person chooses.

> **Answers**
> Helen – spiral, Mike – matching triangles,
> Fiona – square, Lizzie – circle

Tapescript

JAY: Martin. I'm doing a personality test for my psychology homework. Can you look at these shapes and tell me which one you prefer?

MARTIN: Oh, er ... OK. Let me see. The triangle. I think I prefer the triangle.

JAY: Ah. That means you're shy. You don't like meeting new people. And you're very hard-working.

MARTIN: That's me!

JAY: Helen, what about you? Look at these shapes and tell me which one you prefer.

HELEN: Hmm. OK. Well, I <u>don't</u> like the circle. Maybe the ... What's that? The spiral. Yes, I like the spiral.

JAY: That means you're very confident. You never feel nervous or scared. And you're adventurous too. You like doing new and exciting things.

HELEN: I see. How interesting!

JAY: Hey, Mike! Can I ask you a question?

MIKE: OK.

JAY: Which of these shapes do you like the most?

MIKE: Um ... the matching triangles.

JAY: That means you're very friendly. You like meeting new people.

MIKE: Oh yeah?

JAY: Yes. And it means you're clever too.

MIKE: Really! That can't be right. I never pass any exams.

JAY: Fiona, can you help me with this personality test?

FIONA: OK.

JAY: Look at these five shapes and tell me which one you like the most.

FIONA: Hmm ... that one, I think. The square.

JAY: The square. That means you're very honest. You always tell the truth. And you're easy-going too. You don't often get angry.

FIONA: Hey, that's good!

LIZZIE: Hi Jay.

JAY: Lizzie! Great! You can help me. Look at these shapes. Which one do you like the most?

LIZZIE: Oh, er ... the circle, I think. Why?

JAY: Well, that means you're very independent. Do you agree?

LIZZIE: Yes, I suppose so. I like doing things on my own.

JAY: And it means you're generous, too. Is that right?

LIZZIE: Yes, of course it is!

c
- Ask students to copy out the table.
- 🔊 Play the recording again. Once again, pause after the first conversation and elicit the second adjective that Jay uses to describe the 'triangle' personality (*hard-working*). Tell students to write it in the table.
- 🔊 Play the rest of the recording, twice if necessary. Students complete the table with the adjectives.

> **Answers**
>
> | triangle | hard-working |
> | spiral | confident |
> | matching triangles | clever |
> | square | easy-going |
> | circle | independent |

d
- Ask different students to say which shape they chose.
- Look at the example with the class. Point out that they can agree, partly agree or completely disagree with the description given in the 'test'.
- Students write their response to the description of their personality. Encourage them to give reasons or examples of things they do or like.
- Students exchange opinions in pairs.

8 Writing and speaking People I know

- Ask students to think of a person they know quite well (this could be a classmate, a teacher, a friend or a family member). They then look back at their table in 7c and choose one of the five shapes for the person.

Unit 3

- Read out the example or choose a student to do so.
- You could demonstrate further by naming a person that students all know, for example, a popular TV personality. Ask students to suggest the best shape for this person. Then build up a class description on the board, using the example as a model.
- Students write a description of the person they chose.
- In pairs, they describe the person to each other.

Example answer
My grandmother matches the circle. I think she's an independent person because she enjoys living on her own. She's also very generous. When she visits us, she always brings presents and vegetables from her garden.

STEP 3
Reading skills: Using pronouns and possessive adjectives
Word work: Opposites: un- + adjective
Communicative task: Writing a Web page about yourself

1 Share your ideas The Internet

- Students who often use a computer for surfing the Internet will be familiar with words in English. Start by asking if they visit websites in English and invite them to name their favourite sites.
- Look at the two examples and check that students know what they mean. Brainstorm with the class to collect others and write them on the board. These could include: *website, home page, menu, search, search engine, links, connect, contact, download, log in, log off, help.*

2 Reading

BACKGROUND

SeaWorld, in Orlando, Florida, is a huge marine theme park. In different sections of the park, visitors can see whales, dolphins, sharks, sea lions, turtles, penguins and many other sea creatures.

The Matrix (1999) was the first in a trilogy of science fiction adventure films. It was followed by *The Matrix Reloaded* and *The Matrix Revolutions* (both released in 2003). **Keanu Reeves** /kiːˈɑːnuː ˈriːvz/, the star of all three films, was born in 1964. He became internationally famous with his starring role in the big-budget Hollywood film *Speed* in 1994.

Beyoncé Knowles /beɪˈjɒnseɪ ˈnəʊlz/ was born in Houston, Texas in 1981. She is the lead singer and songwriter for the popular girl group Destiny's Child, who have sold more than 33 million records since their first album in 1994. Beyoncé has also made successful recordings as a solo artist and has appeared in several films.

a
- Ask students to read the text quickly to get a general idea of what it is about. Ask: *Who's the boy in the first photo? (Daniel Trent.) What's his Web page about? (It's about Daniel.)*
- Find out what students think of the page Ask: *Does it look good? Is it interesting? Is it easy to follow?* Draw attention to the way the page is organised under topic headings.
- Go through the menu on the left. For each item, ask: *What do you think you'll find if you click here?* and invite students to offer suggestions.

b Comprehension check
- Read the main part of the text aloud. Pause at the end of each section and help with vocabulary (for example, *nearby, untidy, embarrassing*). Students should be able to work out the meanings from other words they know and from the context. Practise the pronunciation, giving special attention to the stress in *embarrassing*.
- Point out that the asterisked words are American English and refer students to the list under the text. Explain that in the USA it's unusual for people to use *have got* – they use the verb *have* instead.
- Choose students to read out the sentences. Emphasise that for some sentences the answer is *?* (= we don't know if it's true or false because the text doesn't tell us).
- Students look back at the text and write their answers. Advise them to use the headings in the text to help them locate the information they need.
- As you check the answers, ask students to correct the false sentences.

Answers
1 T
2 ?
3 F He's better at biology than history.
4 F It's untidy.
5 ?
6 F Simon is his friend.
7 T
8 F He thought he saw Beyoncé, but it wasn't her.

OPTION
You may like to give students examples of other American English words. Write the following columns on the board for students to discuss and complete in their notebooks.

American	British
store	
truck	
fall	
cookie	
candy	
soda	

(*Answers: shop, lorry, autumn, biscuit, sweets, soft drink*)

People 33

c **Reading skills**
Using pronouns and possessive adjectives
- You may want to go quickly through each sentence, asking students to say if the underlined word is a pronoun or an adjective. Remind them that both forms refer to people or things that we have mentioned before. However, a pronoun stands on its own, while a possessive adjective goes with a noun.
- Students find each sentence in the text and look back to find what the pronoun/adjective refers to.
- Point out that the use of pronouns and possessive adjectives means that we can avoid repeating the noun.
- Draw attention to the sentence in the text *It takes only five minutes to get to school*. Note that we sometimes use *It* as an impersonal pronoun which doesn't refer back to a previous noun. Other similar examples:
  – *It's easy to send emails.*
  – *It's important to eat healthy food.*
  – *It was nice of you to come.*
  – *It takes an hour to get to the city centre.*
  Note also the use of the impersonal *It* in expressions for the time and the weather.
  – *It's five o'clock.*
  – *It was raining yesterday.*

> **Answers**
> 2 Daniel's mother   3 Simon and Daniel
> 4 SeaWorld   5 Keanu Reeves
> 6 Daniel's school tennis team   7 Beyoncé's
> 8 Simon and Daniel
> 9 the woman who looked like Beyoncé

3 Word work *Opposites* un- + *adjective*

a
- Students work individually, matching the adjectives with their opposites. They could compare answers with a partner before you check with the whole class.

> **Answers**
> | untidy | tidy |
> | moody | easy-going |
> | confident | shy |
> | friendly | unfriendly |
> | hard-working | lazy |
> | stupid | clever |
> | popular | unpopular |

b
- Draw attention to the *un-* prefix. Go through the list of adjectives and check that the meanings are clear.
- Ask students to decide which of the adjectives can't be used with *un-*. They will probably remember that the opposite of *boring* is *interesting*. (However, the opposite of *interesting* can be <u>un</u>interesting as well as *boring*.)

> **Answer** Boring.

> **OPTION**
> You may want to teach some other common adjectives with *un-*, for example: *unusual, unhelpful, unintelligent, unsure, unfair, unnatural, uninteresting*.
> You may also like to mention that some verbs add the prefix *un-* to form opposites, for example: *uncover, unlock, undo, undress, unpack*.

4 Writing *A Web page*

- This exercise can be started in class and completed for homework.
- Tell students that they are going to write a text for their own Web page. They should use Daniel's Web page as a model, organising their material under the same headings.
- Read through the Writing guide with the class.
- Focus on the questions under the five topic headings in the Writing. You may want to elicit example answers for some of the more difficult questions.
- Ask students to plan their text by choosing topics and writing brief answers to the questions. Ask them to add information as suggested in the Writing guide.
- Students expand their notes into short paragraphs. Some students may want to use all five topics, while others may choose only three or four.
- Ask students to check their text. Encourage them to read each other's work in pairs and to suggest corrections or improvements to their partner.
- You could ask students to design a Web page for the final version of their text. Some students may be able to do this on the computer. Encourage them to add photos and/or illustrations. They can use Daniel's Web page or other pages on the Internet for ideas.
- Collect the finished work to mark, and choose one or two texts to read out in the next lesson.
- If possible, display the Web pages in the classroom and give students time to walk around and look at each other's work.

> **Example answer**
> <u>Cristina Alonso's Web page</u>
> Welcome to my Web page.
>
> **About me**
> I'm fifteen. I'm quite tall and I've got dark brown hair and brown eyes. I'm a confident and independent person.
>
> **My home**
> I live in a flat about three kilometres from the centre of Madrid. I share a room with my sister. It's very small for two people but it looks nice because we've got a lot of posters on the wall.
>
> **My school**
> I go to a school near our flat. My best subjects are English and history, and my worst subject is maths.

My friends

My best friends are Lucia and Ines. We often go shopping or go to the cinema together. Lucia is clever and she's one of the funniest people in our class. Everyone loves Ines because she's very kind and generous.

Fast facts

Sports: I like running and I'm quite good at athletics. I hate volleyball!

Music: My favourite singer is Robbie Williams. He's the greatest! I've got all his records.

Best moment: A year ago I got Robbie Williams' autograph. That was my best moment.

Extra exercises

1
- Students read the questions and choose the correct replies.
- Elicit possible questions for the other three replies. For example: a *What do your cousins look like?* d *What sport does he like?* e *Does she look like you or your brother?*
- You could ask students to practise the conversation in pairs.

Answers 2 g 3 b 4 h 5 f

2
- Ask students to choose the right words.

Answers 1 a 2 b 3 b 4 c 5 b

3
- Students find the correct adjective to complete each sentence.

Answers
1 intelligent 2 generous 3 lazy
4 adventurous 5 moody 6 confident

4
- Do the first sentence with the class as an example.
- Students use the adjectives to complete the sentences.
- When checking the answers, make sure students remember to use *the* with superlative forms. Check the spelling of *laziest* and *friendlier*.

Answers
1 more interesting 2 the best 3 as difficult as
4 the laziest 5 friendlier than

5
- Students use their own ideas to complete the two replies. Explain that there are lots of possible answers here.
- Ask different students to read out their replies.

Example answers
He's quite tall and he's got straight black hair.
He's nice. He's very easy-going and friendly.

6
- Ask students to work on the translations in pairs or small groups, and then discuss with the whole class.

Extra reading

Life and culture The British

Lead in

- Ask students for their ideas about Britain and the British. Write up their ideas on the board in note form. Some of these will probably be questionable or untrue. Put question marks beside all the suggestions, to raise some doubt about making these generalisations, and especially about negative stereotypes.

Task

- Give students time to read through the five texts. Ask them to match any of the topics with the ideas noted on the board.
- Read the texts aloud and help with new vocabulary (for example, *the Royal Family, in the country, common, foreigners, hooligans, scones, jam, delicious*).
- At the end of each text, ask students to identify the popular idea about the British and to say why the writer disagrees with it.
- Ask students to fill in the table, using the common ideas about Britain that are raised in the text.
- You could ask them to make a second column in the table, with contrary facts or ideas that are presented in the texts.
- Ask students to describe some of the ideas that foreigners have of their own country and people. Ask: *What do people expect when they come here? What are some images they have of us? Are these ideas positive or negative? Are they true?* Invite some discussion around these questions.

Example answers

Places to visit: Tower of London
Food: tea and sandwiches
People: English, Royal Family, hooligans
Homes: houses in the country
Weather: cold and wet

People

4 Places

STEP 1

Grammar: Suggestions
Vocabulary: Places
Expressions: Responding to suggestions
Communicative tasks:
  Asking for, making and responding to suggestions
  Talking about a day out

1 Key vocabulary *Places*

BACKGROUND

The Olympic Stadium in Athens was built for the 2004 Olympic Games. It was designed by the Spanish architect Santiago Calatrava, and it has a remarkable steel and glass roof.

The Tate Modern, London's largest gallery of modern art, was opened in 2000. It is by the Thames, opposite St Paul's Cathedral, and occupies a building that was once a power station.

The Ginkakuji (or Silver Pavilion) is a Zen temple at the foot of the Higashiyama (Eastern Mountains) in Kyoto.

Windsor Castle is one of the residences of the Queen. The castle was begun by William the Conqueror after his invasion of England in 1066.

The Blue Mosque in Istanbul was completed in 1616 in the days of the Ottoman Empire. With its six minarets and beautiful domes, it is one of the most famous buildings in Turkey.

Disneyworld was built by Walt Disney, the creator of Mickey Mouse and many animated film classics. Now called Walt Disney World, the theme park is in Orlando, Florida. It opened in 1971.

Selfridges is a large department store in Oxford Street, the busiest shopping street in central London. It has been open since the early 20th century.

- Read out the words in the box and then set the time limit for the matching task. Ensure students realise that the numbers of the descriptions relate to the numbers of the photos. Some of the words should be familiar. For new words, ask students to guess the meaning and to use a dictionary to check if they have time.
- Play the recording. Students listen and check their answers. Point out to students that the places have a capital initial if they are part of a proper name, for example, *a castle*, but *Windsor Castle*.
- Ask them to name the country for each of the places in the photos.

- Play the recording again and ask students to repeat.

Tapescript/Answers
1 The Olympic Stadium in Athens
2 The Tate Modern, an art gallery in London
3 The Ginkakuji Temple in Kyoto
4 Windsor Castle, near London
5 The Blue Mosque in Istanbul
6 Disneyworld in Florida, the world's first theme park
7 Selfridges, a department store in Oxford Street, London

2 Presentation *Shall we go out?*

BACKGROUND

The London Eye is a huge wheel beside the River Thames with a spectacular view over the city. It was built to celebrate the new millennium. The wheel moves very slowly and the ride lasts 30 minutes.

a
- Ask students to say what they can see in the main photo. Make sure they recognise that the city is London. Use the photo to revise or introduce key words in the conversation (for example, *London Eye, Thames, boat trip*).
- In the second photo ask students to identify Jay and Ana. Introduce the two new characters, Martin and Lizzie.

b
- Read out the introduction to the conversation and ask the question.
- Play the recording. Students listen and read. Ask them which places in the conversation appear in the photos, and to identify them.

Answer
Because everyone wants to do something different.

c
- Play the recording again, pausing to help with new vocabulary (for example, *somewhere, look round the shops, exhibition, suggestions*).
- Students look at the conversation and find the answers to the questions.
- Point out that there are several different ways of making suggestions. Drill some sentences containing the target language, for example:
  – *Shall we go out?*
  – *What shall we do?*
  – *Why don't we go on the London Eye?*
  – *How about taking a boat trip?*
  – *Let's take a boat trip.*

36 Unit 4

> **Answers**
> 1 visit Windsor Castle, go shopping in Oxford Street, go on the London Eye, take a boat trip on the Thames, go to the Tate Modern
> 2 Shall we go out somewhere tomorrow?
>   How about visiting Windsor Castle?
>   Shall we go to Oxford Street?
>   Why don't we go on the London Eye?
>   How about taking a boat trip?
>   Let's take a boat trip.
>   Why don't we go to that? (the new exhibition at the Tate Modern)

d • Make sure that students are clear about the meaning of *suggest* and *suggestion*. Practise the pronunciation: /sə'dʒest/, /sə'dʒestʃn/.
• Students read the sentences and look back at the text to decide if they're true or false.

> **Answers**
> 1 True.
> 2 False. She agrees with his suggestion.
> 3 False. She wants to go shopping in Oxford Street.
> 4 True.
> 5 False. He doesn't want to go on the London Eye.
> 6 False. Martin suggests a trip on the Thames.
> 7 True.
> 8 True.
> 9 False. She suggests going to the Tate Modern.

OPTION
You can ask students to practise the conversation in groups of four. Invite one or two groups to perform their conversation for the class.

3 Key grammar *Suggestions*

• Students complete the examples.
• Emphasise the use of the *-ing* verb form with *How about ...?* Explain that the full form of *Let's* is *Let us*.

> **Answers**
> shall
> don't
> take
> about

4 Practice

a • Students match the sentence parts and say/write the sentences.
• For questions 2, 4, 5, 7 and 8, you could ask students to express the same suggestion in a different way, for example, *Let's go to the Tate Modern. Why don't we buy a map? How about asking a policeman?*

> **Answers**
> 1 g Shall we go on the bus or on the tube?
> 2 h How about going to the Tate Modern?
> 3 a What time shall we meet? Is 7.30 all right?
> 4 f Let's buy a map.
> 5 b Why don't we ask a policeman?
> 6 c Where shall we have our lunch?
> 7 d Let's buy some postcards.
> 8 e Shall we sit down?

b • Students write their own sentence with the words in the wrong order.
• Pairs exchange sentences and put the words in the right order.
• Note that there is further work on comprehension and practice of making suggestions in the Module 2 Review at the end of Unit 4.
• 🔊 Pattern drill: TRP page 12 (Unit 4, Step 1)

> **Try this!**
> **Answers:** museum, theatre, cathedral, cinema, palace, aquarium

5 Key expressions
Responding to suggestions

• Read through the responses and ask students to repeat.
• Students match the responses with the meanings.
• Elicit the full form of *I'd (I would)*. Point out that, although we say *I want/I'd like to do something*, *I'd rather* is used without *to*.

> **Answers**
> 1 a 2 d 3 c 4 b 5 a 6 a 7 a

6 Key pronunciation /k/ /p/ /t/

a • Students focus on the sound at the end of each word.
• 🔊 Play the first part of the recording while students listen and read the words.
• Point out that all three sounds are unvoiced – that is, there is no movement of the vocal cords. Ask students to place their fingers on each side of their throat and to say the sounds. There should be no vibration in their throat. Contrast this with the voiced sounds /g/, /b/ and /d/ where the vocal cords vibrate.
• 🔊 Play the recording again and ask students to repeat.

b • 🔊 Play the recording. Students repeat the words and identify the sounds.

> **Tapescript/Answers**
> 1 bat   2 luck   3 jump
> 4 dark   5 cup   6 chocolate

Places 37

7 Speaking A day out

- Read through the instructions and examples with the class.
- Divide the class into groups of four or five. Students make and respond to suggestions.
- Ask different groups to report back on the decision they made, for example, *We're going to the bowling alley.*

STEP 2

Grammar: Expressions of quantity
Communicative tasks:
Describing and expressing opinions about a place

---

1 Share your ideas

BACKGROUND

Most of the population of Australia is concentrated around the coast, especially the east coast. **The outback** refers to the enormous inland area, far from the sea, where not many people live.

Lightning Ridge is in the north of the state of New South Wales. It is an opal mining town, the source of the world's finest 'black' opals, which are the darkest and most valuable form of the stone. It has a population of about 1,800, but an estimated 1,000 tourists come every year for the Easter goat races. Goats pull small carts and race from one end of the main street to the other.

- Give students a few moments to look at the brochure. Explain the meaning of *the outback* in Australia. Ask the questions and brainstorm with the class, collecting ideas and information on the board. General information about Australia could include:
  - *Population: about 20 million*
  - *Original inhabitants: Australian Aboriginals, now about 1.5% of the population*
  - *Capital: Canberra*
  - *Biggest city: Sydney*
  - *Climate: tropical in the north, very hot and dry inland*
  - *Beautiful beaches*
  - *Large areas of desert in the centre*
  - *Animals: kangaroos, wallabies, koalas, wombats, emus, many types of parrots, snakes and lizards*
  - *Some well-known Australians: Kylie Minogue (singer), Mel Gibson (actor), Ian Thorpe (swimmer), Lleyton Hewitt (tennis player), Peter Weir (film director)*
- Use the photos to introduce key vocabulary for the presentation text and the listening (for example, *goat, race, caravan park*).

2 Presentation Too many tourists

a
- Read the introduction and play the recording. Students listen and read.

- Ask for the answer to the question. Ask *Does Brett agree with Cody and Dee? (No, he doesn't.)*

Answer Things they don't like.

b
- Read the text aloud or play the recording again. Pause after Cody and Dee's statements to ask questions, for example: *What happens at Easter? What are some things that Cody doesn't like? Can you play a lot of sports in Lightning Ridge? What are some things that Dee doesn't like? Where does she want to live? Why can't she leave Lightning Ridge?*
- Drill some sentences that contain the target language, for example:
  - *There's too much traffic.*
  - *There are too many people.*
  - *There are a lot of sports facilities.*
  - *There aren't enough shops.*
  - *I haven't got enough money.*
- Students match the sentence parts. They could compare answers with a partner before you check with the whole class.

Answers
1 d 2 f 3 b 4 h 5 c 6 g 7 i 8 a 9 e

3 Key grammar Expressions of quantity

- Students read the examples and complete the explanations.
- Remind the class that *much* goes with uncountable (singular) nouns and *many* goes with plural countable nouns.
- Remind students also that *a lot of* can go with uncountable nouns as well as plural countable nouns, for example, *a lot of traffic*. Ensure that students understand that *enough* can also go with both plural countable nouns and uncountable nouns.
- Emphasise the difference in meaning between *too much/many* and *a lot of*. (Note that *a lot of* simply means 'a large quantity'. *Too much/many* means that the quantity is more than we want / more than what is acceptable.) Ask for translations in the students' language.

Answers too many   enough

OPTION

You may want to refer briefly to the use of *too* + adjective, as a way of reinforcing the meaning of *too*. Students will already be aware of expressions like *It's too hot, I'm too busy, She's too young, This work is too difficult.*

---

38 Unit 4

4 Practice

a
- Students complete the sentences. They can do this orally and/or in writing. Ensure that they use *a lot of* in the first sentence, not *too many* as there is no indication as to the 'right number' of goats.

> **Answers**
> 1 a lot of   2 too many   3 enough
> 4 too much   5 enough

- Pattern drill: TRP page 13 (Unit 4, Step 2, drills 1 and 2)

b
- Students write their own sentences with *too much/many*, *(not) enough* or *a lot of*.
- Encourage students to think of positive as well as negative things to write.
- Invite different students to read their sentences to the class. Ask if other students agree and to give their own opinions if they disagree.
- Note that there is further work on comprehension and practice of expressions of quantity in the Module 2 Review at the end of Unit 4.

5 Listening *It's a fantastic place!*

a
- Remind students of who Brett is.
- Play the recording. Students listen to get a general idea of what Brett says.
- Ask students to say the names of any places or buildings that they heard in the recording. Don't confirm or correct their answers at this stage.

> **Answer**
> He loves it. He thinks it's a fantastic place.

Tapescript

My family sometimes complain about Lightning Ridge, but I think it's a fantastic place. It's only a small town but we've got a five-star Olympic-size swimming pool. I swim there two or three times a week. There's a golf course too, and I play a lot of golf. In the summer the Water Theme Park is open, so I often go there after school with my friends. I also like all the art galleries – there are a lot of art galleries and we've got some really brilliant artists. We get quite a lot of visitors here and in my school holidays I work at the Crocodile Caravan Park.

We don't get much rain here, so if you like trees and flowers, it's not the place for you. But the wildlife is incredible, and you can see a lot of rare birds in this area. We spend a lot of time outside and in the evening we often have a barbie – that's a barbecue – in the garden and invite our neighbours. Everybody knows everybody in Lightning Ridge – it's a very friendly place. And there are about 50 different nationalities here, so it's a really interesting mixture of people.

b
- Read through the sentences with the class. Explain the meaning of *five-star*, *golf course* and *neighbours*.

- Play the recording again once or twice. Students listen and choose the correct answers.
- Play the recording again and pause to elicit answers. Remind the students of the meaning of *rare* and *mixture*.

> **Answers**   1 b   2 c   3 b   4 a   5 b

c
- Students use the words to make sentences. They can do this orally and/or in writing.

> **Answers**
> 1 There isn't much rain.
> 2 There aren't many trees and flowers.
> 3 There's a lot of wildlife.
> 4 There are a lot of art galleries/artists/rare birds/different nationalities/friendly people.

6 Writing and speaking *A place I know*

- Students choose to describe either their town/village or another one, for example, the capital city of their country. They make brief notes about things they like and dislike.
- Ask different students to give their opinions. Invite others to agree/disagree or to add further comments.
- Students write their description.
- Ask some students to read out their work to the class.

> **Example answer**
> [Name of town] is in the south of the country. A lot of people live here and it's got a lot of nice shops and cafés. There's a lot of pollution because there's too much traffic. There aren't enough sports facilities and there aren't enough good pop concerts.

Reading skills: Scanning
Word work: *get*
Communicative task: Writing about a typical day

STEP 3

1 Share your ideas *Student life*

- Invite students to say anything they know about Japanese life and Japanese schools.

2 Reading

a **Reading skills** *Scanning*
- Before looking at the text, read through the questions with the class.
- Point out to the students that the aim here is to find particular information in the text. They aren't expected to understand the whole of the text. Instead, they should look for the part which contains each piece of information and then read to extract it.

Places 39

- Set the time limit. Students read and make a very brief note in answer to each question.
- Ask students for their answers to the second question in Exercise 1.

> **Answers**
> 1 At 8.40.   2 50 minutes.   3 At 3 pm.   4 Yes.

b **Comprehension check**
- 🔊 Play the recording of the text while students follow in their books. Help them with new vocabulary (for example, *cafeteria, classmates, packed lunch*). Pause to ask questions, for example:
  - Did Yumiko get up before 6.15? (Yes.)
  - Where did she have lunch? (In her classroom.)
  - What do students do at three o'clock? (They clean the school.)
  - Do all Japanese students go to a baseball club? (No – but they all go to a club.)
  - Why do students go to 'juku'? (To study for their exams / To get into a good university.)
  - How much sleep does Yumiko get? (Six hours.)
- Choose students to read out the sentences.
- Students put the events in order. They could work on this in pairs.

> **Answers**
> 2 d   3 g   4 b   5 a   6 e
> 7 j   8 c   9 h   10 k   11 f

c
- Discuss the question with the class. Alternatively, you could ask students to discuss in groups and report back to the class.

> **OPTION**
> Before the discussion in 2c, you could ask students to help you write Yumiko's activities in the form of a timetable on the board. It should look something like this:
>
> | | |
> |---|---|
> | 6.00 | get up |
> | 6.45 | homework |
> | 7.30 | leave home |
> | 7.35–8.35 | train |
> | 8.40–12.30 | 4 lessons |
> | 12.30–1.20 | lunch in classroom |
> | 1.20–3.00 | 2 lessons |
> | 3.00–3.30 | tidy classroom |
> | 3.45–5.45 | baseball club |
> | 5.45–6.10 | burger, walk to station |
> | 6.15–6.45 | train |
> | 6.45–9.45 | extra classes |
> | 9.45–10.15 | go home |
> | 10.30–11.30 | homework |
> | 12.00 | bed |

3 Word work *get*

a
- Go through the verbs in the box, indicating their meaning with hand gestures where possible.
- Students complete the sentences. Ask them to start with the ones they are sure of and then to complete the others. They could compare answers with a partner before you check with the whole class.
- Point out that we use *get* a bus/train to mean 'use it to go somewhere', but we use *get on* and *get off* to describe actually entering or leaving the bus/train. Also compare the use of *get on/off* for public transport with *get into/out of* for a car.
- Draw attention to the Remember! box. Make it clear that *get home* is an exception. Normally we use *go/get to* + place, for example, *I'm going to the post office. She got to the station at 8.30.*

> **Answers**
> 1 get up   2 get into   3 get home   4 get off
> 5 get ready   6 get   7 get into   8 get to
> 9 get out of   10 get   11 get dressed   12 Get on

b
- Discuss the translations with the class.

c
- Ask students to write their own sentence and to think about how to translate it into English.
- In pairs, they translate their partner's sentence and discuss the translations together.
- Invite some students to say their sentence for the class to translate.

> **OPTION**
> You could make this into a group activity. Ask each group to write three sentences and to agree on an English translation. They pass their sentences on to the next group to translate into English. Groups then join up to compare translations. Go round the class to check and advise.

4 Writing *A typical day*

- This exercise can be started in class and completed for homework.
- Introduce the topic. Make it clear that students can write about an imaginary situation if they want to.
- Read through the Writing guide with the class. Draw attention to the link words that make a 'bridge' between one event and the next.
- Ask students to make notes in answer to the questions in the exercise.
- Students organise their notes and add details as suggested in the Writing guide.
- Ask them to check their story. Encourage them to read each other's work in pairs and to suggest corrections or improvements to their partner.
- Collect the finished work to mark, and choose one or two stories to read out in the next lesson.

Example answer

I got up at eight o'clock and left home at about half past ten. I met my friend Claudio and we walked to the sports ground for football training.

On the way home we met two English tourists, Sarah and Jack. They wanted to go to the town square, so we walked there with them. I spoke English and they could understand me! I was really pleased.

After that I went home. My grandmother arrived in the afternoon and she brought me a new T-shirt.

At half past five I started my homework. Then I got a text message from Sarah. She invited me to go to the cinema in the evening. I didn't have enough money so I couldn't go. It was very annoying. I watched a boring programme on TV with Mum, Dad and Grandma and then I went to bed.

Extra exercises

1
- Students complete the suggestions. Remind them that they are looking for one-word answers.
- You could elicit alternative ways of making each suggestion.

Answers
1 about   2 Why   3 Shall   4 Let   5 shall

2
- Students choose the correct replies.

Answers   1 c   2 a   3 b   4 b   5 a

3
- Students complete the sentences.
- Ask them to spell the words as you check the answers.

Answers
1 gallery   2 stadium   3 cathedral   4 theme
5 palace   6 aquarium   7 mosque   8 department

4
- Go through the text with the class before students choose the correct words.

Answers   1 c   2 b   3 c   4 a   5 a

5
- Look at the example with the class. Point out to the students that they need to write three or four words for the answers in this exercise.

Answers
2 were too many   3 gave us too much
4 haven't got enough   5 has got too many

6
- Ask students to work on the translations in pairs or small groups, and then discuss with the whole class.

Extra reading

Life and culture Australia

BACKGROUND

The **Australian Aboriginals** were hunter-gatherers who migrated from Asia. The Europeans arrived and took their land and disrupted their culture. Many were deliberately killed and huge numbers died from illnesses introduced to the country by the foreign settlers. About 65% of the remaining Aboriginal population lives in towns and cities, often with low incomes and with high rates of unemployment, alcoholism and suicide. Some communities live in settlements in the outback and have preserved their traditional lifestyle.

The British claimed Australia when James Cook landed at Botany Bay near the present site of Sydney in 1770. The first **convicts** arrived in 1788. Many of the early buildings and roads were constructed by them.

The **dingo fence** stretches from South Australia through New South Wales to Queensland. It was started in the 1880s to keep dingoes from the north out of sheep-grazing land.

Lead in

- Ask the questions about Australia and write short notes on the board as students give their ideas. Use the discussion to introduce the key words *Aboriginals* /æbəˈrɪdʒnlz/ and *convicts* /ˈkɒnvɪkts/.

Task

- Give students time to read through the text. Ask them to add information to the notes on the board.
- Read the text aloud and help with new vocabulary (for example, *Cantonese, Arabic, best-behaved, wool, fence*).
- You could ask some questions to test comprehension:
  - Why don't you see many people in the outback? (Because 85% of the population live in cities.)
  - What happened to the Aboriginals' land? (The European settlers took it.)
  - Where did the prison ships come from? (Britain.)
- Look at the notes in the boxes. Students use these to make some comparisons with their own country.
- Ask them to complete the fact file about Australia. They then make a fact file about their country.

Answers
Population:	20 million
Capital city:	Canberra
Main language:	English
Original inhabitants:	Aboriginals
Currency:	Australian dollar
Coldest months:	July and August
Important dates:	1788, 26th January

Places   41

Module 2 Review

Grammar check

1 Comparatives and superlatives

Work it out for yourself

A
- Ask students to say the adjectives quietly to themselves to work out the number of syllables.

> **Answers**
> a long, short   b curly   c modern   d expensive

B
- Students look at the lines and answer the questions. Remind them of the spelling for adjectives ending in -y: curly – curlier/curliest.
- Students answer the questions about the clocks. Point out the use of *more* and *most* for these longer adjectives.

> **Answers**
> 1 Yes, it is.   2 Yes, it is.   3 No, it isn't.
> 4 No, it isn't.   5 XY   6 XY   7 Yes, it is.
> 8 No, it isn't.   9 A

C
- Ask students to match the sentence parts.

> **Answers**   1 c   2 a   3 d   4 b

1.1
- Look at the example with the class. You may want to go through the whole exercise orally before asking students to write.

> **Answers**
> 2 DVDs are more expensive than CDs.
> 3 Elephants are heavier than rhinoceroses.
> 4 Girls are often more confident than boys.
> 5 Kirsty is moodier than Gemma.
> 6 I'm more easy-going than my brother.

1.2
- Students complete the questions and answer those they can.

> **Answers**
> 1 (In 2005 the oldest man was an Italian aged 112)
> 2 the largest (the blue whale)
> 3 the most popular (American football)
> 4 the most useful [student's own answer]
> 5 the happiest [student's own answer]
> 6 the most difficult [student's own answer]

2 Irregular forms

Work it out for yourself

- Students complete the table.

> **Answers**   good, bad

- Ask students to read through the text. They then complete it with the correct adjectives. You could ask them to compare answers in pairs before you check with the whole class.

> **Answers**
> 2 better   3 the best   4 the worst   5 worse

3 Making suggestions

Work it out for yourself

- If students aren't sure what to look for here, ask them to think about the form of the verb.

> **Answer**
> For *How about ...?* we use the *-ing* form of the verb. (The other expressions use the infinitive.)

- Students write the suggestions using the verbs in the box.
- As you check the answers, you could ask for alternative ways to make the same suggestions.

> **Answers**
> 2 Shall we play cards?
> 3 Let's get a bus into town.
> 4 How about going to the bowling alley?
> 5 Let's look round the shops.
> 6 Why don't we watch the tennis final on TV?
> 7 How about having a barbecue in the garden?
> 8 Shall we make a packed lunch and go to the beach?

4 Expressions of quantity

Work it out for yourself

- Read out the explanations and ask students for some other examples of countable and uncountable nouns.

- Remind them that *too much/many* means 'more than we want' – the meaning is always negative.
- Students answer the questions. Tell them to look back at the examples if they aren't sure.

> **Answers**
> 1 too much   2 too many   3 Yes, we can.
> 4 Yes, we can.   5 No, it doesn't.

- Students look at the pictures and complete the sentences.

> **Answers**
> 1 a lot of   2 too many   3 too much
> 4 enough, enough

Study skills 2   Thinking about learning

- Point out to the students that it's very useful for them to identify their own strengths and weaknesses and to think about things that either help their learning or make it difficult.
- Set the time limit and ask students to respond to the statements.
- In pairs, students exchange their ideas and offer some suggestions to each other.
- Discuss difficulties and elicit positive suggestions for each question.

How's it going?

Your rating

- Students look back at the exercises in the Grammar check and make their own assessment of how well they understand and remember the different language points.

Vocabulary

- Students choose some of the words and ask their partner about them. They can answer by giving a translation in their language.

Test a friend

- Look at the example questions and elicit the correct answers.
- Students refer back to the texts in Units 3 and 4 and write several questions to test their partner. They then ask and answer in pairs.

> **Answers**
> [Student's own answer.]
> It's very hard.

Correcting mistakes

- The sentences listed here contain some common errors. Ask students to rewrite them correctly.
- Some sentences contain more than one error. Make sure students are aware of this, and that they find both errors in questions 1 and 4.
- Emphasise the importance of going back over their work to check for errors when they finish a piece of writing.

> **Answers**
> 1   Alex is the nicest person in the class.
> 2   Megan is taller than her friends.
> 3   I think it is the most beautiful place in our country.
> 4   How about visiting Brighton next weekend?
> 5   She can't come. She hasn't got enough money.

Your Workbook

- Students should complete the Learning diary when they come to the end of each unit.

Coursework 2

My guidebook

Getting around

BACKGROUND

King Arthur is the legendary warrior king who assembled his Knights of the Round Table at Camelot and defended his British kingdom against evil forces. He was assisted by the powerful magician Merlin. Historians believe that these stories are based on the life of a real Celtic chieftain who led local resistance to the Saxon invaders in the 5th century.

According to legend, Arthur's birthplace was at **Tintagel** (/tɪnˈtædʒl/). Although the existing castle ruins are more recent (dating from the 13th century), the remains of an earlier 5th century fortress have been found on the site.

The Serpentine is the name of the lake in Hyde Park. At **Speakers' Corner** you can listen to up to a dozen individuals who each stand on a box to express their opinions to the public on a variety of subjects – often to do with politics or religion, and often controversial.

Brighton Pier opened in 1899. Always a place for enjoying popular entertainment, it now has a funfair, amusement arcades, bars and food stalls.

The **Royal Pavilion at Brighton** (completed in 1823) was built as a seaside residence by King George IV. It is an extravagant Oriental fantasy, with Indian domes and Chinese-style furnishings.

- Look at the photos and map with the class. Referring to Tintagel Castle, tell students that people believe this is where King Arthur was born. Ask them to say what they know about him. If they have studied *Messages* 1, remind them of the story *The Silent Powers*.
- Use the photos and map to revise key words and to introduce new ones (for example, *Frisbee, deckchair, chat, sea front, pier*).
- Tell the class a little about Speakers' Corner and the Brighton Pavilion.
- Give students time to read through the text on their own.
- You can ask some questions to check comprehension, for example:
  - *Where's Cornwall? (In southwest England.) How did Ana get there? (By coach.)*
  - *What are some team sports that people play in Hyde Park? (Rugby, football, Frisbee.) What are some water sports? (Swimming, boating.)*
  - *What do you think a 'travel card' is? (A ticket for all buses, trains and tube trains in London.)*
  - *Does the Queen live in the Royal Pavilion? (No.) Can tourists go there? (Yes.)*
  - *Is Victoria Station in Brighton? (No, it's in London.)*
  - *If you leave London on the 9.30 train, when do you get to Brighton? (At 10.30.)*
- Ask students to suggest some places – either in their own town or not too far away – that they would recommend to visitors of their age. Write their suggestions on the board. Then choose one or two of these places and ask for some information, for example: *Where is it? What can you see/do there? What's the best way to get there?*
- Ask students to plan their text. They should write about at least two places and illustrate them as they wish. Advise them to gather or check information by looking at tourist brochures or Internet websites.
- Set a time limit, allowing one to two weeks for work on the project. If students want to spend longer on this work, you could negotiate an extension of time. Some work may be done in class and some at home.
- Ask students to check their text before they write a final version and design their page. Tell them to use Ana's page as a model.

Module 3 The future

See page 7 of the Introduction for ideas on how to use the Module opening pages.

Answers
1 b 2 a 3 e 4 c 5 d

5 Goals

STEP 1

Grammar:
Present continuous used for the future
The future with *going to*
Communicative tasks:
Talking about arrangements and intentions

1 Share your ideas

BACKGROUND

American football is played by teams of eleven on a field 100 yards (91.44 metres) long. A team has four team moves (or *plays*) to get the ball at least 10 yards (9.14 metres) towards their opponents' goal line. They do this by throwing and running with the ball rather than kicking it. If they can get 10 yards or more, they are allowed another four plays. Otherwise, the ball goes to the other team. If a team can carry the ball over the goal line, they score a *touchdown* (6 points), usually followed by a goal kick (1 extra point). During the play they may also kick a field goal (3 points). The players can bump and block each other and can bring players to the ground when they have the ball. They wear helmets to protect their head and face.

American football is extremely popular in the USA and almost all schools and colleges have teams competing in football competitions.

a
- Ask students to identify the sport in the photo on the left and to give any information they can about American football.
- If your students are sports fans, you could ask: *How is American football different from football in Europe?* (Some possible answers: *Players throw/run with the ball. They don't control the ball with their feet. Players crash into each other. They wear helmets. There isn't a net in the goal.*)
- Ask students if they know which other sports are common/popular in the USA. (Some possible answers: *baseball, basketball, soccer, tennis.*)

- Look at the photo on the right on page 50. Ask: *Who's the man?* (*A football trainer/manager.*) Introduce the alternative word, *coach*. Tell students that the players in the photo belong to a university team and explain that in the USA the word for *university* is usually *college*.

b
- Explain that the diary belongs to the football coach in the photo. Students read the diary page quickly and then say what's happening next weekend (for example, *They're training on Friday. They're going to Kansas City on Saturday. They're going by plane. They're practising before lunch.*).
- Point out that the word *coach* in the diary refers to a bus for long-distance travel. It has a quite different meaning from *(football) coach* (= trainer of a football team).

2 Presentation *Len's diary*

a
- Read out the introduction to Len's speech. Refer back to his diary and make sure students understand that he's speaking at the 'team meeting' mentioned in his diary notes for Friday.
- Ask students to read the text and find the information in the diary.
- 🔊 Play the recording. Students listen and check.

Tapescript/Answers

LEN: OK guys, let's begin. First, I'm going to tell you about tomorrow. Then we're going to talk about our last [1]game. After that, we're going to watch a [2]video of the Zebras.
So here are the arrangements for tomorrow. As you know, we're playing against the Zebras in [3]Kansas City. Kick-off is at 1.30. We're meeting in the [4]college car park and we're leaving at [5]8.30. We're getting the plane at [6]9.45. There's a practice session at 11.15, then we're having [7]lunch at the stadium. Any questions? OK? Well, I've got an important question for you guys: What's going to happen on Saturday?

TEAM: We're going to win!

b
- Read the text aloud. Explain that *guys* is an informal word for 'boys/men', but can also be used to mean 'people', including girls. Ask students to work out the meaning of *arrangements* and *kick-off*.

Goals 45

- Focus on the use of *going to* at the beginning of the text. Point out that here Len is talking about how he intends to organise the meeting.
- Then focus on the use of the present continuous. Point out that tomorrow's activities are fixed and definite arrangements. (They've already ordered the coach, got the plane tickets, organised the lunch etc.)
- Drill some sentences with both verb forms.
- Read through the questions. Ask students to look at the text and make brief notes for the answers.
- Choose students to read out the questions and then elicit the answers. Encourage students to answer in full sentences, following the form of the questions.

> **Answers**
> 1 They're going to talk about their last game.
> 2 They're going to watch a video of the Zebras.
> 3 They're playing in Kansas City.
> 4 They're playing against the Zebras.
> 5 They're leaving at 8.30.
> 6 They're getting to the airport by coach.
> 7 No, they aren't. (They're having lunch at the stadium in Kansas City.)
> 8 He's going to buy a present for Kim. He's going to mend his motorbike.

3 Key grammar *The future with the present continuous and* going to

- Students complete the explanations.
- Note that it's often very hard to distinguish an intention from an arrangement, and it's sometimes possible to use either verb form. For example, in the presentation text Len says *We're having lunch at the stadium* but he could also say *We're going to have lunch at the stadium*. Don't let students get anxious about the rules. Put the main emphasis on the use of the present continuous for actions that are fixed: they usually involve an arrangement with another person or organisation, i.e. the coach/flight has been booked etc.
- Discuss translations with the class.

> **Answers**
> present continuous
> going to

4 Practice

a
- Students write the sentences. Make sure they use the present continuous form of the verbs.

> **Answers**
> 2 It's Tamsin's birthday on Friday but she isn't having a party.
> 3 I must go. I'm meeting my sister at the school gate.
> 4 My pen friend's coming next week. He's arriving at the airport at 2.30 on Tuesday.
> 5 Martin's going out with Lizzie this evening. They're going to the cinema.
> 6 The Raiders aren't playing on the 4th. They've got a free weekend.

b
- Students write their own sentence for their partner to complete.
- You could ask some students to report back on their partner's arrangement (for example, *Gina's meeting Pablo after school*).
- Pattern drill: TRP page 13 (Unit 5, Step 1, drill 1)

c
- Look at the example with the class. Elicit the question: *What's he going to do?* Point out that Len knows what he wants to do and intends to do it.
- Elicit the questions for the other four pictures. Then choose different students to ask and answer the questions across the class.
- You may want to ask students to write down the answers.

> **Answers**
> 2 What's she going to do?
>   She's going to paint the room.
> 3 What are they going to do?
>   They're going to play cards.
> 4 What's he going to do?
>   He's going to mend his bike.
> 5 What's she going to do?
>   She's going to wash her car.

- Pattern drill: TRP page 13 (Unit 5, Step 1, drill 2)

5 Listening and speaking
That's a long way!

BACKGROUND
Oxfam is a British charity which raises money to help people suffering from poverty and hunger in countries all over the world.

a
- Look at the photo and ask: *Who is she?* Make sure that students recognise Mrs Grant, the mother in Ana's host family in London.
- Read out the sentences under the photo and help students with the new vocabulary: *cycle, raise money, charity*. Use the map to show that Mrs Grant is going to cycle from one end of Britain to the other.
- Play the first part of the recording. Students listen for the answer to the question.

46 Unit 5

> **Answer** 1,400 kilometres.

Tapescript

TEACHER: So let's give a warm welcome, everyone, to Penny Grant.
PENNY: Thank you, and thanks very much for inviting me. Well, I'm going to cycle across Britain – at least, that's my plan. I'm going to cycle from Land's End to John O'Groats. As you may know, Land's End is the farthest point south in England and John O'Groats is the farthest point north in Scotland – a total distance of nearly 1,400 kilometres. I'm doing it to raise money for the charity Oxfam. So first, I'd like to tell you about Oxfam …

b
- Read through the questions with the class.
- 🔊 Play the second part of the recording. Students listen and put the questions in order (1–5). Don't confirm or correct their answers yet.

> **Answers** 4, 2, 5, 3, 1

c
- 🔊 Play the recording again. Students listen and check their answers to 5b.
- 🔊 Go through the questions in order and ask students to say anything they can about Penny's replies. Then play the recording again. Pause after each reply and elicit the main information.
- In pairs, students ask and answer. Explain that they don't have to repeat Penny's words exactly, but they should give the correct information.
- Ask pairs to change roles and repeat the activity.

Tapescript/Answers

PENNY: … So now you know all about Oxfam. Well, has anyone got any questions? Is there anything else you'd like to know?
GIRL 1: When are you leaving?
PENNY: You mean, leaving on my trip?
GIRL 1: Yes.
PENNY: I'm leaving next month.
BOY 1: How long is it going to take?
PENNY: About two weeks, I think. I'm going to do about 100 kilometres a day.
GIRL 2: Where are you going to stay?
PENNY: In youth hostels. There are lots of youth hostels on my route, so finding somewhere to stay won't be a problem, I hope.
BOY 2: How much money are you going to raise?
PENNY: I want to raise about £3,000 – that's my goal, anyway.
BOY 3: What's Oxfam going to use the money for?
PENNY: They're going to build a new school in a village in Afghanistan.

6 Writing and speaking Making plans

- Ask students for some other ideas about how to raise money for charity.
- In pairs, students plan their own charity activity and write sentences.
- Ask pairs to report back to the class about their plans.

> **Example answer**
> We're going to have a rock concert. It's taking place on 3rd June at the town hall and 15 musicians are coming. We're going to try to raise £10,000.

OPTION You could extend this activity by playing the 'Information memory game' (see Games, page 110 in the Teacher's Book). After four or five pairs have described their plans, teams try to remember and reproduce the information they heard.

Grammar:
   The future with *will* and *going to*
   will for offers
Vocabulary: Sports clothes
Expressions: Shopping
Communicative tasks:
   Talking about the future
   Making offers
   Making a conversation in a shop

STEP 2

1 Key vocabulary Sports clothes

- Read out the words in the list and then set the time limit for the matching task. Some words will be familiar. For the others, ask students to guess what they can from English words they know, and to use a dictionary to check if they have time.
- 🔊 Play the recording. Students listen and check.
- Point out that *shorts* and *trunks* are plural (like *jeans*, *trousers*).
- You may want to introduce the word *suit* here. Note that we normally pronounce it /suːt/ but it can be pronounced /sjuːt/.
- 🔊 Play the recording again and ask students to repeat. Pay attention to the stress on the first syllable in compound nouns: *tracksuit*, *swimsuit*, *swimming trunks*, *wetsuit*.

Tapescript/Answers

1 boots   5 swimming trunks
2 swimsuit   6 socks
3 wetsuit   7 shorts
4 tracksuit   8 goggles

Goals 47

Try this!
Answers could include: *trainers, football shirt, sweatshirt, skis, skates, rollerblades, skateboard, basketball, tennis ball, baseball, tennis racket.*

2 Presentation *Of course I will*

a
- Give students a moment to look at the photos.
- 🔊 Read the introduction. Ask the question, then play the recording. With books closed, students listen for the answer to the question.

Answer Blue.

b
- 🔊 Play the recording again while students listen and read.
- Explain or elicit the meaning of new vocabulary (for example, *expert, try on, medium, fitting room*). You could tell students that the three basic clothes sizes are *small, medium* and *large*.
- Point out the use of the pronouns *one* and *ones*. Ask students to say what these words refer to. (*I like this one* = this tracksuit. *Have they got any green ones?* = green tracksuits.)
- Make sure that students understand the meaning of *offer* (verb). Then read through the sentences with the class. Ask students to find the false sentence.

Answer Sentence 6 is false.

c
- For the true sentences, students find the part of the conversation that gives the answer.
- Drill some of the sentences with *will* and *won't*.

Answers
2 Lizzie says, 'I'll give you my expert opinion!'
3 Ana says, 'I'll try it on.'
4 Lizzie says, 'I'll hold your bag for you.'
5 Lizzie says, 'I'll ask the assistant.'
7 Ana says: 'I'll get this blue one.'
8 Lizzie says, 'I think I'll try them on.'

OPTION
You can ask students to practise the conversation in groups of three. This is a good opportunity to include a shyer student in the role of the shop assistant, as this is only one line.

3 Key grammar *The future with* will *and* going to

a
- Look at the examples in the Grammar box. Focus particularly on the use of *will* for spontaneous decisions. Discuss translations of the examples with the class.

- Remind students that *will* and *won't* have the same form for all subjects. They are followed by the infinitive of the main verb.

b
- Students complete the example and read the explanation.
- Point out that we usually use the short form *I'll* (or *We'll*) in offers.

Answer 'll

4 Practice

a
- Look at the example. Make it clear that the speaker has just seen the trousers. He hasn't planned to try them on – he's deciding to do it as he speaks.
- You could go through the rest of the sentences and ask: *Is this a plan or a decision at the time of speaking?*
- Students complete the sentences. They can do this orally and/or in writing.

Answers
2 are you going to   3 'll show   4 're going to
5 'll walk   6 'm going to

- 🔊 Pattern drill: TRP page 14 (Unit 5, Step 2)

b
- Students make offers to go with the pictures. They can do this orally.
- Choose pairs of students to say the dialogues in the pictures.
- You could give the class some other situations and ask them to respond with offers. For example:
  – I'm thirsty. (I'll get you some water.)
  – It's hot in this room. (I'll open the window.)
  – I'd like to hear some music. (I'll play / put on a record.)
  – I'd love an ice cream. (I'll buy you one.)
- Note that there are is work on further comprehension and practice of future forms in the Module 3 Review at the end of Unit 6.

Answers
1 (I'll) answer it.
2 (I'll) cook the dinner.
3 (I'll) carry that for you.
4 (I'll) do it.

5 Key expressions *Shopping*

- Students match the sentences with the replies.
- Drill each sentence with the class.
- Students can practise the dialogues in pairs.

Answers 1 d   2 a   3 e   4 b   5 c

Unit 5

6 Key pronunciation /aɪ/ /ʊ/ /æ/

- 🔊 Play the recording while students listen and read the words.
- 🔊 Play the recording again and ask students to repeat the words.
- Students say the words to themselves and find the odd one out in each group. Ask them to say why it is the odd one out.

Answers
1 give (The vowel sound is /ɪ/, not /aɪ/.)
2 boot (The vowel sound is /uː/, not /ʊ/.)
3 play (The vowel sound is /eɪ/, not /æ/.)

OPTION
If you have time, you could write up one or two sentences with a mixture of the three vowel sounds, for example:
Put that black sock on your right foot.
Ask students to identify the three sounds and to repeat the sentences.

7 Writing and speaking Buying clothes

- You could ask pairs (or groups of three – see below) to think about these questions to help plan their conversation:
  - *What do you want to buy?*
  - *What do you see in the shop?*
  - *What's it like? Size? Colour?*
  - *Will you try it on?*
  - *Will you buy it?*
- Pairs write their conversation and then practise it together.
- Ask some pairs to act out their conversations for the class.
- Students could also do this role play in groups of three: the third person is the shop assistant, who can either be helpful and offer to get a bigger size etc., or unhelpful, like the one in the presentation conversation.

Example answer
A: I want to get some football shorts.
B: OK, let's have a look. What colour?
A: White. These look OK, but I'm not sure if they're the right size.
B: Why don't you try them on? I'll wait outside the fitting room.
A: OK. I think I'll try on this sweatshirt too. I won't be a minute …
No, the shorts are too small. Have they got any bigger ones?
B: I'll have a look …
No, they're all small.
A: Oh. Well, I won't get any shorts. But I think I'll get the sweatshirt. It's cool.

STEP 3

Reading skills: Skimming
Word work: Adjective/verb + preposition
Communicative task: Writing an interview

1 Share your ideas Sport

- Discuss the questions with the class. Write words for sports and other useful vocabulary on the board. If possible, use the discussion to revise or introduce key words from the reading text (for example, *athletics/athlete, Olympic (Games), gold medal, champion*).

2 Reading

BACKGROUND
Steve Redgrave was a champion British rower. He won gold medals in five consecutive Olympic Games: in Los Angeles (1984), Seoul (1988), Barcelona (1992), Atlanta (1996) and Sydney (2000). He has now retired from professional sport.

a Reading skills Skimming
- Focus on the photo and introduce the words *high jump* and *high jumper*.
- Set the time limit (one minute only!) and ask students to read the text very quickly. Make it clear that they're looking for quite general information here – they shouldn't stop to puzzle over details.
- Read through the questions with the class and make sure that students understand them. Help them to guess the meaning of *in particular, well-paid* and *forgetful*.
- Ask students to answer the questions. Point out that we can pick up a lot of information by reading through a text quickly, without taking in every detail.

Answers
1 b 2 a 3 b 4 a
5 ambitious, positive, forgetful

b Comprehension check
- Look at the list with the class. Explain the meaning of *irritating*.
- Point out to students that this time they need to look more carefully at the text to find particular information. Draw attention to the questions in the text that will show them where to look.
- 🔊 Play the recording of the text while the students read it. They can work individually or in pairs to complete the exercise.
- Draw attention to useful expressions in the text: *I guess …, I've got a good/bad/terrible memory, It drives me/them mad, the greatest … of all time, incredibly successful.*

Goals 49

Answers
1 Sausage sandwiches, curry.
2 The high jump, chess.
3 Getting up early, remembering names, birthdays etc.
4 People who talk loudly, the rain.
5 Snakes.
6 He interrupts people.
7 Steve Redgrave.
8 Competitions.

c • Look at the questions. Point out to students that here they are being asked for accurate names and figures. Again, they should use the questions in the text to work out where to look. They could complete the exercise orally or in writing.

Answers
1 The English Schools Championship.
2 Two metres and five centimetres.
3 Because it's got a High Performance Centre for athletics.
4 The European Junior Championship.
5 To be the World Champion high jumper.

3 Word work *Adjective/verb + preposition*

a • Students complete the sentences with the prepositions.
  • Look at the Remember! box with the class.

Answers
1 at   2 in   3 of   4 about   5 at   6 to

OPTION
You could add other associated adjectives which take the same prepositions. For example:
good/bad at: brilliant at, terrible at
afraid of: scared of, frightened of, terrified of
worry about: worried about, anxious about, sad about, (un)happy about, confident about, optimistic about, pessimistic about

b • You could begin by inviting students to ask you some of the questions and giving your own answers.
  • In pairs, students ask and answer.

4 Speaking and writing *An interview*

• This exercise can be started in class and completed for homework.
• Read out the instructions and look at the example. Point out that the notes are very short, recording only important words.
• Students choose three or more questions and interview their partner. Encourage them to follow up with further questions or explanations.
• Look at the Writing guide with the class.
• Students expand their notes into a paragraph about their partner.
• Ask them to check their work. Encourage pairs to read each other's paragraphs and to suggest corrections or improvements to their partner.
• Collect the finished work to mark, and choose one or two paragraphs to read out in the next lesson.

Example answer
I spoke to Eva. She's good at music and she loves playing the keyboard. She's also good at writing stories and drawing. Her brother often annoys her because he's lazy and he makes stupid jokes. She worries about her grandfather because he's ill and he's getting old.

Extra exercises

1 • Explain that the conversation is taking place in a shoe shop. Speaker A is a shop assistant.
  • Students read the assistant's sentences and choose the correct replies from the customer.

Answers 1 c   2 f   3 e   4 b   5 d

2 • Remind students of the use of *will* for either offers or spontaneous decisions.
  • Ask them to choose the correct words.

Answers
1 I'm going to   2 I'll   3 We're going to
4 Are you going to   5 I'll   6 are going to

3 • Students choose the correct words to complete the conversation.
  • You could ask them to practise the conversation in pairs.

Answers 1 a   2 a   3 b   4 c   5 a

4 • Ask students to find the words for sports clothes.

Answers
1 swimsuit   2 trunks   3 goggles
4 wetsuits   5 tracksuit

5 • Students choose the right words.

Answers 1 b   2 a   3 c   4 b   5 a

6

- Ask students to work on the translations in pairs or small groups, and then discuss with the whole class.

Extra reading

Life and culture The history of the Olympics

> **BACKGROUND**
>
> **Olympia** is in the western Peloponnese in southern Greece. It was once a very important religious sanctuary, dominated by the enormous temple of the god Zeus. Extensive remains of the ancient site still exist at Olympia, including the stadium for foot races and the hippodrome for horse races. Other events included wrestling, boxing, javelin, discus, long jump and pentathlon.
>
> Some events were held here in the 2004 Olympics, hosted by Athens. Medal winners at these Games were crowned with wreaths of green leaves, following the practice of the ancient Games.
>
> **The modern Olympic Games** have been held every four years since 1896, except for breaks during the two World Wars.

Lead in

- Brainstorm with the class to suggest as many Olympic sports as possible, and write them on the board. Include the word *wrestling* in the list and help with the pronunciation: /ˈreslɪŋ/.

Task

- Briefly discuss the last Olympic Games. Ask students to say when/where it took place and to mention any notable events or achievements that they remember.
- Teach or revise the word *ancient* (/ˈeɪnʃnt/). Ask students what they know about the ancient Olympic Games: *When did they start? Where did they take place? Who competed? Did women compete? Which of the events on the board were in the ancient Olympics?* If students aren't sure of the answers, ask them to guess, but don't confirm or correct their answers yet.

- Give students time to read through the text themselves.
- Read the first half of the text aloud and help with new vocabulary (for example, *historians, event, religious*). Check the answers to the pre-reading questions.
- Read the second half of the text. Ask students to use the context to work out the meaning of *restart, design, flag* and *represent*.
- Ask some questions to test comprehension, for example:
  - *Who organised the first modern Olympics? (Pierre de Coubertin.)*
  - *What was his nationality? (French.)*
  - *Did the Games take place in France? (No, in Greece.)*
  - *What's on the Olympic flag? (Five rings.)*
  - *Why are the colours important? (There's at least one colour from every country's flag.)*
  - *What colours are there from our flag?*
- Read out the questions or choose students to do so. Ask students to say which questions go with the first half of the text and which with the second. Remind them to look carefully at the question words to make sure they select the right information.
- Students answer the questions. They could work on this individually or in pairs.
- Ask about the time and place of the next Olympic Games. If bids are being prepared or considered for the city to host the Games after the next ones, you could also ask students to predict which city will win, and to say why.

Answers

1. In 776BC.
2. Only one (Greek).
3. Coroebus of Elis.
4. Wrestling, horse racing.
5. He was a Frenchman. He organised the first modern Olympic Games.
6. In Athens.
7. Nearly 300.
8. They represent the five continents.
9. Over 11,000.

Goals

6 Choices

STEP 1

Grammar: First conditional
Vocabulary: At the table
Expressions: Polite requests
Communicative tasks:
 Talking about results
 Making a conversation in a restaurant

1 Key vocabulary *At the table*

a
- Read out the words in the box and then set the time limit for the matching task. Some of the words should be familiar and most should be fairly easy to guess.
- Play the recording. Students listen and check.
- You may want to mention the words for different types of spoon: *soup spoon, dessert spoon, teaspoon, tablespoon*.
- Play the recording again and ask students to repeat. Make sure they say the long /uː/ in *spoon*. Note that *salt* can be pronounced /sɔːlt/ or /sɒlt/ and note the pronunciation of *serviette* /sɜːvɪˈjet/.

Tapescript/Answers

1 salt and pepper   5 fork
2 menu   6 plate
3 glass   7 knife
4 spoon   8 serviette

b
- Students match the words and the definitions.

Answers
2 glass 3 salt and pepper 4 spoon
5 plate 6 knife 7 menu 8 serviette

c
- Read out the example definition to the class and elicit the answer.
- In pairs, students take turns to choose a definition from 1b and read it out. The other student provides the word without looking at his/her book.

2 Presentation
You'll be ill if you eat all that

BACKGROUND
Basmati rice is a firm, long-grain white rice that comes from India or Pakistan. It is usually eaten with curries.

a
- Look at the photo with the class and ask students to identify the people and where they are.

- Read through the menu. Elicit the meaning of *starter*, *main course* and *dessert* and help with the new words for food on the menu. Give special attention to the pronunciation of *dessert* /dɪˈzɜːt/, and draw attention to the /ə/ sound in *melon* /ˈmelən/ and *carrot* /ˈkærət/.
- Ask the question and then play the recording. Students listen and read.
- Ask: *Who isn't having a starter? (Ana and Charlie.) What are the others having? (Mr Grant's having pâté. Mrs Grant's having soup.)*

Answer Two people.

b
- Play the recording again. Pause to check comprehension. Elicit the meaning of new words (for example, *starving, pass, order, certainly*).
- Point out the use of *I'll have* as Mr and Mrs Grant decide what they want to order. Compare this with the requests from Ana and Charlie: *Could I have ...? I'd like ....*
- Drill some of the useful expressions in the conversation:
  – *What do you fancy?*
  – *I think I'll have pâté.*
  – *I'm starving.*
- Students read the sentences and look back at the text to decide if they're true or false.

Answers
1 True.
2 False. He's going to have steak.
3 False. He's going to have pâté.
4 True.
5 False. She isn't going to have a starter.
6 True.
7 True.
8 True.
9 False. She isn't going to have a dessert.

3 Key grammar *First conditional*

- Students complete the explanation.
- Emphasise the use of the present simple in the *if* clause, even though it's referring to a possible event in the future.
- Point out that the *if* clause can come before the result clause or vice versa. The meaning is the same.
- Note that when the *if* clause comes first, it is followed by a comma. When the result clause comes first, we don't use a comma.
- Focus on the Remember! box. Make it clear that we never say *will/won't can*. *Can* and *can't* change completely to *will/won't be able to* in the future.

Answer present

52 Unit 6

4 Practice

- Look at the example. You may want to go through the whole exercise orally with the class.
- Students write the full sentences.
- You could ask students to say the sentences with the clauses in the opposite order. (For example: *Jay will give you Ana's address if you ask him.*)
- Note that there is further work on comprehension and practice of the first conditional in the Module 3 Review at the end of Unit 6.

Answers
2 If you ask Jay, he'll give you Ana's address.
3 You won't be healthy if you don't eat enough fruit.
4 If we visit Lightning Ridge, we'll be able to watch the famous goat races.
5 If I don't do my homework now, I won't be able to go out later.
6 Charlie will eat your chips if you don't finish them.

- Pattern drill: TRP page 14 (Unit 6, Step 1, drill 1)

OPTION
Start some conditional sentences for students to finish, for example:
- *If it rains at lunchtime, ...*
- *If we get too much homework next week, ...*
- *If the school library isn't open tomorrow, ...*
- *[Teacher's name] will be pleased if ...*
- *[Football team] won't win next Saturday if ...*

5 Key expressions *Polite requests*

a
- Students match the sentence parts.
- Ask students to translate the sentences into their language. Point out that *Could I ...?* is a little more formal and polite than *Can I ...?*
- Say the requests and ask students to repeat.

Answers 1 d 2 f 3 e 4 a 5 c 6 b

b
- Elicit other endings for the sentence openings (1–6).

Example answers
1 Could you help me with this exercise, please?
2 I'd like a cheese sandwich, please.
3 Could I have a glass of water, please?
4 Could I ask a question, please?
4 Could we have a table by the window?
5 Can I have some bread, please?

- Pattern drill: TRP page 14 (Unit 6, Step 1, drill 2)

6 Key pronunciation /e/ /eɪ/ /ʌ/

- Play the recording while students listen and read the words.
- Play the recording again and ask students to repeat the words.
- Students say the words to themselves and find the odd one out in each group. Ask them to say why it is the odd one out.

Answers
1 plaice (The vowel sound is /eɪ/, not /e/.)
2 said (The vowel sound is /e/, not /eɪ/.)
3 goat (The vowel sound is /əʊ/, not /ʌ/.)

OPTION
If you have time, you could write up one or two sentences with a mixture of the three sounds, for example:
Fred ate a plate of steak and some onion curry for lunch.
Ask students to identify the three sounds and to repeat the sentences.

7 Speaking *At a restaurant*

- Ask students to work in groups.
- Remind them of the use of *(I think) I'll have ...* for decisions about the meal, and the expressions for polite requests (*I'd like ..., Could I/we have ...?*) when they're talking to the waiter. Ask the person playing the waiter to repeat back the orders to check them.
- You could ask one or two groups to act out their conversation for the class.

Grammar: *will* and *might*
Communicative tasks:
  Making promises
  Talking about uncertainty and probability in the future

STEP 2

1 Share your ideas

- Look at the map and the photo of Kenya. Ask the question and invite students to give their ideas in sentences using *will*. You could prompt them with questions, for example: *What animals will you see? What will the weather be like? What will the houses be like? Will life be very different from life here?*

Choices 53

2 Presentation *You might not enjoy it!*

BACKGROUND

British students often take a year off, known as a *gap year*, between finishing school and starting university. Many travel during this period, and some participate in community service projects specially organised for young people in different parts of the world. They often work closely with local people on projects which may include the construction and repair of buildings, setting up electricity and water supplies and teaching or sports training at primary school.

a • Ask students about the photos of people. Make sure they recognise Lizzie from Unit 4 and explain that she's going to Kenya during her 'gap year' when she finishes school.
   • Read out the questions and the introduction. Play the recording. Students listen and read.

   Answers
   Lizzie's father and mother are worried. Her father is negative about the trip. Lizzie is positive and excited.

b • Read the texts aloud or play the recording again. Pause to elicit or explain the meaning of new vocabulary (for example, *go clubbing, malaria, tablets, promise, miss*).
   • Focus on the difference between *will* and *might*. Ask: *Is Lizzie's father sure about the heat and the mosquitoes?* (Yes.) *Is her mother sure that Lizzie will feel homesick?* (No – but it's a possibility.) Explain that *You never know* means 'You can't be sure – it might happen'.
   • Focus on Lizzie's speech and point out that we use *will* when we're making promises.
   • Drill some sentences with the target language, for example:
     – It'll be very hot.
     – You probably won't like the food.
     – You might feel homesick.
     – You might not enjoy it.
     – I'll take my tablets.
     – I won't forget.
   • Read through the questions with the class. Ask students to match them with the answers.
   • Play the recording. Students listen and check.
   • Choose pairs of students to ask and answer the questions across the class.

   Tapescript/Answers
   1 e Will it be very hot in Kenya?
        Yes, it will.
   2 h Will there be many mosquitoes?
        Yes, there will.
   3 d Will Lizzie be able to go clubbing?
        No, she won't.
   4 c Will she like the food?
        She might like it. She might not like it.
   5 f Will she feel homesick?
        She might miss her family. She can't be sure.
   6 a Is Lizzie's mum sure she'll be ill?
        No, she isn't, but it's possible.
   7 i What will Lizzie take every day?
        Some special tablets.
   8 g What other promises does she make?
        She'll contact her parents regularly.
   9 b Will Martin forget about Lizzie?
        No. He'll write to her every week.

3 Key grammar *will* and *might*

a • Discuss translations with the class.
b • Point out that here the examples with *will* are predictions about the future.
   • Remind students that we use *probably* if we think the event is very likely (but not certain) to happen. Explain that we use *probably* with *will*, <u>not</u> with *might*.
   • Students complete the explanations.
   • Remind students of the word order when we use *probably* with *will* and *won't*: *You'll probably like it* but *You probably won't like it*.
   • Focus on the use of *might/might not*. Emphasise that we use this verb to talk about something we think is possible in the future – but we don't really know.
   • Students complete the explanation.
   • You could mention that it's possible to use the contracted form (*mightn't*) for *might not*.

   Answers
   will, won't
   will, won't
   might, might not

4 Practice

a • Make sure it's clear that all these sentences are promises that Lizzie makes before her trip to Africa.
   • Ask students to complete the sentences. They can do this orally and/or in writing.

   Answers
   2 'll be   3 won't go out with   4 'll wear
   5 'll send   6 won't forget

   Try this!
   The missing letters are all vowels: *a, e, i, o* and *u*.
   Answers: swim in the Indian Ocean, study wild animals, learn another language, go on safari

54 Unit 6

b
- Students complete the sentences. Remind them to be careful with the word order.

> **Answers**
> 2 probably won't like 3 probably won't have
> 4 'll probably win 5 'll probably study

c
- Read out the example dialogue. Use intonation to suggest the enthusiasm of the first speaker and the negativity of Lizzie's dad.
- In pairs, students work out the replies and then practise the dialogues.
- Ask different pairs to say the dialogues. Encourage them to say their parts as expressively as possible.

> **Answers**
> 2 might not like it 3 might bite us 4 might rain
> 5 might crash

d
- Students can prepare by writing sentences using *will (probably)* or *might* about their future.
- In pairs, students talk about their future.
- Note that there is further work on comprehension and practice of *will* and *might* in the Module 3 Review at the end of Unit 6.

5 Listening *Song*

a
- 🔊 Ask students to close their books. Play the song. The first time through, let students simply listen and get a sense of the rhythm and melody.
- 🔊 Ask the question and play the song again.

> **Answer** The singer's girlfriend.

b
- Ask: *What's happening tomorrow?* (*The singer's going away.*) Make it clear that he's making promises to his girlfriend before he leaves.
- 🔊 Play the song again. Ask students to listen for what the singer says about the future and the promises they hear, and write them on the board. Point out that *true* means 'faithful' in this context. Explain the meaning of *kiss* and *lips*.
- 🔊 Ask students to turn to page 144. Play the song again and encourage the class to sing along.

> **Answers**
> I'll kiss you.
> I'll always be true.
> I'll write home every day,
> I'll send all my loving to you.
> I'll pretend (that I'm missing ...)
> ... hope that my dreams will come true.

6 Writing and speaking *Going abroad*

- Give the example of a trip to Britain. Ask students for some responses to the questions.
- Ask students to choose a country and to imagine what it will be like to spend a month there. Ask them to make quick notes first and then to write sentences.
- In pairs, students tell each other about their trip. Encourage them to speak without reading aloud, referring to their written sentences when they need to.

> **Example answer**
> I'm going to spend a month in Japan. It'll be very different from [student's country] and I might meet some interesting people. I won't miss school, but I'll probably miss my family and friends. Also, I might have some problems because I won't be able to speak Japanese and people might not understand me. But I think I'll enjoy the trip.

STEP 3

Reading skills: Identifying the topic
Word work: Compound nouns
Communicative task:
  Making predictions about the future

1 Share your ideas *Artificial intelligence*

- Look at the photos with the class and use them to establish the meaning of *robot*. Practise the pronunciation: /ˈrəʊbɒt/.
- Ask the questions and invite different students to answer. Briefly discuss films that students mention. Ask: *What are the robots like? What do they do? How are they different from the humans in the film? Are they good or bad?*

2 Reading

a
- Ask students to read through the text quickly to find the answer to the question.

> **Answer** Hal is a robot.

b **Comprehension check**
- 🔊 Play the recording of the text. Help with new vocabulary (for example, *chairman, computer chip, oven, laboratory, common, smart, develop, grow up, language level*). Wherever possible, ask students to work out the meanings from the context. Give special attention to the pronunciation of *oven* /ˈʌvən/ and *laboratory* /ləˈbɒrətri/.
- Read through the questions and ask students to find the answers in the text. They could work on this in pairs.
- Ask students for their responses to the last question in the text.

Choices 55

> **Answers**
> 1 No, he wasn't.
> 2 No, they weren't.
> 3 Coffee makers, fridges, washing machines and ovens.
> 4 They're getting smarter. They're starting to think.
> 5 He's learning to speak.
> 6 Anat Treister-Goren. She talks to Hal and reads him children's stories.
> 7 His language level is improving quickly.
> 8 Yes, he will.

c **Reading skills** *Identifying the topic*
- Ask students to think about the main idea of the text. Point out that although the writer talks a lot about Hal, this is only one part of a more general idea about the present and future development of computer technology.
- Remind students that paragraphs are 'steps' in the organisation of a text. The paragraphs are all related to the main idea of the text, but each one develops its own set of thoughts.
- Ask students to identify the topic of each paragraph.

> **Answers**
> Paragraph 2 c   Paragraph 3 a
> Paragraph 4 e   Paragraph 5 b

3 Word work *Compound nouns*

a
- Look at the example. Point out that in compound nouns two words are put together to give the meaning.
- Students match the words to form compound nouns.
- Read out the list and ask students to repeat. Check that they put the main stress on the first syllable of each compound, except for *mobile phone*, where the main stress is on *phone*.

> **Answers**
> 2 dining room   3 traffic jam   4 car park
> 5 bus stop   6 mobile phone   7 alarm clock
> 8 washing machine   9 computer chip   10 pop star

b
- Students can work individually or in pairs to think of more compound nouns. There are many examples, which could include: *art gallery, living room, fitting room, clothes shop, golf course, heart attack, boat trip, disc jockey*. They could also include nouns where the two parts are joined together to form a single word, for example, *bedroom, classroom, wetsuit, beefburger, bookshop*.

4 Speaking and writing
My future predictions

- Read out the questions. Check that students know the meaning of *hope*.

- Read through the Writing guide to give them ideas for expressing different kinds of opinions.
- Look at the examples with the class. Ask students to say if they agree with these statements. Invite them to offer their own opinions about the future and to discuss them together.
- Students write sentences. Encourage them to use a variety of language to express their opinions, as suggested in the Writing guide.
- Take in the finished work to mark.

> **Example answer**
> The Earth's climate will change and we probably won't be able to stop it.
> I think we might discover life on another planet.
> Computers will become incredibly fast and powerful.
> I don't think I'll be famous, but I hope I'll have a happy life.

OPTION
You could type out and photocopy a selection of the class's predictions (choosing one from each student if possible) and hand them out in the next lesson. Ask the class to decide which prediction is
– the most optimistic
– the most pessimistic
– the funniest
– the most likely to come true.

Extra exercises

1
- Students read the questions and choose the correct replies.
- You could choose pairs of students to ask and answer the questions across the class.

> **Answers** 1 b   2 b   3 c   4 b   5 c

2
- Students choose the correct alternatives to complete the conditional sentences.

> **Answers** 1 b   2 a   3 b   4 a   5 a

3
- Look at the example and remind students of the word order: *will probably* but *probably won't*.
- Students put the words in the correct order.

> **Answers**
> 2 I might study French next year.
> 3 We'll probably go shopping on Saturday.
> 4 Will you be able to finish your homework?
> 5 I probably won't go out tonight.
> 6 They might not come to our party.

Unit 6

4

- Ask students to read through the text. Tell them that the missing words are all things we use at the table.
- Students work out the words and use them to complete the text.

Answers
1 menu   2 spoon   3 plate   4 knife
5 pepper   6 serviette   7 fork

5

- Students use their own ideas to complete the four replies. Explain that there are lots of possible answers here.
- Ask different students to read out their replies.

Example answers
Can I have melon, please?
Could I have chicken and mushrooms?
Yes, I'd like some mineral water, please.
No, thank you.

6

- Ask students to work on the translations in pairs or small groups, and then discuss with the whole class.

Extra reading

Life and culture   Journey into space

BACKGROUND

The International Space Station has been developed by 16 nations: the USA, Canada, Japan, Russia, Brazil and 11 nations of the European Space Agency. It orbits the Earth at an altitude of 250 miles (400 km) and is staffed by international crews of astronauts who carry out research in solar-powered laboratories.

The first 'space tourist' was American businessman Dennis Tito, who was flown to the Russian Mir space station in 2000. Two years later a South African millionaire, Mark Shuttleworth, spent ten days on the International Space Station. The cost of each flight was approximately $20 million.

Lead in

- Ask students to name the planets in our solar system, using their own language. Then ask them to say any of the names that they know in English. Help them with those that they don't know. (Mercury, Venus, Earth, Mars, Jupiter, Saturn, Uranus, Neptune, Pluto.)
- Elicit information about the planets, for example:
  - The planets move round the sun.
  - Mercury is the closest to the sun.
  - Earth is between Venus and Mars.
  - Jupiter is the largest planet.
  - Pluto is the smallest planet.
  - Saturn has got coloured rings of gas.
  - Some people think there might be life on Mars.

- If there have been any interesting news stories recently about space flights or discoveries about outer space, encourage students to talk about them. Make sure that they understand the meaning of *space*.

Task

- Look at the pictures with the class. Elicit or provide some basic information about the International Space Station.
- Give students time to read through the text themselves. Then ask them to say what they think the main idea is.
- Read the text aloud and help with new vocabulary (for example, *extremely, zero-gravity, wedding*). Ask students to say what they think a *space plane*, a *space hotel* and a *spacewalk* might be.
- Ask questions to test their understanding of the tenses, for example:
  - Does space tourism exist now?
  - Is it cheap now?
  - Is the writer sure about cheaper space travel in the future?
  - Is the writer sure that a space hotel will exist?
- Read out the sentences or choose students to do so. Students look back at the text to find the answers. They could do this individually or in pairs. Remind them to correct the false sentences.
- Ask: *Do you think you'll take a trip into space one day? Would you like to go?* Discuss the questions with the class.

Answers
1 False. They can go into space if they're rich.
2 True.
3 False. Tourists can stay there.
4 False. The richest people travelled by plane.
5 False. They are planning to build space planes.
6 True.
7 False. A Japanese company is building a space hotel now.
8 False. You'll be able to go for a spacewalk.

OPTION

You could ask students to identify the topic of each paragraph of the text and suggest a heading for each one. For example:
Paragraph 1: How about a holiday in space?
Paragraph 2: Space tourism – but only for the rich
Paragraph 3: Cheaper space travel in the future?
Paragraph 4: A hotel in space

Choices

Module 3 Review

Grammar check

1 The future with the present continuous, *going to* and *will*

Work it out for yourself

A
- Students look at the sentences in 1–3 and decide which of the two meanings is the right one.

Answers 1 b 2 a 3 a, a

B
- Students choose the verb form for each explanation. Ask them to look back at the sentences in 1A if they aren't sure.
- You could ask them to suggest some more example sentences for each verb form.

Answers
1 will 2 present continuous
3 going to 4 will

1.1
- Ask students to choose the right words. Remind them to look carefully at the context to decide which verb form is correct.

Answers
1 I'm starting 2 I'm going to 3 I'll 4 we'll
5 He isn't working 6 I'll try 7 I'm going to phone

1.2
- Students write the correct form of the verb in brackets.
- Ask them to compare and discuss answers with a partner before you check with the whole class.
- You could ask students to match the sentences with the explanations in 1B.

Answers
1 won't like 2 're playing 3 'll phone
4 'm going to do 5 'll write

2 The first conditional

Work it out for yourself

A
- Students look at the conditional sentence and match the two clauses with the explanations.

Answers 1 a 2 b

B
- Students answer the questions and complete the explanation of the form of the first conditional. Ask them to look back at the example in 2A if they aren't sure.
- Emphasise the use of the present simple in the *if* clause, even though we're referring to a possibility in the future.

Answers
1 present simple 2 the future with *will*
present simple, *will*, *won't*

- Look at the example with the class. Make sure it's clear that the first sentence describes the possible future action and the second describes the result of that action. Remind students of the comma after the *if* clause.
- Students rewrite the sentences using the first conditional. You may want to go through the exercise orally before asking them to write.
- Remind students that we can put the clauses in the opposite order. Ask them to do this with the sentences they have written.

Answers
2 If I'm late, will you wait for me?
3 If you wear your boots, your feet won't get wet.
4 If I do my homework now, I'll be able to go out later.
5 If my brother doesn't get a ticket, he won't be able to go to the match.
6 If you don't put salt in the soup, it won't be nice.

3 *will*, *might* and *probably*

Work it out for yourself

- You could ask students to read through the sentences and say which speakers are sure about the result of the race and which are not sure.
- Students put the sentences in order 1–6, from the most optimistic (1) to the most pessimistic (6). You could ask them to discuss this in pairs.

Answers
1 Tom 2 Jack 3 Dave
4 James 5 Pete 6 Mark

3.1
- Students rewrite the sentences using *might* and *might not*.

Answers
2 I might discover the secrets of the universe.
3 I might not pass my exams.
4 My dreams might not come true.
5 I might not be successful.

3.2
- Look at the example and elicit the negative form of the sentence. Remind students of the difference in word order: *I'll probably go* but *I probably won't go* (not *I won't probably go*).
- Students rewrite the sentences using *probably*.

> **Answers**
> 2 I probably won't buy anything.
> 3 England probably won't beat Brazil tonight.
> 4 But it'll probably be an exciting match.
> 5 I probably won't go out this evening.
> 6 I'll probably stay at home.

Study skills 3
Making a vocabulary notebook
- Read through the suggestions for recording vocabulary.
- Choose a selection of new words from Module 3 and write them on the board. Ask students first to help you organise them alphabetically with translations and then to put them in thematic groups. In both cases, elicit the part of speech and the main stress.
- Discuss the advantages of each method of recording.
- Ask students to keep a vocabulary notebook and to add to it throughout the course.

How's it going?
Your rating
- Students look back at the exercises in the Grammar check and make their own assessment of how well they understand and remember the different language points.

Vocabulary
- Students practise some of the recording techniques discussed in Study skills 3.
- When they have written their words, ask them to compare what they have done with a partner.

Test a friend
- Look at the example questions and elicit the correct answers.
- Students refer back to the texts in Units 5 and 6 and write several questions to test their partner. They then ask and answer in pairs.

> **Answers**
> Because she's going to join a sports club.
> *All My Loving.* (See page 144.)

Correcting mistakes
- The sentences listed here contain some common errors. Ask students to rewrite them correctly.

- Some sentences contain more than one error. Make sure students are aware of this, and that they find both errors in questions 1 and 3.
- Emphasise the importance of going back over their work to check for errors when they finish a piece of writing.

> **Answers**
> 1 I'm going shopping tomorrow. I'm going to buy some swimming trunks.
> 2 We're going to leave at nine thirty.
> 3 I'll be free next week.
> 4 If Charlie's late, Penny will be annoyed.
> 5 I might come tomorrow. I'm not sure.

Your Workbook
- Students should complete the Learning diary when they come to the end of each unit.

Coursework 3
My guidebook
Shopping in London
- Ask students to say what they can see in the photos on Ana's guidebook page. For each shop, ask: *What sort of shop is it?* or *What do they sell?*
- Give students time to read through the text on their own.
- Focus on some of the new vocabulary in the text (for example, *optician, travel agent, colourful, jewellery, souvenir*). Help students to work out or guess the meanings.
- You can ask some questions to check comprehension, for example:
  – *What can you buy at Davenport's?* (Jokes and puzzles.)
  – *What's the best shop for clothes, in Ana's opinion?* (Topshop.)
  – *Is the Virgin Megastore open every day?* (Yes, it is.)
  – *What's the largest shop in Ana's list?* (Selfridges.)
  – *Where can you buy scary books?* (Forbidden Planet.)
- Ask students to suggest some shops and markets that they would recommend on their own shopping page. Encourage them to think about a range of different businesses and elicit some information about each one (for example, location, opening hours, the best products for sale). Invite some discussion here, including agreement and disagreement about the best places to go.
- Ask students to plan their text. They should write at least four paragraphs and illustrate them as they wish. They may want to gather some extra information by visiting the shops or checking their websites on the Internet.
- Set a time limit, allowing one to two weeks for work on the project. Some work may be done in class and some at home.
- Ask students to check their text before they write a final version and design their page.

Module 4 Your world

See page 7 of the Introduction for ideas on how to use the Module opening pages.

Answers
1 c 2 b 3 a 4 e 5 d

7 Achievements

STEP 1

Grammar: Present perfect
Communicative tasks:
Describing achievements and changes

1 Share your ideas

- Focus on the photos and ask students to say what they can see.
- Use the photos to revise key words (for example, *environment, pollution, destroy, medicine*) and to introduce new ones (for example, *satellite, communication, to pollute*). You may need to help with other new words that students want to use here. Collect useful vocabulary on the board as they comment on each photo.

Example answers
There are some beautiful cities.
The air is very dirty/polluted now.
We can prevent a lot of illnesses.
We haven't got enough food for everyone.

2 Presentation *I've changed the world*

a
- Make sure students understand that the conversation is an imaginary conversation between the human brain and the Earth.
- Students read to get a general idea of the two sides of the debate. Ask them to answer the question. Ask: *What does the Earth think?* (*That a lot of things in the world are worse.*)

Answer No – the brain is sure, but the Earth isn't.

b
- Read through the conversation. Pause after each speech to check comprehension and to help with vocabulary. Give special attention to the new verbs: *produce, save (lives), take care of, improve*. For irregular past participles, elicit the infinitive form of the verbs.
- You may want to draw attention to the use of *the* + singular noun to talk in general about products and inventions (*I've produced the car, I've invented the telephone*).

- Read through the sentences and explain that they are missing parts of the conversation. Elicit or explain the meaning of *selfish* and remind students of the negative prefix *un-* (Unit 3 Step 3) to elicit the meaning of *unkind*. For each sentence, ask: *Who do you think says this, the human brain or the Earth?*
- Ask students to look carefully at the context to find the right place for each sentence in the conversation.
- 🔊 Play the recording. Students listen, read and check their answers.
- Drill some sentences from the text, for example:
  - *I've changed the world.*
  - *Have you forgotten about me?*
  - *You've made some amazing machines.*
  - *Medicine has saved their lives.*
  - *People haven't learnt to share.*
- Discuss the conversation with the class. Ask them to say who they think is right – or are both sides right?

Answers 1 c 2 e 3 d 4 b 5 a

OPTION You can ask students to practise the conversation in pairs.

3 Key grammar *Present perfect*

a
- Read through the table with the class. Ask students to say the full form of the contracted forms.
- Focus on the examples of the present perfect. Draw attention to the use of *have* and explain that the verb form that follows is called the *past participle*.
- Draw attention to the past participles. Explain that the *-ed* ending is the regular form. *Learn* is an irregular verb and the past participle has a different ending.
- Ask students to turn to the irregular verb list on page 143. Point out that the form of the past participle is often the same as the past simple – but not always.
- Students complete the questions and short answers and the explanation of the form of the present perfect.

Unit 7

- Read through the rest of the explanation. Explain the meaning of *achievement*. Point out that we often use the present perfect to refer to something that happened at some time in the past <u>and is still important now</u>. The action(s) happened in the past but we're seeing it/them in relation to the present. For example:
  - *I've changed the world. (It's a different place now.)*
  - *I've built some fantastic cities. (I'm proud of this now.)*
  - *Your technology hasn't produced enough food. (It's a problem now.)*

> **Answers**
> Have, haven't
> has
> has, haven't

b
- Students find the past participles in the text and list them with their infinitive forms.
- Ask students to say which verbs are regular and which are irregular. You could ask them to say the past simple forms as well as the participles.

> **Answers**
>
> | Verb | Past participle |
> |---|---|
> | forget | forgotten |
> | produce | produced |
> | make | made |
> | pollute | polluted |
> | destroy | destroyed |
> | take | taken |
> | save | saved |
> | invent | invented |
> | put | put |
> | improve | improved |
> | learn | learnt |
> | do | done |

OPTION
Help students to make some sentences about achievements, using verbs from the text in the present perfect. For example:
Brazil has produced some great footballers.
My maths results have improved.
They've built a new sports centre in our town.

4 Practice

a
- Students put the words in the correct order.
- Choose students to ask and answer across the class.
- In pairs, they ask and answer the questions.

> **Answers**
> 2 Have people walked on Mars?
>   No, they haven't.
> 3 Has the climate changed?
>   Yes, it has.
> 4 Have we protected the environment?
>   No, we haven't.
> 5 Has pollution destroyed a lot of trees?
>   Yes, it has.
> 6 Has the world stayed the same?
>   No, it hasn't.

b
- Look at the example with the class. Note that here the present perfect verb refers not to an achievement, but to a recent event. Here again, the event is in the past but we're seeing it in terms of its effect on the present. (*My watch has stopped – it isn't working now.*)
- You may want to go through the whole exercise with the class and then ask them to write the answers. Tell them to use contracted forms with pronouns.
- Note that there is further work on comprehension and practice of the present perfect in the Module 4 Review at the end of Unit 8.

> **Answers**
> 2 've lost   3 's made   4 haven't done
> 5 hasn't arrived   6 've built   7 has changed
> 8 haven't put

- Pattern drill: TRP pages 14-15 (Unit 7, Step 1, drills 1 and 2)

OPTION
Ask students to think of a sentence giving a present situation and the reason for it, for example: *I'm not very happy because I've lost my jacket.* Remind them not to use a past time expression because the present perfect refers to an indefinite time in the past.
Students write their sentence, gapping the present perfect verb, for example, *I've lost*, for their partner to complete. Students work in pairs and complete each other's gapped sentences.

5 Listening and speaking
What a difference!

a
- Keep the work on this listening text light-hearted. The advert is obviously not a real one and it should generate some fun.
- Look at the picture and explain to students that they are going to hear an advert for the CD-ROM on the radio. Explain the meaning of *tame* and *tamer* (as in *lion-tamer*).
- Play the recording once and check the answer to question 1.

Achievements

- 🔊 Play the recording again up to ... *you'll be amazed at the difference* and ask for suggestions for adjectives to describe Eddie before his parents bought *Teentamer*. Then play the rest of the recording and elicit adjectives to describe Eddie after *Teentamer*. Introduce the new adjective *rude*.

Answers
1 Parents with difficult teenage children.
2 Example answers:
Before: difficult, moody, rude, lazy, selfish
After: polite, helpful, tidy, hard-working, serious, kind, generous

Tapescript
PRESENTER: Parents, have you got a difficult teenager? Is your house like this?
MOTHER: Eddie! Turn that computer off and do your homework.
EDDIE: Oh, Mum! Leave me alone. I haven't finished this game!
MOTHER: Eddie! Do as I say!
EDDIE: Yeah, yeah. All right. In a minute ...
PRESENTER: Parents, are your kids a problem? Are they moody and rude? Do they refuse to help at home? Well, buy our new *TeenTamer* CD-ROM! *TeenTamer* is full of ideas on how you can train your teenager to be polite and helpful. Follow our programme and you'll be amazed at the difference.
MOTHER: Eddie? Where are you?
EDDIE: I'm upstairs, Mum. I've tidied my room and now I'm doing my homework.
MOTHER: That's great, Eddie.
I can't believe it! The *TeenTamer* programme has changed him so much! Look! He's done the shopping, and he's washed the car. We haven't argued at all, and he's even bought me some flowers! He's a completely different boy!
EDDIE: I've finished my homework, Mum. Shall I do the washing up?
MOTHER: Yes, please!
PRESENTER: A happy mother! The *TeenTamer* CD-ROM has improved the lives of thousands of families. Buy it! Try it! It'll change your world.

b
- Read through the sentences with the class. Draw attention to the irregular participles *come* and *bought*.
- 🔊 Tell students to focus on the second half of the advert. Play the recording again. Students write down the sentence numbers when they hear the actions described.
- Pick out and practise some useful expressions for the writing and speaking task in Exercise 6. For example: *You'll be amazed at the difference. I can't believe it. He's a completely different boy. It'll change your world.*

Answers 4 and 6

c
- Make sure students understand the meaning of *perfect*. Give them a few moments to gather some ideas.
- Ask different students to say sentences with *I've* and *I haven't*.

6 Writing and speaking *An advert*

- Read out the instruction and look at the example. Make sure students understand that this time the CD-ROM is for teenagers who want to change their parents. Elicit a few more example sentences to describe the marvellous effects of the product.
- In groups of three, students write their own advert and practise it together. They take the roles of a delighted teenager, a perfect parent and the presenter. Encourage them to use their imagination and their sense of humour.
- Walk round the class, giving help where necessary, especially with the formation of present perfect verbs.
- Invite different groups to perform their advert for the class.

Example answer
PRESENTER: Hello, teenagers! Have you got moody, difficult parents? Listen!
GIRL: Mum, can I have chips with dinner tonight?
MUM: No, they're bad for you. Have you tidied your room?
PRESENTER: Is your house like this? Buy our new *ParentTamer* CD-ROM and train your parents! We've got lots of useful ideas. You'll be amazed at the difference.
MUM: Your dinner's ready. It's beefburger and chips. I'll tidy your room after dinner – you can watch TV. Or I can help you with your homework if you want.
GIRL: Thanks, Mum.
This is amazing! I've tried *ParentTamer* and it's changed my life. Look! My mum has cooked beefburgers and chips for me. She's going to tidy my room and she hasn't asked me to help.
PRESENTER: Buy *ParentTamer*! You'll be amazed at the difference!

Grammar: Present perfect and past simple
Vocabulary: Using a machine
Expressions: *I think so. / I don't think so.*
Communicative tasks:
Talking about what people have done and when they did it
Talking about using a machine

STEP 2

1 Key vocabulary *Using a machine*

- Focus on the pictures and ask students to say what they are about (*using a CD player*). Read out the verbs under the pictures.
- Set the time limit. Students put the pictures in order (1-6) of playing and then removing a CD and match them with the verbs. With the example *plug in* supplied, they should be able to guess the other verbs.
- 🔊 Play the recording. Students listen and check.
- Point out that the five phrasal verbs must be used with both parts to give the intended meaning. Draw attention to the verb *unplug* (not *plug out*). You could tell students that we can use *switch on/off* instead of *turn on/off*.
- Note that these phrasal verbs are separable. We can say either *turn the machine on* or *turn on the machine*. However, when we are using a pronoun, only one order is possible: we must say *turn it on* (not *turn on it*).

Tapescript/Answers

1 c plug in   2 a turn on   3 e put in
4 f take out   5 b turn off   6 d unplug

> **OPTION**
>
> You could give some sentences to practise the use of *turn on/off* and *put in/out*. You may also like to add *turn up/down*. Ask students to supply the right verbs. For example:
>
> *I want to cook a chicken, so I'm going to ..... the oven ..... .* (turn on)
>
> *The oven's too hot. You need to ..... it ..... .* (turn down)
>
> *I think the chicken's ready now. I'm going to ..... it ..... .* (take out)
>
> *It's bedtime, so I'm going to ..... the TV ..... .* (turn off)
>
> *You can use the washing machine for those clothes. Open the door and ..... them ..... .* (put in)
>
> *I can't hear the music very well. Would you ..... the radio ..... ?* (turn up)
>
> *It's dark in here. Why don't you ..... the light ..... ?* (turn on)

2 Key pronunciation /ɪ/ /ɒ/ /aʊ/

- Ask students to read the sentences.
- 🔊 Play the recording and ask students to repeat. Make sure they pronounce /ɪ/ and /ɒ/ as short vowels, and that they link up consonant word endings with the following vowels.
- Give attention to the /aʊ/ sound. Accentuate the two separate vowels and then run them together. Ask students to do the same.
- Practise the sound with some other words, for example, *how, shout, town, about*.

3 Presentation *Have you plugged it in?*

a
- Look at the photo and ask: *Where are they? What are they doing?*
- Read out the introduction to the listening. Point out that in this sentence the verb *work* means 'function or operate'. You could mention the common expressions *How does it work?* and *It doesn't work*.
- 🔊 Ask the question, then play the recording. With books closed, students listen for the answer to the question.

> **Answer** He's forgotten to turn the TV on.

b
- 🔊 Play the recording again while students listen and read. Elicit the meaning of *instructions* and *connected*.
- Point out that some sentences are in the past simple while others are in the present perfect. Draw attention to the use of past time expressions with the past simple verbs.
- Drill sentences with the target language, for example:
  - *I've bought a DVD player.*
  - *I bought it yesterday.*
  - *Have you looked at the instructions?*
  - *Yes, I have. I looked at them last night.*

  You could also drill other useful expressions, for example:
  - *That's strange.*
  - *Wait a minute!*
  - *How stupid of me!*

- Read through the questions and ask students to answer in full sentences. They can do this orally and/or in writing. Tell them to look carefully at the verbs in the question and to answer in the same tense.

> **Answers**
>
> 1 He's bought a DVD player.
> 2 He bought it yesterday.
> 3 No, it wasn't.
> 4 Yes, he has.
> 5 He looked at them last night.
> 6 He's connected the DVD player to the TV, he's plugged it in and he's put a DVD in.
> 7 He hasn't turned the TV on.

> **OPTION**
>
> You can ask students to practise the conversation in groups of three, if possible by improvising their own version without reading from the book. You may want to invite one or two groups to perform their conversation for the class.

Achievements

4 Key grammar
Present perfect and past simple

- Ask students to read the examples and complete the explanations.
- Make it clear that the past simple refers to a definite, finished time in the past. However, the present perfect refers to an indefinite time in the past (so there are no past time expressions) and it also relates that time to the present.

Answers
present perfect
past simple

5 Practice

a
- Students match the sentences. Draw attention to the irregular past participle of *break*: *broken*.

Answers   1 b   2 d   3 e   4 a   5 c

b
- Ask students to choose the correct verb form. They could work on this in pairs and then write down the sentences. Alternatively, you could do the exercise orally with the class.
- As you go through the answers, ask students to pick out words that helped them to decide which tense to use. Draw attention to the references to the present on the one hand and the past time expressions on the other.
- Check the spelling of *stopped*.

Answers
2 We can go out now. Look! The rain has stopped.
3 An Englishman invented the World Wide Web in 1991.
4 They aren't ready. They haven't finished their breakfast.
5 Where's my bike? Someone has taken it!
6 What's the matter? Have you lost something?
7 I bought a tracksuit at the market last Saturday.
8 I've done my homework. I did it before dinner.

c
- Ask a pair of students to read out the short conversation.
- Make sure students understand they have to change the name of the book and A's response.
- Students practise the conversation in pairs.
- Note that there is further work on comprehension and practice of the present perfect and past simple in the Module 4 Review at the end of Unit 8.

Try this!
Answers: changed, broken, taken, tidied, stopped, bought, plugged, forgotten

OPTION
For more practice with past participles, you could play 'Bingo'. Ask students to write six irregular participles from Unit 7 in a grid. Call out verbs in their infinitive form. Students cross out the matching participles when they hear the verbs. The winner is the first person to cross out all their words and to call out *Bingo!*
Irregular participles: forgotten, built, made, taken, put, done, learnt, lost, come, bought, broken

6 Key expressions
I think so. / I don't think so.

- Ask students to read the sentences and put them in order.
- Make it clear that *I think so* and *I don't think so* are usually responses to a question. We use them to mean: 'The answer is probably *yes/no*, but I'm not quite sure.'
- Say the two expressions and ask students to repeat. Make sure they put the main stress on the word *think*.
- Students practise the conversation in pairs.
- You may want to mention that we can also use these expressions for agreeing or disagreeing. For example:
A: This music is awful.
B: I think so too. / I don't think so.

Answers
I don't understand how this works.
Are there any instructions with it?
Yes, I think so. But I can't find them.
Did you leave them in the shop?
No, I don't think so. They might be in the box somewhere.

7 Writing and speaking *How does it work?*

- Read through the example with the class and elicit some suggestions for the missing parts of the conversation.
- Pairs write their conversation and then practise it together. Walk round the class, helping where necessary.
- Ask some pairs to act out their conversation.

Example answer
A: I've got a problem. I've bought a new video recorder.
B: Great! When did you buy that?
A: I bought it on Thursday at Electromart. Anyway, I'm not sure how it works.
B: Well, have you connected it to the TV?
A: Yes, I have.
B: And have you turned it on?
A: Yes, but nothing's happening.
B: Well, that's strange. Have you plugged it in?
A: Oh! No, I haven't done that. How stupid of me!

Unit 7

STEP 3

Reading skills: Understanding the main idea
Word work: The infinitive of purpose
Communicative task: Writing a letter about a campaign

1 Share your ideas *Our endangered planet*

BACKGROUND

The **Siberian tiger** is the largest member of the cat family. These magnificent animals are now only found in a small area in northeast Russia and it is estimated that there are only about 400 surviving in the wild.

Some other examples of endangered animals: all types of tiger, mountain gorilla, giant panda, rhinoceros, Asian elephant, cheetah, blue whale.

- Read the dictionary definition with the class. Then ask students to give other examples of endangered animals. Help them with vocabulary where necessary.
- Ask for students' ideas about dangers to the environment. Make sure that the destruction of the world's rainforests is raised and use the discussion to revise key words from the reading text (for example, *rainforest, environment, protect, save*). Write brief notes on the board as students suggest ideas.

2 Reading

BACKGROUND

Kids Saving the Rainforest was started in 1998 when Janine Licare and a school friend, Aislin Livingstone, began selling their own artwork to try to raise money. With contributions from friends, classmates and volunteers, the small shop that they set up in Janine's mother's hotel grew into a much larger idea. Now the weekend activities and summer camps run by KSTR are especially to educate and invite support from young people. Children come to learn about the rainforest environment and to help with projects like tree-planting and to care for injured or abandoned animals. They also contribute artwork to sell in the KSTR shop, which operates online.

Preservation of the **Mono Titi monkey** population is one of KSTR's main aims. They build 'monkey bridges' high above the roads to stop the animals being killed on electric wires or by traffic. They also plant trees that provide food and shelter for the monkeys.

The idea of **'Adopt-a-tree'** is that people make a donation and have a new young tree raised under their name, before transplantation into the forest.

a
- Ask students to look at the photos. Tell them that the place is Costa Rica and, if possible, use a map to show the location of the country.
- Introduce the word *monkey*. Ask some questions about the photos, for example: *What kind of place do these monkeys live in? (A rainforest.) How old do you think the girl is? What do you think the children are learning about in the third photo?*
- Explain the meaning of *campaign*.
- Ask students to read the text to find the answers to the questions.

Answers
She started a campaign to protect the rainforest environment around her home.
She decided to start this campaign because the rainforest and its wildlife were disappearing.

b **Comprehension check**
- Play the recording of the text, pausing to help with new vocabulary (for example, *take action, achieve, injured, variety, adopt*). Ask questions to check comprehension, for example: *Why were the animals and birds disappearing? (Because people were destroying the rainforest.) Is the Mono Titi monkey the main animal they're interested in? (Yes.) What do you think the 'Adopt-a-tree' project is?*
- Students read the sentences and complete the true/false exercise. You could ask them to correct the false sentences. Remind them that some sentences should be answered *?* because the information isn't in the text.

Answers
1 T
2 F It was disappearing, but it's still there now.
3 F She started it with a friend.
4 T
5 F They were volunteers.
6 ?
7 T
8 ?

c **Reading skills** *Understanding the main idea*

1
- Read out the topics and ask students to choose the right one.
- Ask them to say why the other two are wrong. What sort of information would we get in a text about Costa Rica or about famous kids?

Answer b

2
- Read out the sentences and ask students to say which gives the main idea of the text.

Achievements   65

- Point out that although protecting trees and helping animals are important in the text, they are parts of the explanation of the work that Janine has done. Neither of them on its own is the main idea (and in fact the last paragraph doesn't mention either of them).

Answer a

OPTION

You may want to ask students to suggest the topic of each paragraph in the text.
Example answers:
1 How Janine's campaign started
2 Aims of the campaign
3 Janine's achievements
4 Janine's international fame

3 Word work *The infinitive of purpose*

- Read the explanation and examples with the class.
- Ask students to match the sentence parts.

Answers 2 f   3 a   4 e   5 c   6 b

4 Writing *A letter*

- This exercise can be started in class and completed for homework.
- Introduce the topic. Explain to the students that they are going to write their letter to *Take Action*, the newsletter which produced the article about Janine Licare.
- Read through the questions and examples. You could choose one of the campaign topics and ask students to suggest ideas for the things that the campaign has achieved.
- Read through the Writing guide with the class. You could sketch the layout of the letter on the board. Point out that if we know the name of the person we're writing to, we use that in the greeting. For people we don't know personally, it's usually best to say *Dear Mr/Mrs/Miss/Ms ...*
- Emphasise that *Yours sincerely* is a formal ending. Note that formal endings like *Yours truly* are becoming increasingly rare, even in business correspondence.
- Tell students that they should end their letter by signing their full name.
- Ask students to decide on a campaign and to think of a name for it. They then make notes in answer to the three questions.
- Students expand their notes into a letter, using the writing guide to organise it and set it out correctly.
- Collect the finished letters to mark and choose two or three to read out in the next lesson. You may want to display the letters in the classroom.

Example answer

14 Parkdale Road
Glastonbury
BA6 9TD

2nd March

Dear Take Action!

I'm writing to tell you about our campaign to clean our neighbourhood. My friends and I started this campaign two months ago and it's called *TeenCleaners*.

We've achieved a lot. For example, we've cleaned the area round our school and we've collected rubbish in the city centre. We've found a lot of volunteers to help us and we've organised a big cleaning day for the whole town on 16th March.

I hope you will tell people about *TeenCleaners* in your next newsletter.

Yours sincerely

[name]

OPTION

If students have become interested in the work of Kids Saving the Rainforest, you might like to help them build up a class letter to the organisation. It could explain how they heard about KSTR and express general support. Ask for a volunteer to send the letter to the KSTR website and, if it gets a reply, to bring it in for the class to read.

Extra exercises

1 • Students complete each reply with a one-word answer.

Answers
1 so   2 stopped   3 did   4 think   5 works

2 • Ask students to read through the text. They then complete it with the words given.

Answers
1 took out   2 turned off   3 put in   4 turned on
5 turned it off   6 unplugged   7 plugged it in
8 turned it on

3 • Students read the questions and choose the correct replies.
• As you go though the answers, you could ask students to suggest example questions for some of the alternative replies.

Answers 1 b   2 a   3 a   4 b   5 c

Unit 7

4
- Students read through the conversation and the possible replies. They choose the best ones.
- You could discuss with the class why the remaining three options don't work in the conversation.

> **Answers** 1 d   2 b   3 h   4 e   5 f

5
- Look at the example. Make sure students understand that they need to use the present perfect for the questions and replies. You may want to go through all the questions with the class.
- You could choose students to ask and answer the questions across the class.

> **Answers**
> 2 Have they built a new gym?
>   No, they haven't built a new gym. They've built a new swimming pool.
> 3 Has Sam bought a coat?
>   No, he hasn't bought a coat. He's bought a shirt.
> 4 Has Julie argued with her parents?
>   No, she hasn't argued with her parents. She's argued with her best friend.
> 5 Have they learnt Spanish?
>   No, they haven't learnt Spanish. They've learnt Italian.
> 6 Have you done Exercise 6?
>   No, I haven't done Exercise 6. I've done Exercise 5.

6
- Ask students to work on the translations in pairs or small groups, and then discuss with the whole class.

Extra reading

Life and culture Saving Gwrych Castle

BACKGROUND

Gwrych Castle /ˈgʌrɪx ˈkɑːsl/ is in the north of Wales, close to the coast of Colwyn Bay and not far from the town of Llandudno. It has had many different uses since the original family sold it in 1946. It was closed to the public in 1985 and has been uninhabited since 1989. Weather and vandalism have brought the building to a very poor condition.

Caernarfon Castle (widely known by its anglicised pronunciation /kəˈnɑːvn ˈkɑːsl/) dominates the town of Caernarfon in north Wales. This enormous castle was built by the English king Edward I in 1283 as a military fortress and the seat of English government in Wales. It was also used as a royal residence.

The Prince of Wales is Prince Charles, the Queen's eldest son and the heir to the throne.

Lead in
- Discuss the questions with the class. If there aren't any notable buildings in the students' own town, they could talk about those they know in a nearby town or city.
- Ask some questions about the building, for example: *How old is it? Who built/used/lived in it? Has it changed a lot in the last ... years?* Use the discussion to revise or introduce key words (for example, *castle, medieval, in good/poor condition, fall down*).

Task
- Look at the photos with the class and explain that the castle is in Wales. If possible, show the location of Gwrych (near Llandudno in north Wales) on a map. Explain that the name is in Welsh (the Celtic language of Wales) and help with the pronunciation.
- Give students time to read through the text themselves. Ask them to read quickly, to get the main idea.
- Read the text aloud and help with new vocabulary (for example, *location, preservation, prince*). Draw attention to the use of the present perfect and ask students to say or guess the infinitives for irregular participles (*been, fallen, gone, done, held, given, written, met*). Explain that *gone* in paragraph 3 means 'disappeared'.
- Read out the sentences. Students look back at the text to find the answers. They could do this individually or in pairs. Remind them to correct the false sentences.
- Ask students if they know of any old buildings that are in poor condition. Are there any reasons to save these buildings? Is it possible to save them?

> **Answers**
> 1 F He was seven when he first saw the castle.
> 2 F It's nearly 200 years old.
> 3 ?
> 4 F It isn't a hotel.
> 5 F Some of the walls have fallen down.
> 6 ?
> 7 ?
> 8 F Nobody has lived there for a long time.
> 9 T
> 10 T

OPTION

If students all have access to a computer at home, you could ask them to access the Gwrych Castle website and find out one more piece of information about the castle. Ask them to report what they have learnt at the start of the next lesson. Alternatively, you could choose one of the buildings that they were interested in during the lead-in discussion. Ask them to find an English-speaking website with information about the building and to collect one or two facts in English to report in the next lesson.

Achievements   67

8 Experiences

STEP 1

Grammar:
  Present perfect + *ever* and *never*
  Present perfect + *just*
Vocabulary: Outdoor activities
Communicative tasks:
  Talking about experiences
  Describing things that happened a short time ago

> **Try this!**
> Answers
> Indoor: bowling, table tennis, snooker
> Outdoor: golf, fishing, running
> Both: athletics, swimming

2 Presentation *I've never done that!*

> **BACKGROUND**
>
> The wreck of the *Titanic* was discovered in 1985 at a depth of 3,669 metres off the coast of Newfoundland, Canada. A number of companies have run tours over the wreck but there has been a lot of concern about looting and damage. There is now an international agreement between the USA, the UK, Canada and France to protect the site.
>
> **The Mig 25** is a Russian military jet that can fly at enormous speed and almost three times higher than a normal passenger plane. At this altitude, you see the curved surface of the Earth below and the blackness of space. It is possible to book a flight in one of these jets and even to fly it!
>
> **Zorbing** was developed in New Zealand, where bungee-jumping also started. A zorb is a plastic ball which bounces down a steep slope. The person inside it (the 'zorbonaut') is either strapped in by a harness or stands up and runs, like a hamster in its wheel, with the aim of keeping upright all the way to the bottom.

1 Key vocabulary *Outdoor activities*

a
- Read out the key words and ask students to match them with the photos. Most of the activities should be familiar or easy to guess from the related verbs.
- 🔊 Play the recording. Students listen and check.
- Use the photos to elicit some words for equipment used in these activities, for example:
  sailing: boat/yacht
  canoeing: canoe (/kəˈnuː/)
  snowboarding: snowboard
  skateboarding: skateboard
  surfing: surfboard
  scuba-diving: wetsuit, goggles
  You could teach the word *rope* for climbing and bungee-jumping.
- 🔊 Play the recording again and ask students to repeat. Give special attention to the pronunciation of *canoeing* /kəˈnuːɪŋ/ and to the stress on the first syllable in the compounds <u>snow</u>boarding and <u>skate</u>boarding.

Tapescript/Answers
  1 skateboarding
  2 sailing
  3 bungee-jumping
  4 climbing
  5 snowboarding
  6 surfing
  7 canoeing
  8 scuba-diving

b
- Make sure that students know what *outdoor* means. Set the time limit. Students write all the words they can think of. These could include: *football, tennis, baseball, hockey, athletics, swimming, running/jogging, riding, cycling, rollerblading, skiing.*
- Remind students that we use *go* with the activities ending in *-ing*.

a
- Ask students to look at the photos and say what they can see.
- Look at the name of the organisation in the website address and introduce the word *extraordinary* (/ɪksˈtrɔːdənri/). Ask students what they think the advert is about.
- 🔊 Play the recording while students listen and read.
- Ask students to say which activity they would like to try.

b
- 🔊 Play the recording again. Pause after each section and ask some questions, for example:
  – Where is the Titanic? (*At the bottom of the Atlantic.*)
  – How high does the Mig 25 fly? (*25 kilometres above the Earth.*)
  – How fast does a zorb go down the hill? (*60 kilometres an hour.*)
  – Can Emily swim? (*Yes.*) Can she drive? (*Yes.*) Does she like zorbing? (*She's never tried it.*)
- Focus on the present perfect verbs and ask students to say them in the infinitive form. Draw attention to the pronunciation of the past participle *read* /red/ (as in the past simple).
- Focus particularly on the use of *have/has been*. Explain that *been* is the past participle of *be* – but it's also often used as the past participle of *go*.

68 Unit 8

- Drill some of the sentences with the target language, for example:
  - *You've read about the Titanic.*
  - *You've never seen the real ship.*
  - *I've never tried zorbing.*
  - *Have you ever been in a Mig 25?*
  - *Have you ever been to the edge of space?*
- Ask students to read the questions and match them with the answers.
- Choose different students to ask and answer the questions across the class.

> **Answers** 1 d 2 c 3 e 4 a 5 b

3 Key grammar
Present perfect + ever *and* never

- Read through the examples and explanations with the class. Ask students to translate the examples.
- Point out that when we say *I've done a bungee-jump*, we mean that we've done it at some time(s) during our life. If we want to say what happened at a certain time, we use the past simple, for example, *I did a bungee-jump a year ago/in 1998/when I was younger. Has he ever ...?* means 'at any time in his life up to now'. *She's never ...* means 'at no time in her life up to now'.
- Emphasise that we use *ever* in questions. It can't be used in affirmative sentences (except in the expression *hardly ever*) and is only very rarely used in negative ones.
- Remind students that *never* is used with an affirmative verb: *Emily has never tried zorbing* (not *Emily hasn't never ...*).
- Note that in American English *ever/never* can also be used with the past simple.

4 Practice

a
- Point out that most of the verbs in this exercise are irregular. You may want to start by asking students to say the past participle for each verb. Introduce the participle *ridden* for *ride*. Remind the class that there is a list of irregular verbs on page 143 of the Students' Book.
- Students make true sentences with *ever* and *never*. They can do this orally and/or in writing.
- Note that *gone* is the true past participle of *go*, but it has a different usage. *She's gone to Mexico* means that she's still away. *She's been to Mexico* means that she went and returned, either recently or at some time(s) during her life. However, there is no need to explain this to the class at this stage.

> **Answers** Students' own answers.

b
- Go through some or all the sentences in 4a and elicit the question forms. Remind students to use *been* as the past participle for *go*.

- Choose students to demonstrate by asking and answering across the class.
- In pairs, students ask and answer the questions.

> **Answers**
> The questions are as follows:
> 1 Have you ever tried zorbing?
> 2 Have you ever been to England?
> 3 Have you ever climbed a mountain?
> 4 Have you ever been sailing?
> 5 Have you ever done a bungee-jump?
> 6 Have you ever ridden a horse?
> 7 Have you ever been skateboarding?
> 8 Have you ever swum in a river?

OPTION
For revision of irregular past participles and the present perfect, you can play 'Use the verbs' (see Games, page 110 in the Teacher's Book). For each team in turn, say one of the irregular verbs from Units 7 and 8. The team first has to say the past participle form of the verb. They then have to make a question using it with *Have you ever ...?*

5 Key grammar *Present perfect* + just

- Read through the example and explanation with the class. Ask students to translate the example.

6 Practice

- In pairs, students ask and answer the questions about the pictures.
- Check by choosing different students to ask and answer across the class.
- Note that there is further work on comprehension and practice of the present perfect with *ever, never* and *just* in the Module 4 Review at the end of Unit 8.

> **Answers**
> 1 What have they just done?
>   They've just got off the plane.
> 2 What's she just done?
>   She's just done the washing up.
> 3 What have they just done?
>   They've just arrived at the station.
> 4 What's he just done?
>   He's just dropped the eggs.

- 🔊 Pattern drill: TRP page 15 (Unit 8, Step 1)

Experiences

OPTION

For further practice of the present perfect with *just*, you can play this game. Ask students to close their eyes, and then make some change that they will be able to notice (for example, turn off the lights, move your chair, put your book on the table, open your bag, write something on the board). Ask students to open their eyes and say what you've just done. Then invite individual students to take your place at the front and keep the game going.

7 Writing and speaking *My experiences*

- Look at the examples with the class. You could give students some more ideas by making statements about things you've done and haven't done.
- Students write their own sentences and questions.
- Ask different students to tell the class about their experiences and to ask their questions. Encourage them to talk rather than to read aloud, referring to their written work only when necessary.

Example answers

I've had a holiday in Greece. I've read all the *Harry Potter* books. I've learnt how to ride a skateboard.
I've never been skiing and I've never seen snow.
Have you ever ridden a motorbike? (No, I haven't.)
Have you ever been camping? (Yes, I have.)

STEP 2

Grammar: Present perfect + *for* and *since*
Expressions:
   How long ...? + time expressions (with *for* and *since*)
Communicative tasks:
   Talking about present situations and how long they have continued

---

1 Share your ideas

- Ask students to look at the photo and say what they can see. They should be able to identify the London Eye and the River Thames. They then discuss the other questions. Elicit that Ana and Charlie are in the London Eye.

2 Presentation *We've been here for hours!*

a
- Read out the introduction to the conversation. Use the photo to teach the word *pod* for the individual compartments on the London Eye. They are also called *capsules*.
- Ask the question, then play the recording. With books closed, students listen for the answer to the question.

Answer No, she isn't.

b
- Play the recording again while students listen and read.
- Explain or elicit the meaning of new vocabulary (for example, *I bet, shut up, for ages*). Explain that *shut up* is not very polite. Also explain that the question *Are you doing anything this evening?/ tomorrow night?/ on Saturday?* nearly always comes before an invitation – it implies 'Would you like to do something with me if you're free?'
- Draw attention to the use of the present perfect. Point out the irregular past participle *known*. Also make it clear that *been* (used at the beginning of the conversation) is the past participle here of *be*, not *go*.
- Drill some sentences with the target language, for example:
   – *We've been here for five minutes.*
   – *We've been here since quarter past three.*
   – *I haven't seen you for ages.*
   – *How long have you known Jay?*
   – *Since I arrived in London.*
- Students read the sentences and look back at the text to decide if they're true or false. Remind them to correct the false sentences.

Answers
1 True.
2 True.
3 False. They've been there for five minutes.
4 False. He hasn't seen her for ages.
5 True.
6 False. She's known him since she arrived in London.
7 False. He's just telephoned her.

3 Key grammar
Present perfect + for *and* since

- Focus on the use of *for* and *since* in the conversation. Explain that *since* marks the time when something started to happen in the past – it's still happening now.
- Look at the time line and ask students to complete the examples. Emphasise that in both sentences Ana and Charlie are still there (at the top of the wheel) *now*. The present perfect can be used to talk about an action that started in the past and is still happening in the present. Ask students to translate the sentences into their language and compare the tense used.
- Go through the explanations of *for* and *since*. Point out that *since* goes with a particular point in time (*since 3.15, since last Wednesday, since 2001, since Ana arrived in London*). *For* goes with a period of time which can be specific (*for five minutes, for three weeks, for 20 years*) or vague (*for hours, for ages, for a long time*).

Answers
for
since

Unit 8

4 Practice

a
- Look at the example with the class. Draw attention to the two different tenses.
- Students make sentences, one with the present simple and the other with the present perfect. They can do this orally and/or in writing.

> **Answers**
> 2 My sister is married to a football coach. They've been married since December.
> 3 Jay has known Martin for ages. He knows him very well.
> 4 Ana plays the piano. She's played it since she was four.
> 5 Sue has worked in a language school since 1998. She works with students from all over the world.
> 6 Lizzie really likes listening to modern jazz. She's liked it for a long time.

OPTION
As preparation for 4b, you could ask students to make a present perfect question with *How long ...?* for each of the situations in 4a, for example:
1 How long have the Grants lived in London?
2 How long has your sister been married?
3 How long has Jay known Martin?

b
- Look at the example. Ask students to make the same reply using *since*. (*I've known him since [year]*.)
- Elicit some more example questions using the verbs from 4a.
- Students think of suitable questions for their partner, and then ask and answer in pairs. Remind them that they can answer with *for* or *since*.
- Ask different students to report back on some of the information they got from their partner.

c
- Choose two students to read out the example conversation.
- Draw attention to the use of the past simple for the second question and answer. This is because we're talking about a finished action that happened at a particular time in the past.
- Ask students to suggest some replacements for the underlined words in the conversation. They can ask about any of their partner's clothes or possessions.
- In pairs, students ask and answer.
- You could invite some pairs to say one of their conversations for the class.
- Note that there is further work on comprehension and practice of the present perfect with *for* and *since* in the Module 4 Review at the end of Unit 8.
- Pattern drill: TRP page 15 (Unit 8, Step 2)

5 Key expressions
Time expressions with for *and* since

a
- Go through the expressions in the list. Remind students of the difference between *a couple of* (about two) and *several* (about three or four).
- Ask them to work out what is meant by *the Friday before last* and explain that we can also say *the week/weekend/month/year before last*. Contrast this with *the day before yesterday* (not *the day before last*).
- Ask students to list the expressions. Tell them to think carefully about whether the expression describes a period of time or a certain point in time.

> **Answers**
>
> | for | since |
> | --- | --- |
> | a long time | Christmas |
> | a few weeks | last term |
> | several years | the day before yesterday |
> | hours | quarter past three |
> | five minutes | the Friday before last |
> | a couple of days | the nineteenth century |

b
- Students write their own gapped sentence for their partner to complete.
- Ask pairs to compare answers.

6 Key pronunciation *Stress in words*

a
- Ask students to read the words and say them aloud quietly to themselves. Then play the recording while they listen and read.
- Play the recording again for students to repeat.
- Remind them that the *-ed* verb ending is a separate syllable only if the final sound is /d/ or /t/.

b
- Ask students to copy the list of sound patterns 1–4 in their notebooks, leaving plenty of space after each one.
- Play the recording. After each word, ask students to repeat and to identify the sound pattern (1–4).
- Play the recording again. Students write the words beside the correct sound patterns in their list, and identify the odd one out.
- Ask students to say the words for each sound pattern, without the recording.

> **Answers**
> 1 changed, helped, stopped, washed, looked
> 2 taken, argued, finished, shouted, broken
> 3 arrived, become
> 4 invented, protected, connected
> The odd one out is *visited*. The stress pattern is ●●●.

Tapescript
invented   changed   protected   helped
arrived   stopped   taken   washed   argued
finished   shouted   looked   connected
broken   become   visited

7 Listening and speaking
My favourite people

a
- Ask students to look at the three people in the photos. Ask: *What does he/she look like? How old do you think he/she is?*
- 🔊 Play the recording. Students match the descriptions with the photos.
- 🔊 Ask the question about Mike's relationship to the three people. Tell students that Mike doesn't actually say the answers – they have to work them out from his descriptions. Play the recording while they listen for the answers.

> **Answers**
> 1 B 2 A 3 C
> Lily is Mike's girlfriend. George is Mike's grandfather (or possibly his uncle). Vlad is Mike's pen friend/e-friend.

Tapescript

1 He's my favourite person in the whole world. He's always in a good mood and he's always interested in what I've done. Of course, he's known me since I was born. He's lived in the same house for nearly 50 years, and I often go and see him on my way home from school.

2 I haven't known her for very long. I met her at a friend's house. We've been out together four times now. She's great. I haven't seen her since the Friday before last, but I hope I'll be able to see her next Saturday.

3 He comes from Prague in the Czech Republic. I've known him since we were both at primary school. I've been to Prague once and he's been here a couple of times. I haven't written to him for ages, so I must remember to send him an email soon.

b
- Ask students to read through the questions.
- 🔊 Play the recording again. Pause at the end of each description to give students time to write their answers.
- In pairs, they ask and answer the questions.
- 🔊 Play the recording again. Students listen and check.
- Choose different students to ask and answer across the class.

> **Answers**
> 1 Since Mike was born.
> 2 For 50 years.
> 3 No, he hasn't.
> 4 At a friend's house.
> 5 Four times.
> 6 The Friday before last.
> 7 When they were both at primary school.
> 8 A couple of times.
> 9 No, he hasn't.

8 Writing and speaking *Who is it?*

- Read the example description with the class and ask students to work out who the person is (*the writer's great-grandmother*).
- Ask students to choose a person to describe. This person could be a family member, a neighbour, a teacher or a friend. Tell them not to include the person's name or describe their relationship with him/her, but to give some clues that will help their partner to guess. Remind them to use the present perfect with *for* and *since*.
- Students write their description. Walk round the class, giving help where necessary.
- In pairs, students read each other's descriptions and try to guess who their partner has described.
- You could invite some students to read out their description and ask the class to guess.

> **Example answer**
> He's 21 years old. I've known him since I was born, but I haven't seen him for about six months. He's been at university in Bologna for two years, so he hasn't lived with my uncle and aunt since [year]. He's just got brilliant results in his university exams.

STEP 3

Reading skills: Guessing meaning from context
Word work: Prepositions of time
Communicative task: Writing a biography

1 Share your ideas *Music*

- Ask the questions and invite students to discuss the concerts they've been to (or seen on TV/listened to on the radio). Help with the use of tenses, for example: *I've been to a lot of concerts/I've seen [band/singer] but I saw them in 2005/I went to two concerts last year.*

2 Reading

> **BACKGROUND**
> U2 is best known for a hard rock sound with thoughtful lyrics. As well as Bono, the members of the band are David Evans, known as 'The Edge' (guitar and keyboards), Adam Clayton (bass) and Larry Mullen (drums). After gathering a big following in Ireland and Britain, U2 became established as international superstars with the release of *The Joshua Tree* in 1987. The song *I still haven't found what I'm looking for* comes from this album.

a
- Look at the photos and ask students to identify the band.
- Ask what they know about U2. If necessary, you can prompt them with questions, for example: *Who's in the band? Where are they from? Who's the lead singer? What records have they made?* Write notes on the board as students give information.

Unit 8

- Students read the text. Ask them to find some new information to add to the notes on the board.

b **Reading skills** *Guessing meaning from context*
- Students look through the text for the words in the list. Don't explain or discuss any of the target vocabulary, but help with the meanings of *international human rights*, *fight* and *AIDS* in the last paragraph, if necessary.
- Ask students to find the word *released* in paragraph 1. Ask the questions to help them guess the meaning.
- Students study the context and think about the part of speech for each of the other words. They could discuss this in pairs, or you may prefer to do the exercise orally with the whole class.
- You can ask students to do the same with other words in the text, for example, *supergroups*, *live* and *numerous*. Note the pronunciation of the adjective *live* /laɪv/, and contrast it with the verb /lɪv/. You can ask students to provide either a paraphrase of the word in English, or, if easier, a translation.
- Say all the new words in the box in 2b and ask students to repeat them.

c **Comprehension check**
- Read out the questions or choose students to do so.
- 📷 Play the recording of the text while students listen and read.
- Students look back at the text and answer the questions.

> **Answers**
> 1 They won a local music competition.
> 2 In September 1979.
> 3 For [25] years. / Since 1979 or 1980.
> 4 Ireland.
> 5 More than 100 million.
> 6 Yes, they are.
> 7 Yes, you can.
> 8 Paul Hewson.
> 9 Campaigns for international human rights and to fight AIDS in Africa.

OPTION

With a strong class, you may want to do a little more on parts of speech. Write some or all of the following words on the board: *1 record 2 hit 3 live 4 lead 5 right 6 campaign*. For each one, ask students to identify the part of speech in the text.
Answers: 1 noun 2 noun 3 adjective
4 adjective 5 noun 6 verb

Then ask them to give an example of its use as a different part of speech:

record: verb (for example, *They're going to record a new song.*) Note the stress on the second syllable of the verb /rɪˈkɔːd/.

hit: verb *live*: verb *lead*: verb *right*: adjective
campaign: noun

3 Word work *Prepositions of time*

a
- Explain or elicit the meaning of *Easter*.
- Ask students to read the paragraph and then to fill in the prepositions. You may want to go through all the sentences orally with the class and then ask them to write the answers.

> **Answers**
> 1 in 2 in 3 at 4 in 5 on
> 6 On 7 at 8 at 9 in

b
- Students complete the explanations. Ask them to find an example in the text for each use of the prepositions.

> **Answers**
> 1 at: at 10.45 / at one o'clock; at Easter
> 2 in: in the morning; in December; in 1992; in the spring
> 3 on: on Saturday; on 15th April

4 Writing *A biography*

- This exercise can be started in class and completed for homework.
- Introduce the topic. Ask students about the purpose of a biography. Ask: *What do people want to find out when they read a biography? What information should it include?*
- Read out the list of questions. Add any other ideas that the students may have about topics that their biography should cover.
- Read through the Writing guide with the class. Explain the meaning of *chronological order*.
- Use the examples to point out to students that some of their information about past events should be given in the past simple. However, when describing events that have just happened or things that have happened over a period of time up to now, they will need to use the present perfect.
- Ask students to write down everything they know about their chosen band/singer. They may want to check information at home from magazines or Internet fan sites. However, emphasise that this is <u>their</u> biography — it mustn't be copied from other sources.
- Students use the Writing guide to organise their material and write their biography.
- Collect the finished work to mark. You may want to make a classroom display of the biographies or ask some students to use their work for a class presentation.

Extra exercises

1
- Students choose the correct alternatives to complete the sentences.

> **Answers** 1 c 2 b 3 b 4 c 5 a

Experiences

2
- Remind students that *ever* and *never* go between *have/has* and the past participle.
- Students put the words in the correct order.

> **Answers**
> 1 Have you ever been to a rock concert?
> 2 Gillian has never played table tennis.
> 3 Thomas has just bought a new car.
> 4 I've never been riding.
> 5 How long have you had your washing machine?
> 6 We've just come back from our holiday in Switzerland.

3
- Students read the questions and choose the correct replies.
- You could choose pairs of students to ask and answer the questions across the class.

> **Answers** 1 c 2 b 3 b 4 a 5 b

4
- Students read the text and choose the right words.
- As you check the answers, ask students to explain why the alternatives aren't correct.

> **Answers** 1 b 2 b 3 a 4 c 5 c

5
- Students use their own ideas to complete the four replies. Explain that there are lots of possible answers here.

> **Example answers**
> Have you ever been to Berlin?
> Yes, I went there with my father.
> Last summer.
> It was a really interesting holiday.

6
- Ask students to work on the translations in pairs or small groups, and then discuss with the whole class.

Extra reading

Life and culture Poem

Lead in

- Look at the picture. Ask students to say what they can see and what they think the poem is about. Encourage them to suggest a variety of answers. Use the picture to introduce the words *curtain*, *flapping* (i.e. in the wind) and *rag-doll* (= a doll, often home-made, which is made from pieces of fabric stitched together and stuffed with soft material).

Task

- Give students time to read through the poem. Were they right? Establish that the room in the picture belongs to a girl called Lulu and that she's no longer there.
- Read the whole poem aloud while students follow in their books. Then read it verse by verse and help with key vocabulary (for example, *wide*, *money-box*, *crumple*, *engine*, *roar*, *gust*, *wander about*).
- Discuss the first question with the class. Make sure students understand that the mother addressed in the poem is also Lulu's mother. Ask: *Do you think the speaker is older or younger than Lulu?* (Younger.)
- Divide the class into small groups and give them time to discuss the other three questions. Make it clear that the poem doesn't directly state an answer to question 2, so they will have to look for clues and make up their own minds.
- Ask the groups to report their conclusions and discuss the questions with the class. Ask them to refer to the poem to support their answers. As the discussion develops, you can ask other questions, for example:
  - *What do we learn from the wide-open window?* (Lulu was probably looking out of the window.)
  - *What did the child hear in the night?* (Voices and the roar of an engine.) *Whose voices were they?* (Lulu's and perhaps her boyfriend's.) *What was the engine and why did it roar?* (It was probably a car and it roared because it was driving away quickly.)
  - *Who do you think cried and when?* (The mother, perhaps when she found Lulu's note.)
  - *How do you think the speaker is feeling?* (Confused, anxious, worried.)
  - *How is the mother feeling?* (Shocked and unhappy.)

> **Example answers**
> 1 Lulu's little sister or brother.
> 2 Lulu has left home – perhaps with her boyfriend or with some other friend.
> 3 She's taken her money box.
> 4 She wrote a note to her mother.

OPTION

Ask the groups to practise reading the poem aloud. They could do this in any way they like – reading all together, reading different parts individually, or a combination of both. Encourage them to read as expressively as possible. Tell them to look carefully at the punctuation to work out where to pause and when to run on from one line to the next. Ask some groups to read out the poem to the class.

Alternatively, you could practise with the whole class. Ask them to say the first two and last two lines all together, and divide the rest up between different sections of the class.

Module 4 Review

Grammar check

1 Present perfect

Work it out for yourself

A
- Students match the sentence with the correct picture.
- Elicit another sentence using *change* in the present perfect.

> **Answers**
> 1 Picture B.
> 2 He's changed his name.

B
- Students choose the correct explanation.
- Point out that in the sentences in 1A the 'present results' are that he's now got short hair, new clothes and a new name.

> **Answer** b

- Students write the complete sentences for 1–6.
- They then match their sentences with the present results expressed in a–f.

> **Answers**
> 2 Someone has taken my book. b
> 3 I haven't finished my dinner. e
> 4 Have you seen my keys? a
> 5 My watch has stopped. d
> 6 Pete has broken his leg. f

2 Present perfect and past simple

Work it out for yourself

A
- Students match sentences 1 and 2 with pictures A and B.
- If they have difficulties here, point out that in the first picture the bus has just left – the girl is talking about a recent action and its effect on her situation now. However, in the second picture the boy is talking about something that happened some time ago – it's a finished action in the past.

> **Answers** 1 picture B 2 picture A

B
- Ask students to match the sentences and complete the explanations.

> **Answers**
> 1 b 2 a
> present perfect, past simple

- Students choose the correct form of the verbs. Remind them to look carefully for past time expressions, which go with the past simple.

> **Answers**
> 1 has arrived 2 has polluted 3 invented
> 4 saw 5 haven't touched 6 Have you finished

3 Present perfect + *ever/never*

Work it out for yourself

A
- Remind the class that we can use the present perfect to describe someone's experiences in their life up to now.
- Ask students to complete the sentence.

> **Answer** 's won

- Students complete the sentences with the present perfect and *ever/never*.

> **Answers** ever won, 's never won

3.1
- Students make sentences using the present perfect. They could work on this in pairs. Remind them to look at the irregular verbs list on page 143 if they aren't sure of the past participles.
- Emphasise that there are no dates or times given in these sentences – they are about experiences that have happened at some time in Dean's life up to the present.

> **Answers**
> 2 He's met the Queen.
> 3 He's travelled to China and Japan.
> 4 He's made a video called *Training with Dean*.

3.2
- Elicit the questions with *ever*.
- Choose different students to ask and answer across the class.

> **Answers**
> 2 Have you ever won a competition?
> 3 Has your school ever been on TV?
> 4 Have you ever written a poem?

4 Present perfect + just

Work it out for yourself

- Ask students to look at the picture and choose the correct alternative.

> **Answer** b

- Students identify the meaning of *just*.
- You could ask them to say what else has just happened in the picture. (For example, *The man has just put his hand on the wet paint.*)

> **Answer** b

- You could elicit some examples from the class before asking students to write their own sentences.

> **Answers** Students' own answers.

5 Present perfect + for/since

Work it out for yourself

A
- Students look at the example and identify the tense.

> **Answer** present perfect

B
- Students think of the replies to the question in 5A.

> **Answers**
> I've been here for 20 minutes.
> I've been here since 3.15.

- Look at the unfinished examples for number 1. Ask students to complete the question with *have*. Then elicit a range of suggestions for the answers.
- Students write the other question and give their own answers.
- You could choose pairs of students to ask and answer across the class.

> **Answers**
> 1 Seth, how long have you had your computer?
>   I've had it for two years. I've had it since [year].
> 2 Sally, how long have you lived in London?
>   I've lived here for ten years. I've lived here since [year] / since I was six.

Study skills 4 Learning to listen

- Read through the sentences and make sure that students understand them. Help with the meaning of *relax* and *concentrate*.

- Set the time limit. Students grade the importance of the suggestions for listening. They then exchange opinions in pairs, giving reasons for their answers.
- Discuss the answers with the class. Point out that all the suggestions in the list are worthwhile and helpful. However, the students' grading should make them aware of some strategies that are especially useful for them.

How's it going?

Your rating

- Students look back at the exercises in the Grammar check and make their own assessment of how well they understand and remember the different language points.

Vocabulary

- Students choose some of the new words and read them out for their partner to write and use in a sentence. They then check whether the word has been spelt and used correctly.
- Point out that it can be useful to write example sentences for difficult words in their vocabulary notebook.

Test a friend

- Look at the example questions and elicit the correct answers.
- Students refer back to the texts in Units 7 and 8 and write several questions to test their partner. They then ask and answer in pairs.

> **Answers**
> No, he didn't.
> They come from Ireland.

Correcting mistakes

- The sentences listed here contain some common errors. Ask students to rewrite them correctly.
- Some sentences contain more than one error. Make sure students are aware of this, and that they find both errors in question 4.
- Emphasise the importance of going back over their work to check for errors when they finish a piece of writing.

> **Answers**
> 1 I bought some fruit at the market yesterday.
> 2 We can play football now. The rain has stopped.
> 3 Has she ever been to the USA?
> 4 I haven't seen my uncle for three years.
> 5 I've known Carla for a long time.

Your Workbook

- Students should complete the Learning diary when they come to the end of each unit.

Coursework 4

My guidebook

Useful information

- Ask students to say what they can see in the photos on Ana's guidebook page. For the different items and places, ask *What do people use this for?* or *What do people do here?* Use the pictures to introduce key words (for example, *stamp, letter box, public telephone, telephone box, emergency, ambulance, bureau de change*).
- Give students time to read through the text on their own.
- Focus on other new vocabulary in the text. Help students to work out or guess the meanings.
- You can ask questions to check comprehension and activate information about the students' country, for example:
  - *How much is a normal stamp in our country?*
  - *What colour are our letter boxes?*
  - *Are there lots of public telephones in our town? Where's the nearest one?*
  - *Where can you buy telephone cards here?*
  - *What's the emergency number in the UK? What is it here?*
  - *Are the opening hours for shops the same here?*
  - *Have you ever stayed in a Youth Hostel? What was it like?*
  - *Is there a tourist information centre here? Where is it? / Where's the nearest one?*

- Ask students to plan their text. They should write at least four paragraphs, using some of Ana's topics to organise their page. Encourage them to illustrate their text as they wish.
- Set a time limit, allowing one to two weeks for work on the project. Some work may be done in class and some at home.
- Ask students to check their text before they write a final version and design their page.

Module 4 Review   77

Module 5 — The way it's done

See page 7 of the Introduction for ideas on how to use the Module opening pages.

Answers 1 a 2 e 3 c 4 d 5 b

9 Getting it right

STEP 1

Grammar: *have to, don't have to, mustn't*
Communicative tasks:
 Talking about rules and obligations
 Describing school rules

1 Share your ideas

- Ask students to describe the school in the photos and to compare it with their own. Make it clear to them that this is an unusual school in the USA. During this discussion, introduce the word *rules*. Ask questions about the photos, for example, *What are the students doing outside? Are they wearing school uniform?*

2 Presentation
They don't have to go to lessons!

BACKGROUND

The Sudbury Valley School was founded in 1968 in Massachusetts, using a large house with a barn set in 10 acres of land. The school works on the basis that children are naturally curious and will learn most effectively when they pursue their own interests, deciding for themselves what they want to learn and how. There is no curriculum and no timetable at Sudbury Valley and there are no formal classes or grades. Students from four to 19 mix freely with one another and with the teachers, who are there as resources for them to call on as they need them. They have a lot of freedom but at the same time are given great responsibility, both for their own learning and behaviour and for the operation of the school itself. Decision-making is democratic. For decisions about rules of behaviour, the use of facilities and all the practical business of running an institution, there is a weekly School Meeting, where each student and staff member has one vote. Any complaints about individuals' behaviour are investigated by a committee of students and may be followed by a trial where both sides of the case can be heard.

There are now other 'Sudbury schools' operating in the USA and in other parts of the world. The most famous 'alternative school' in the UK is probably Summerhill, started by A. S. Neill in 1921.

a ● 🔊 Ask the question, then play the recording. With books closed, students listen for the answer.

Answer Yes, she does.

b ● 🔊 Play the recording again while students listen and read.
- Pause to explain or elicit the meaning of new vocabulary (for example, *obey, think for yourself*).
- Focus briefly on the use of *have to* and *don't have to*. Make it clear that *have to* is similar to *must*, but *don't have to* means 'it isn't necessary'.
- Ask some questions to test comprehension, for example:
 – *Does Jodie follow a timetable of lessons?* (No.)
 – *Who decides what things the students will learn?* (The students.)
 – *How often do they do exams?* (Never – there aren't any exams.)
 – *Are there any rules at all at this school?* (Yes.)
 – *Who makes the rules and how?* (Everyone makes the rules. They discuss them and then vote at the School Meetings.)
- Supply other information that students might want to know about Sudbury Valley.
- Drill some sentences with the target language, for example:
 – *You don't have to do tests.*
 – *You don't have to sit in a classroom.*
 – *Everyone has to obey the rules.*
 – *We have to help with the cleaning.*
 – *You mustn't interrupt.*
- Explain the meaning of *choice*. Then ask students to match the sentence parts. They could work on this in pairs.

Answers 1 d 2 a 3 c 4 e 5 b 6 f

Unit 9

> **OPTION**
> Discuss Jodie's school with the class. You can ask questions, for example: *Does this seem like a good school? Can students learn things if they don't have to go to classes? Do you think students can make good decisions and rules? Would you like to go to this school?* You may find that students want to say more than they can express in English in response to these questions – if so, discuss them in the students' own language.

3 Key grammar
have to, don't have to, mustn't

a
- Look at the examples, drawing attention to the use of *has* in the third person singular and the use of *to* before the main verb.
- Explain the meaning of *obligations* and ask students to complete the explanation.
- Note that there is a slight difference between *must* and *have to*. We can use either of them for requirements that are imposed on us from outside, but *must* is used more often than *have to* for requirements that we feel inside ourselves (for example, *I must remember Julie's birthday. I really must clean my room. You must come to our party.*). There is no need to explain this to the class at this stage, however.

> **Answers**
> have to, has to

b
- Look at the examples and ask students to complete the explanation.
- Focus on the difference between *don't have to* and *mustn't*. Elicit some other example sentences using these forms.
- Discuss translations of the forms with the class.

> **Answers**
> don't have to, doesn't have to

4 Practice

a
- Students complete the sentences with the correct form of *have to* and the verbs in the list. They can do this orally and/or in writing.

> **Answers**
> 2 has to do 3 have to stay 4 have to shout
> 5 has to work 6 have to wear

- Pattern drill: TRP page 15 (Unit 9, Step 1, drill 1)

b
- Remind students to think about whether the signs mean 'Don't do it!' (*You mustn't*) or 'It isn't necessary to do it.' (*You don't have to*).
- Students complete the sentences.

> **Answers**
> 1 mustn't 2 don't have to 3 don't have to
> 4 mustn't 5 mustn't 6 don't have to

- Pattern drill: TRP page 16 (Unit 9, Step 1, drill 2)

c
- Read the examples with the students and find out if these 'rules' apply to any of them.
- Ask students to write at least one sentence with *have to* and one with *don't have to* about their duties at home. They can write more if you wish.
- Students compare with a partner. Ask them to report back on their partners, using *has to* and *doesn't have to*.
- Note that there is further work on comprehension and practice of *have to, don't have to* and *mustn't* in the Module 5 Review at the end of Unit 10.

5 Speaking and listening *Making a pizza*

a
- Read out the introduction to the listening and use the photo to introduce the words *ready-made* and *pizza base*.
- Read through the words in the list. Elicit or explain the meaning of *olives*.
- Ask students to predict the ingredients that the speakers will use for their pizza. Don't confirm or correct their answers yet.

b
- Play the recording. Students listen and check their predictions.

> **Answers** 5, 4, 1, 6

Tapescript

JODIE: I'm hungry. Let's make a pizza.
ROSS: OK. So first of all we must make a base.
JODIE: We don't have to make it. There are some ready-made pizza bases in the cupboard. Look!
ROSS: Oh, OK then. So we need to make some tomato sauce.
JODIE: No, we don't have to do that either. We can use a jar of ready-made sauce. It'll be much quicker. Look! There's one here.
ROSS: Oh, all right. I'll put the sauce on the base. What else do we need?
JODIE: Let's add some onion. We don't have to cook it first. And we need some pieces of ham and some cheese.
ROSS: I've done the sauce.
JODIE: Right. Now the cheese?
ROSS: Yes. You have to put the cheese on before the ham.
JODIE: OK. Mmm, lots and lots of cheese. And now the ham. There. Finished!
ROSS: Great. Let's put it in the oven. Have you turned the oven on, Jodie?

Getting it right

JODIE: Yep. It has to be 220 degrees. Great! It'll take about 15 minutes.
ROSS: So it'll be ready about half past one. We mustn't forget about it.
JODIE: Don't worry, I won't forget. I'm starving.

c
- Read through the recipe card with the class. Explain or elicit the meaning of *add*, *jar* and *degrees* (°).
- Play the recording again. Pause after each step in the recipe to ask about the things the speakers have to and don't have to do.
- Students complete the recipe card. They could work on this in pairs.

Answers
1 tomato sauce   2 (pizza) base   3 onion
4 don't have to   5 cheese   6 ham   7 oven   8 15

OPTION
You could ask students to rewrite the instructions on the card to fit with their own favourite pizza.

6 Writing and speaking An ideal school?

- Look at the instructions and examples. Check that everyone understands the meaning of *ideal*.
- Ask students to suggest one or two example sentences about their school and about their ideal school.
- Students write their own sentences.
- Invite different students to read out their sentences and discuss the answers with the class.

Example answers
We have to get to school before eight o'clock. We have to read a lot of boring books. We have to do homework every night. We have to be polite to the teachers.
You don't have to study maths if you don't want to. You don't have to be quiet in class. You don't have to do much homework.

STEP 2
Grammar: *should, shouldn't*
Vocabulary: Illness and injuries
Expressions: Thanking people and responding to thanks
Communicative tasks:
 Understanding and giving advice
 Making suggestions

1 Key vocabulary Illness and injuries

- Read out the sentences. Ask students to guess what they can from English words they know or from similar words in their language and to use a dictionary to check if they have time.

- Set the time limit for the matching task. Students could work on this in pairs.
- Play the recording for students to listen and check their answers.
- As you check, you might want to ask students to translate the words *faint* and *first-aid box* into their language.
- Read out the sentences and ask students to repeat.
- You could ask them to think of other words to substitute in some of these sentences, for example:
  2 He's broken his arm/finger/nose.
  3 I've hurt my hand/back/knee.
  4 I've got a sore foot/leg/finger.
  5 He's got toothache/stomach ache/a headache.

Tapescript/Answers
1 e She feels sick.
2 a He's broken his leg.
3 d Ow! I've hurt my finger.
4 g I've got a sore throat.
5 b She's having an injection.
6 f She's just fainted.
7 h He's got earache.
8 c Here's the first-aid box.

Try this!
Answers: hand, eyes, arm, hair, nose, teeth, mouth, face

2 Presentation What should we do?

a
- Ask students to identify the three young people in the photo (*Lizzie, Ana and Martin*) and to say what's happened to the woman. (*She's fainted.*) Ask: *Who do you think Martin's calling on the phone? (An ambulance.)*

Answer The woman's fainted.

b
- Read out the introduction to the conversation. Ask the question, then play the recording. With books closed, students listen for the answer.

Answer No, they don't.

c
- Play the recording again. Help with new vocabulary (for example, *like that*, *first-aid course*, *You're welcome*) and remind students that 999 is the phone number for emergencies.
- Focus on the first half of the conversation. Ask students to look at the use of *should/shouldn't* and ask some questions to check comprehension, for example:
  – What does the man want to do? (*Move the woman.*)
  – Then what does he want to do? (*Put her head between her knees.*)

80 Unit 9

- Drill some sentences with *should/shouldn't*, for example:
  - *What should we do?*
  - *You shouldn't leave her on the ground.*
  - *We shouldn't move her.*
  - *No, we shouldn't.*
  - *Yes, we should.*
- Read through the sentences and check that the meaning of *advice* is clear.
- Students look back at the conversation to decide if the sentences are true or false. Ask them to correct the false ones.

> **Answers**
> 1 False. A woman has just fainted.
> 2 False. He wants to phone for an ambulance.
> 3 True.
> 4 True.
> 5 True.
> 6 False. She doesn't follow his advice.
> 7 False. She feels a bit sick.
> 8 True.

3 Key grammar should, shouldn't

- Students complete the examples and the explanation.
- Make sure that they understand the difference in meaning between *must/mustn't* and *should/shouldn't*.
- Point out that the form of *should* and *shouldn't* remains the same for all subjects.

> **Answers**
> should
> shouldn't
> should, shouldn't

4 Practice

a
- In pairs, students complete the matching task and complete the advice.
- You could ask pairs to practise the six dialogues.

> **Answers**
> 1 d sit   2 f play   3 a go
> 4 b take   5 e eat   6 c do

b
- Ask students to write a piece of advice, but to leave a gap for the main verb, as in the example. Encourage them to make sure that the problem is included in the context, for example, the use of *It's raining* in the example. Pairs then complete each other's sentences.
- Pattern drill: TRP page 16 (Unit 9, Step 2)

c
- Use the examples to explain the meaning of *bad habits*. Ask the class to give some other examples.

- Students write about their own bad habits. Encourage them to use both *should* and *shouldn't* in their sentences. If you think it's possible, ask your students to do this without writing first.
- Invite different students to read out one or two of their sentences for the class to compare with their own.
- Note that there is further work on comprehension and practice of *should* and *shouldn't* in the Module 5 Review at the end of Unit 10.

5 Key expressions Thanking people

a
- Direct students to the second half of the conversation in 2b to find the expressions for thanking people. (*Thank you very much* isn't in the conversation, but students are familiar with it.)
- Explain that *Thanks* and *Thank you* can both be used in formal or informal conversations. However, when writing formally we use the full form, *Thank you*.
- Say the expressions and ask students to repeat.

> **Answers**
> Thanks. Thanks very much. Thank you.
> Thank you very much.

b
- Ask students to look at the conversation again and to find another expression they can use to thank people (without the word *thank*).
- Explain that *That's very kind of you* is a fairly formal expression. You could mention that *nice* is also often used: *That's (very) nice of you.*
- Draw attention to the replies to the woman's thanks in the conversation: *You're welcome, No problem*. You can add the other common replies *That's all right* and *That's OK*.
- In pairs, students complete the conversation and then practise it together.
- Ask them to think of a different situation and make another conversation.

> **Answers**
> you, very, you
> welcome, problem

6 Key pronunciation /s/ /ʃ/

a
- Play the recording while students listen and read the words.
- Play the recording again for students to repeat.
- You can accentuate the difference between the two sounds by saying the words in pairs (*Sue – shoe, see – she* etc.) and asking students to repeat.
- Point out that the most common spelling for the /ʃ/ sound is *sh*. (Words like *sure* and *sugar* are exceptions.) Another common use of /ʃ/ is in the *-tion* noun ending (for example, *station* /ˈsteɪʃn/, *competition* /kɒmpəˈtɪʃn/).

Getting it right   81

b • 🔊 Play the recording. Students repeat the words and identify the sounds.

Tapescript/Answers

should (2), sun (1), shirt (2), ship (2), sock (1), shorts (2), seat (1), shop (2), shark (2)

> **OPTION**
> If you have time, you could write up one or two sentences with a mixture of the two consonant sounds, for example:
> *Sally should wash her socks.*
> *Does this shop sell T-shirts?*
> Ask students to identify the /s/ and /ʃ/ sounds and to repeat the sentences.

7 Writing and speaking *Problems!*

• Work on an example conversation with the class. Describe a problem, for example: *I've lost my jacket. / Someone's taken my bag.* Elicit appropriate advice and expressions of thanks for the rest of the conversation.

> **Example answer**
> A: I think I've left my glasses at the library.
> B: You should go and look for them.
>   I'll come with you.
> A: Oh, thanks.
> B: No problem.

STEP 3

Reading skills: Identifying the topic
Word work: Adverbs
Communicative task: Writing about customs

---

1 Share your ideas *Different customs*

• Introduce the word *customs*.
• Ask students to answer the questions about expressions in their language.
• You can ask questions to help prepare for the quiz, introducing the word *rude* as part of this discussion. For example: *What's polite when we're eating with people? What's rude? What do we take when we visit someone's home for a meal?*

2 Reading

a • Look at the pictures and ask students to say what the people are doing. Use the pictures to introduce the key words *walk into (someone), bowl, nod* and *thumb/thumbs up*.
  • 🔊 Play the recording while students listen and read. Elicit or explain the meaning of *upset, burp, lick, bowl, wedding* and *funeral*.

• Ask students to choose the answers they think are correct. They could discuss this in pairs.
• Students check their answers with the key on page 99.

> **Answers**
> See key on page 99 in the Student's Book.

b **Comprehension check**
  • Read through the quiz with the class. Ask about the customs in the students' country, for example:
  1 What do we say?
  2 Is it polite to eat noisily here? Do you ever lick your soup bowl?
  5 What do you mean when you nod your head?
  6 Do colours of flowers have any special meanings in our country?

  • For question 4, you could explain that in English (especially in American English) we sometimes say *Enjoy!* and a waiter may say *Enjoy your meal* before people start to eat, but these are much less common than the expressions used in some other languages.
  • Read out the sentences or choose students to do so. Make sure that the meanings of *apologise* and *occasions* are clear.
  • Students look back at the quiz and answer *T, F* or *?*. You could ask them to correct the false sentences.

> **Answers**
> 1 T
> 2 F It isn't rude in Japan.
> 3 T
> 4 ?
> 5 T
> 6 T
> 7 T
> 8 F You shouldn't touch them on the head. It's rude.
> 9 T
> 10 ?

c **Reading skills** *Identifying the topic*
  • Look at the topics with the class. Elicit or explain the meaning of *physical*.
  • Students match the questions with the topics.

> **Answers**
> Food: 2, 4*
> Particular occasions: 6
> Language: 1, 3, 4*
> Physical actions: 5, 7, 8
> * 4 could be considered as either food or language, so accept either answer.

82 Unit 9

3 Word work *Adverbs*

a
- Read through the explanation with the class. Use the example to point out the difference between an adverb and an adjective:
  She's a clear speaker. (The adjective describes the noun, *speaker*.)
  She speaks clearly. (The adverb goes with the verb, *speaks*, and describes how she does it.)
- Emphasise the regular *-ly* ending, and then draw attention to the list of irregular adverbs.
- Look at the spelling rules in the Remember! box.
- Ask students to find the adverbs in the quiz. Note that *usually* is given as an example here, but most other frequency adverbs aren't formed by adjective + *-ly*.

Answers
often, accidentally, politely, noisily

b
- Check that students understand the meaning of the adjectives in the box.
- Ask them to form adverbs from these adjectives.
- As you go through the answers, check the spelling of *angrily, carefully, easily* and *luckily*.

Answers
angrily, anxiously, badly, calmly, carefully, easily, loudly, luckily, nicely, quickly, quietly, sadly, slowly

c
- Ask students to complete the sentences with adverbs from their list. Explain that there are sometimes several possible answers, but they should choose the one that fits best.
- Ask students to compare answers with a partner before you check with the whole class.

Answers
(Other answers are possible.)
1 anxiously   2 carefully   3 angrily   4 badly
5 quietly   6 slowly   7 easily   8 quickly

OPTION
For further practice, you can play 'Adverbs' (see Games, page 110 in the Teacher's Book).

4 Writing *A visit to my country*

- This exercise can be started in class and completed for homework.
- Introduce the topic. Explain to the students that they need to think about information that will help their pen friend to communicate and feel comfortable when he/she comes to visit.
- Read through the questions and ask students to suggest answers and ideas.
- Read through the Writing guide with the class. You could sketch the layout of the email on the board, starting with the lines *To: ..., From: ...* and *Subject: ...*
- Tell students that *Hi* is the most common way to start an email to a friend. Explain that, as well as using the abbreviations listed, they can sign off with the following:
  Fairly formal: *Best wishes, All the best*
  Informal: *Bye, See you soon*
  For a close friend: *Love, Lots of love*
  In an email it's also possible to sign off just with your name.
- Point out that although emails to friends are informal and conversational, it helps the reader to follow what we're saying if we start a new paragraph for a new topic or idea.
- Ask students to make notes in answer to the questions under the topics of *Food* and *Language*.
- Students expand their notes into an email, using the Writing guide to organise it.
- Ask them to check their work. Encourage pairs to read each other's emails and to suggest corrections or improvements to their partner.
- Collect the finished emails to mark and choose two or three to read out in the next lesson.

Example answer
To: danny.rogers@online.co.uk
From: vs.blanc@tiscali.fr
Subject: Your visit

Hi Danny
Before you come next month, I'd like to tell you a few things about our customs here.

We usually have breakfast at about seven o'clock. Lunch is the main meal and everything stops for two hours at lunchtime. We usually eat meat and a salad, then we have a dessert. We have dinner at about eight in the evening.

It's polite to say 'Bonjour' when you go into a shop or a post office and you should say 'Au revoir' when you leave. We only use the word 'tu' for people we know really well, so you should use 'vous' in shops. If you accidentally walk into someone, you should say 'Pardon' and if someone thanks you, you should say 'Je vous en prie.'

It'll be great to see you.
Bye for now
Virginie

OPTION
It may be possible to ask the students to send their work as real emails to pen friends in a British school or, if that isn't possible, addressed to you at the school email address.

Getting it right

Extra exercises

1
- Students complete each reply with a one-word answer.
- Choose students to say the dialogues across the class.

> **Answers**
> 1 kind 2 welcome 3 problem 4 much 5 OK

2
- Students choose the correct replies.

> **Answers** 1 b 2 a 3 b 4 a 5 a

3
- Ask students to complete the sentences. Make it clear that some answers are two words.
- Check the spelling of some of the more difficult words, for example, *headache, stomach, throat, injection*.

> **Answers**
> 1 headache 2 sick 3 hurt 4 first-aid
> 5 toothache 6 stomach ache 7 sore throat
> 8 injection

4
- Students match the questions with the answers.

> **Answers** 1 b 2 d 3 a 4 e 5 c

5
- Explain the meaning of *aspirin*.
- Students read the sentences and choose the correct replies.
- You could ask them to practise the dialogue in pairs.

> **Answers** 1 f 2 a 3 h 4 g 5 d

6
- Ask students to work on the translations in pairs or small groups, and then discuss with the whole class.

Extra reading

Life and culture Mardi Gras

> **BACKGROUND**
>
> In the Roman Catholic calendar, **Lent** is the 40-day period of fasting before Easter, starting on Ash Wednesday. The day before Ash Wednesday used to be called **Mardi Gras**, or 'Fat Tuesday', because people used up all the fat in the household before the fasting began. (It is called Shrove Tuesday in English.) Because Easter is not on a fixed date, Mardi Gras (the day) can be any time from early February to early March.
>
> **Mardi Gras in New Orleans** started in 1837. The festival season opens on 6th January, when private masked balls begin. Most of the city's parades, each organised around a certain theme by a carnival club, start taking place a fortnight before Mardi Gras Day, with some of the biggest held on the Tuesday itself.
>
> Some parades have thousands of participants including bands, dance groups, clowns and motorcycle groups, as well as the people on the gigantic floats that tour the streets.
>
> **King Cakes** are usually ring-shaped, cinnamon-flavoured cakes, covered with coloured sugar. A small plastic baby is baked in the cake and whoever gets the slice with the baby is supposed to buy the next King Cake or host the next party. The tradition originally comes from the Christian festival of Epiphany, celebrating the arrival of the three kings to worship the new-born Christ.

Lead in

- Introduce the word *festival* and ask students to discuss their own favourite festivals. Ask some questions about each one, for example: *When is it? What's the reason for it? What do people do?* Write up brief notes as students give information.

Task

- Look at the photos and tell the class that this festival is in New Orleans in the USA. If possible show the location of the city on a map.
- Ask students what they can see in the photos and use them to introduce key words (for example, *carnival, parade, jazz, costumes, masks, cake*). You could write up the name Mardi Gras and ask students to say anything they know about this festival.
- Give students time to read through the text themselves. Ask them for any other information they have picked up about the New Orleans Mardi Gras.
- Read the text aloud and help with other new vocabulary (for example, *fat, fill, sweets, fireworks*). Either translate or briefly explain *Lent* and *Ash Wednesday*. Explain that a *ball* is a big formal party where people dress up and dance.
- Ask students to read the questions and look back at the text to find the answers. They could do this individually or in pairs.
- Ask the class to say what festival in their country is the most similar to Mardi Gras in New Orleans. What things are similar? What things are different?

> **Answers**
> 1 'Fat Tuesday'.
> 2 Because it's the last day before Catholics have to stop eating and drinking certain things for Lent.
> 3 In January or February.
> 4 On the Tuesday before Ash Wednesday.
> 5 In New Orleans.
> 6 Purple, green and gold costumes.
> 7 Jazz.
> 8 Coins, flowers, necklaces and sweets.
> 9 There's a big party.
> 10 King Cakes.

10 Where is it made?

STEP 1

Grammar: Present simple passive
Vocabulary: Materials
Expressions: Expressing a reaction
Communicative tasks:
 Describing what things are made of
 Talking about where things are produced

1 Key vocabulary Materials

- Read out the words in the box. Set the time limit and ask students to match the words with the pictures. Most of the words should be familiar or easy to guess.
- 🔊 Play the recording. Students listen and check.
- 🔊 Play the recording again and ask students to repeat.
- Explain that the names of materials are uncountable nouns. Point out that *a glass*, the object we drink from, is countable, but *glass*, the material, is uncountable.
- You may want to mention that the same words can also be used as adjectives (*a gold ring, plastic cups* etc.).

Tapescript/Answers
1 cotton 2 metal 3 silver 4 leather
5 gold 6 wood 7 plastic 8 glass

2 Presentation Is it made in England?

BACKGROUND

Portobello Road is in Notting Hill in north London. There is a general market here every day of the week, but the antiques market is on Saturdays, with dealers selling antiques of every description. In the general section of the market there are stalls selling almost everything – food, clothes, kitchenware, souvenirs etc.

a • Ask students what they can see in the photo. You can prompt them with questions, for example: *Where are they?* (At a market.) *Who's looking at the teapot?* (Jay.) *What's Ana holding?* (Little buses/London souvenirs.) *What else is the man selling?* (Dishes, vases etc.) Use the photo to introduce some key words from the text (for example, *antiques, teapot, souvenir*).

b • 🔊 Read out the introduction to the conversation. Ask the question, then play the recording. With books closed, students listen for the answer.
  • Ask them to name the three things that Ana and Jay look at.

Answer
Three things (watches, a teapot, London buses).

c • 🔊 Play the recording again while students listen and read.
 • Pause to explain or elicit the meaning of new vocabulary (for example, *bargain, imported, these days*).
 • Explain that *quid* is an informal word for *pound(s)* (like *bucks* for *dollars* in US English). Ask what the man means by *four ninety-nine* (four pounds and ninety-nine pence).
 • Focus on the use of the present passive. Take the first example, *They're made in Taiwan*, and ask *What's 'they'?* (*The watches.*)
 • Ask students to find other examples of passive verbs in the conversation. Read them out and ask students to repeat.
 • You could also drill other expressions, for example:
   – *They're a real bargain.*
   – *That's expensive!*
   – *They're four ninety-nine each.*
 • Students read the sentences and look back at the text to decide if they're true or false.
 • When checking the answers, help students to use the passive to correct the first two false sentences.

Answers
1 False. Lots of other things are sold there.
2 True.
3 False. They're made in Taiwan.
4 True.
5 False. He thinks it is expensive.
6 True.
7 True.
8 True.
9 True.

3 Key grammar Present simple passive

- Refer students back to the example from the conversation: *They're made in Taiwan*. Establish that the watches don't do the making – they are made by people in Taiwan. You could write the following pair of sentences on the board to compare the active and passive:
 People in Taiwan make the watches.
 The watches are made in Taiwan.
- Ask students to complete the examples of the passive in the Grammar box. Point out that the verb *be* is followed by the past participle form of the main verb.
- Make sure that students recognise that these passive verbs are in the present tense. We're talking about actions that happen in the present time, not in the past.
- Read through the explanations and ask students to complete them.

Answers
are
aren't
isn't, are

Where is it made? 85

4 Practice

a
- Look at the example exchange and elicit the questions and answers for all the pictures in Exercise 1.
- Choose students to ask and answer across the class. Alternatively, they could ask and answer in pairs.

Answers
A: What's the shirt made of?
B: It's made of cotton.
A: What's the box made of?
B: It's made of metal.
A: What's the necklace made of?
B: It's made of silver.
A: What's the belt made of?
B: It's made of leather.
A: What's the ring made of?
B: It's made of gold.
A: What's the bowl made of?
B: It's made of wood.
A: What are the cups made of?
B: They're made of plastic.
A: What's the bottle made of?
B: It's made of glass.

b
- Look at the example. Then hold up or point to two or three objects in the classroom to elicit similar sentences.
- Invite students to say their own sentences about other objects.

c
- Go through the list of participles and ask students to work out what the verbs are. Say them aloud and ask students to repeat.
- Look at the example. Emphasise that we aren't talking about who does the stealing, but about the fact that this happens to the phones.
- Ask students to make sentences using the present passive. They can do this orally and/or in writing.
- Note that there is further work on comprehension and practice of the present simple passive in the Module 5 Review at the end of Unit 10.

Answers
2 The swimming pool in Central Park isn't used in the winter.
3 About 350,000 babies are born every day.
4 Penguins aren't found in the Arctic.
5 In Sri Lanka, two people are killed by poisonous snakes every day.
6 English is spoken by about 1.5 billion people.

OPTION
Help students to revise the irregular verb forms they have learnt in Units 7, 8 and 10. Say the infinitive of each verb and ask students to say the past simple and the past participle.
Alternatively, you can write up a list of infinitives and ask students to write the other forms, listed under these headings:
Past participle ending -n or -en
Past simple and past participle the same
Others

5 Key expressions *Expressing a reaction*

- Read through the sentences. Elicit or explain the meaning of *lottery* and *waste*.
- Say the responses and ask students to repeat. Make sure they say them expressively, with the intonation rising on the stressed syllable of the adjective.
- Point out that *amazing* usually means 'surprising in a positive way'. (Note that this adjective is often used in conversation simply to mean 'really good'.)
- In pairs, students take it in turns to say a sentence and make a response.
- If there's time, you could ask pairs to make more dialogues using other adjectives, for example, *nice, awful, interesting, great*.

Answers 1 c 2 a 3 e 4 b 5 d

6 Speaking and writing *Around the world*

- Look at the examples and make sure that students understand the meaning of *grown* and *imported*. Point out that we use *import from* + country of origin.
- Ask for example sentences using *made in* and *built in*.
- Divide the class into groups and set the time limit. Students write down as many sentences as they can. Encourage them to use brand names to make the sentences more natural where possible.
- Point out that we usually use *make* for everyday and small machines, for example, stereos, TVs, but that we usually use *build* for structures and bigger machines, for example, bridges, aeroplanes, ships. We can use *make* or *build* for racing cars.

Example answers
(Rolls Royce) cars are made in Britain.
Coffee is grown in Brazil.
A lot of our stereos are made in Asia.
(BMW) motorbikes are imported from Germany.
Our tea is imported from India.
Oranges are grown in Spain.
Grapes are grown in Australia.
Aeroplanes are built in France.
(Ferrari) racing cars are made/built in Italy.

Unit 10

STEP 2

Grammar:
  Past simple passive
  Passive + *by*
Communicative tasks:
  Doing and making a quiz
  Talking about when things were built, made or produced

1 Share your ideas

- Focus on the photos and ask students to say what they can about them. Help with key vocabulary to identify the items (for example, *Statue of Liberty, skyscraper, president, lift, cartoon characters*), but don't confirm or correct any information that will be tested in the quiz.

2 Presentation *Where was it built?*

BACKGROUND

The Statue of Liberty was designed and made in France – the internal frame was designed by Gustave Eiffel, who designed the Eiffel Tower. It was completed and shipped to New York as a gift to the USA in 1884.

The first skyscraper was the Home Insurance Building (now demolished) in Chicago. It was built in 1885 and had ten storeys, with another two storeys added in 1890. Construction of the famous skyscrapers of Manhattan in New York started in the 1890s.

President Kennedy was shot by Lee Harvey Oswald in Dallas, Texas in 1963. **Ronald Reagan** was President from 1980 to 1988. He died in 2004 after suffering from Alzheimer's disease. **President Lincoln** was assassinated in a Washington theatre in 1865.

The first machine-powered lift was commissioned by the French king Louis XV for his personal rooms at Versailles.

Walt Disney's **Mickey Mouse** first appeared in the short cartoon *Plane Crazy* in 1928. Spiderman and Bugs Bunny are not Disney creations.

Vincent Van Gogh (1853–1890) was born in Holland but lived much of his life in France. He did 11 paintings of sunflowers.

The **Star Wars** film trilogy was directed by George Lucas. It began with *Star Wars* in 1977 and continued with *The Empire Strikes Back* (1980) and *Return of the Jedi* (1983). Lucas then made three 'prequels' to the Star Wars story between 1999 and 2005.

a
- Read out the quiz questions. Explain or elicit the meaning of *assassinated* and *created*. Say these words and ask students to repeat. You could also help them with the pronunciation of the names *Reagan* /ˈreɪgən/ and *Lincoln* /ˈlɪŋkn/.
- Set the time limit and ask students to choose the answers they think are correct.
- 🔊 Play the recording. Students listen and check their answers.

Tapescript/Answers
1 b France
2 b Athens
3 c Chicago
4 c John F. Kennedy
5 a in France in 1743
6 c Mickey Mouse
7 c Van Gogh
8 a George Lucas

Try this!
Answer: The Eiffel Tower.
Encourage student to write similar clues and then to read them out for the class to guess.

b
- Point out that all the quiz questions are about things that happened in the past. Focus on the past passive verbs. Show that the form is the same as for the present passive, except that the verb *be* is now in the past.
- In question 2, draw attention to the use of *hold* for organised events. Draw attention to the past participle, *held*.
- Focus on the use of *by* in questions 6–8. Explain that we use *by* if we want to identify the person/people who did the action.
- Students read the sentences and decide if they are true or false. Ask them to make two sentences to correct the ones that are false, as in the example.
- As you check the answers, you could ask some other general knowledge questions, for example:
  2 When were the last Games held?
  3 Are there any skyscrapers in our town/capital city?
  4 Where was Kennedy assassinated? (In Dallas, Texas.)
  5 Who was it used by? (The king of France.)
  6 Which other cartoon characters were created by Disney? (Examples: *Donald Duck, Minnie Mouse, Bambi, Snow White.*)
  7 Can you think of any famous paintings by Monet or Picasso? (Examples: *Water Lilies* by Monet, *Guernica* by Picasso.)
  8 What's a famous film that was directed by Steven Spielberg? (Examples: *Jaws, Jurassic Park, Schindler's List,* the Indiana Jones films.) Which films did Peter Jackson direct? (*The Lord of the Rings* trilogy, *King Kong*.)

Where is it made? 87

Answers
2 False. They weren't held in Rome. They were held in Athens.
3 True.
4 True.
5 False. It wasn't used in Italy. It was used in France.
6 False. He wasn't created in 1922. He was created in 1928.
7 False. It wasn't painted by Monet. It was painted by Van Gogh.
8 False. They weren't directed by Peter Jackson. They were directed by George Lucas.

3 Key grammar *Past simple passive*

- Students complete the examples and the explanations.

Answers
built
were
directed
was, weren't

4 Practice

a
- Ask students to read through the text. They then complete it using the verbs in the past simple passive. They can do this orally and/or in writing.

Answers
1 was created   2 was called   3 was needed
4 weren't used   5 was followed   6 were sold

b
- Students make their own sentence using the past simple passive. They then write it down with the words in the wrong order for their partner to work out.
- You could invite some students to come to the front and write their sentence on the board for the class to work out.
- Note that there is further work on comprehension and practice of the past simple passive in the Module 5 Review at the end of Unit 10.
- Pattern drill: TRP page 16 (Unit 10, Step 2)

OPTION
For revision of the passive, you can play 'Use the verbs' (see Games, page 110 in the Teacher's Book). For each team in turn, say one of these verbs: *grow, make, build, produce, use, direct, find, play, eat, sell, create, speak, write*. The team first has to say the past participle form of the verb. They then have to make a sentence using the verb in the present or past passive.

5 Key pronunciation
Weak forms /wəz/ /wə/

- Ask students to read the sentences.
- Play the recording while students listen and follow in their books. Point out that the words/syllables in bold type are the ones that are stressed.
- Play the recording again and ask students to repeat. Beat time with your hand to show the stress. Give special attention to the unstressed /ə/ sound for *was* and *were*.
- Practise the sentences in 'chunks', for example:
  – *was made*
  – *It was made*
  – *It was made in America.*

6 Reading and listening *Song*

BACKGROUND
In the children's film *The Wizard of Oz*, the young heroine Dorothy dreams of a place beyond the farm in Kansas where she has grown up. She is transported to a magical world where she is joined in adventures by a cowardly lion, a tin man and a scarecrow. In the end she learns that 'there's no place like home' and returns to the farm. The film has become a classic, especially because of the performance of the young Judy Garland.

The song *Over the Rainbow* comes from this film. It was written by Harold Arlen and Yip Harburg. It was nearly removed from the film because the producers felt it was too slow. However, it was included and it won an Oscar for the film.

a
- Introduce the word *rainbow*. Use the picture to illustrate.
- Look at the photo with the class. Ask if any students can identify the film (*The Wizard of Oz*) and to say anything they can about it.
- Ask students to read the text and find the answer to the question.
- Ask: *Who wrote the song?* (*We don't know – the text doesn't say.*) *Who first sang it?* (*Judy Garland.*) *Who chose it as the best movie song?* (*The American Film Institute.*) Draw attention to the passive verbs and the new participles *sung* and *chosen*.

Answer Yes, it is.

b
- Tell students that they're going to hear the same text but with some mistakes in it. Ask them to follow the text and listen for the details which are wrong in the recording.
- Play the first two sentences and pause. Ask students to complete the example.
- Play the whole recording once or twice. Students make a note of the mistakes they hear.
- Ask students to identify the mistakes and correct them as in the example.

Unit 10

Answers

It was written more than half a century ago.
(It wasn't first sung in 1949.) It was first sung in 1939.
(It wasn't chosen as 'the best movie song of all time' in 2005.) It was chosen in 2004.
(It wasn't chosen by the British Film Institute.) It was chosen by the American Film Institute.
Judy Garland's life wasn't a happy one.

Tapescript

The song *Over the rainbow* is perhaps the most famous movie song in history. It was written more than a century ago. It was first sung by Judy Garland in the film *The Wizard of Oz* in 1949. A number of different singers have recorded the song and, in 2005, it was chosen as 'the best movie song of all time' by the British Film Institute. Judy Garland's life was a happy one. So the place 'over the rainbow' remained a dream, in her song and in her real life too.

c
- Play the song. The first time through, let students simply listen and get a sense of the melody and feeling of the song.
- Ask students to read the sentences and then play the song again. Students complete the sentences with the words from the list.
- Ask students to turn to the song words on page 144. Play the song again and encourage the class to sing along if they want to.

Answers

1 singer's 2 place, rainbow 3 dreams
4 happy, problems 5 bird, fly

7 Writing and speaking *A quiz*

- Look at the example with the class and elicit the answer (a – Picasso).
- In pairs, students write their own quiz items, including a choice of three answers, as in the example. Remind them that the sentences must be about the past and tell them that they must be sure of the correct answers.
- In turn, pairs read out their quiz items. The other pairs confer and write down the answers they think are correct (a, b or c). After each batch of questions, the writers give the correct answers.

OPTION
You can conduct this as a full-scale class quiz with students in teams of four or five. See 'Team quiz', page 110 in the Teacher's Book.

STEP 3

Reading skills: Using pronouns and possessive adjectives
Word work: Parts of speech
Communicative task: Describing a film

1 Share your ideas *Animated films*

BACKGROUND

Although computer animation was already widely used, *Toy Story* (1995) was the first completely computer-animated feature film. Other later ones include *Shrek* (2001) and *Shrek 2* (2004), *Monsters, Inc.* (2001), *Finding Nemo* (2003), *The Incredibles* (2004) and *Cars* (2006).

- Explain the meaning of *animated film*.
- Ask the questions and invite students to discuss the animated films they've seen. Introduce the word *image(s)* during this discussion.

2 Reading

a
- Look at the photos and ask students if they recognise the films (*Snow White and the Seven Dwarfs* and *Shrek 2*). Ask them to say when they think the two films were made and to say anything they can about the differences between them.
- Ask the question. Students read the text to find the answer. Make sure they understand that a *feature film* is the main (full-length) film that we go to see at the cinema.

Answer

It's an award for the best animated feature film.

b **Reading skills**
Using pronouns and possessive adjectives

- You may want to go through each sentence quickly, asking students to say if the underlined word is a pronoun or an adjective. Remind them that both forms refer to people or things that we have mentioned before. However, a pronoun stands on its own, while a possessive adjective goes with a noun.
- Students find each phrase in the text and look back to find what the pronoun/adjective refers to.

Answers

2 *Toy Story* 3 *Toy Story* 4 today's films
5 *Shrek* 6 *Shrek 2* 7 animated films

Where is it made?   89

C **Comprehension check**
- Read out the questions or choose students to do so.
- 🔊 Play the recording while students listen and read. Pause to help with new vocabulary (for example, *advanced, realistic, muscles, variety, emotions, animators, software developers, engineers, script, play a part, category*). Explain that *big business* means something that brings in a lot of money.
- Students answer the questions.
- As you check the answers, you can add other questions, for example:
  - *Is Shrek a character or an actor? (A character.)*
  - *Was he drawn by hand? (No.)*
  - *Does he look more realistic than the characters in Snow White? (Yes.)*
  - *Does it save a lot of time to use computers for animation? (No.)*

Answers
1 Yes, they were.
2 No, he didn't.
3 They're made on computers / with the most advanced technology.
4 Yes, it was.
5 Yes, they have. They've become much more powerful.
6 Because the actions and characters are more realistic.
7 Years. (It took three years to make *Shrek 2*.)
8 Because hundreds of people are used, and because famous stars are paid millions of dollars to read the parts of the main characters.

3 Word work *Parts of speech*

- Say the three listed words and ask students to repeat. Then elicit an example sentence for each one and write them on the board. For example:
  - *The concert was a great success.*
  - *It was a very successful concert.*
  - *We wanted to raise a lot of money and we succeeded.*
  Point out how each part of speech is used.
- Look at the example in the table and again demonstrate with sentences (for example, *The length of the table is three metres. It's a long table*).
- Ask students to complete the table. Tell them to fill in all the words they can (many of them are in the text) and then to use a dictionary if necessary. They can work on this in pairs.
- As you go through the answers, elicit example sentences for some of the words.

Answers
2 animated   3 success   4 power   5 wide
7 created   8 introduce, introduced
9 draw, drawn   10 paint, painted

4 Writing and speaking *Famous films*

- This exercise can be started in class and the writing can be completed for homework.
- Introduce the topic and read through the questions.
- Read through the Writing guide with the class. Use the examples to show that we use the past tense to say when/where a film was made and who directed it. However, when we tell the story, we normally use the present simple.
- Students may recognise that the examples refer to the 1997 film *Titanic*. If they know the film, you could ask them for suggestions about how to complete the description of the story. Help them to select only the most important events to make a brief outline.
- Ask students to make notes in answer to the questions in the exercise. They may want to check information or spelling at home from a film site on the Internet.
- Students expand their notes into a paragraph, using the Writing guide for help with language and organisation. Remind them not to mention the name of the film and to avoid names of characters that might give it away.
- In pairs, students read their description and guess their partner's film. Encourage them to exchange opinions about the films.
- Collect the finished descriptions to mark and choose two or three to read out in the next lesson. Choose ones which describe different films and ask the class to guess the titles.

Example answer
It's a computer-animated film and it was made in 2003. The heroes are two fish: a young boy fish and his father. At the beginning of the film they live in the sea near Australia. But then a diver catches the young fish and he's put in a dentist's aquarium in Sydney. His father is very nervous, but he decides to go and find his son, with the help of another fish called Dory. They have lots of adventures with other sea animals. Finally, the young fish escapes from the aquarium and the story has a happy ending. The animation is fantastic and it's a great film for kids – my little brother loves it.
[Answer: *Finding Nemo*]

Extra exercises

1
- Students read the sentences and choose the correct replies.
- You could elicit example sentences for some of the other replies.

Answers
1 c   2 b   3 b   4 a   5 b

Unit 10

2
- Look at the example with the students. Elicit how we know the verb should be in the present passive. (*Every year.*)
- You might want to go through the whole exercise before asking students to write.
- You could focus on the sentences with *by* and ask students to change them to the active forms. (*Pollution kills thousands of trees every year. Shakespeare wrote the play* Hamlet etc.)

> **Answers**
> 2 was written   3 are made   4 was painted
> 5 were discovered   6 are killed   7 is grown
> 8 are sold

3
- Students write the sentences using the verbs in the past simple passive.

> **Answers**
> 2 My bicycle was stolen last night.
> 3 St Paul's Cathedral was designed by Christopher Wren.
> 4 Why were the pyramids built?
> 5 Our old house was destroyed by fire.
> 6 The new rules were introduced last week.

4
- Look at the example. Point out that in the second version, the subject of the sentence is the 'receiver' of the action, so the verb must be passive. Remind students that we use *by* if we want to identify the 'doer' of the action.
- You might want to go through the whole exercise before asking students to write.

> **Answers**
> 2 is written by my brother.
> 3 was released yesterday.
> 4 was seen by several people.
> 5 is grown in Thailand.
> 6 were stolen from that bank last night.

5
- Remind students that the words for materials can be either nouns (*My bag's made of leather*) or adjectives (*I've got a leather bag*).
- Ask students to read the text and write the words for materials.

> **Answers**
> 1 glass   2 plastic   3 cotton
> 4 metal   5 silver   6 gold

6
- Ask students to work on the translations in pairs or small groups, and then discuss with the whole class.

Extra reading

Life and culture
Living in an international world

Lead in
- Ask the question and brainstorm with the class to produce a list of common objects on the board. Ask students what they know about where these things were made. Which of the objects were made in their country?

Task
- Look at the pictures and tell students that the young woman's name is Joanne. Ask them to say what she's doing in each picture.
- Give students time to read through the text themselves.
- Read the text aloud and help with new vocabulary (for example, *advertises, silk*). Ask where salsa dancing comes from (*Cuba*). Note the pronunciation of the Irish name *Sean*: /ʃɔːn/.
- Ask questions to check comprehension, for example:
  - *How does Joanne get to work* (By car.)
  - *What's her job?* (She's a clothes designer.)
  - *Is she successful? How do you know?* (Yes, she is. Her coats are sold all around the world.)
  - *What does she do before dinner?* (She takes her dog for a walk.)
  - *Does she cook dinner on Saturday?* (No, she eats at a restaurant.)
- Read out the questions or choose students to do so. Explain the meaning of *manufactured*.
- Students look at the text and the illustrations to find the answers. They could do this individually or in pairs.
- When checking the answers, ask students to say them in full sentences.

> **Answers**
> 1 It comes from Colombia.
> 2 It was grown in Canada.
> 3 It was produced in France.
> 4 It was manufactured in Germany.
> 5 It was made in Korea.
> 6 It's imported from Italy.
> 7 It was made in Japan.
> 8 Natasha was born in Russia and Sean was born in Ireland.
> 9 They do salsa/Cuban dancing.

Where is it made?

Module 5 Review

Grammar check

1 have to/don't have to, must/mustn't

Work it out for yourself

A

- Ask students to match the sentences with the pictures. Remind students that *must* and *have to* have the same meaning, but *mustn't* and *don't have to* mean two different things.

> **Answers**
> Picture A: 1, 3, 4   Picture B: 2

B

- Students match the sentences with the explanations.

> **Answers**
> 1 c (must)   2 b (don't have to)
> 3 c (have to)   4 a (mustn't)

1.1 • Students read the sentences and choose the correct words.

> **Answers**
> 1 must   2 mustn't   3 have to
> 4 has to   5 mustn't   6 has to

1.2 • Look at the example. Make it clear to the students that they need to use the words in brackets in their sentences.
- Ask them to compare answers with a partner before you check with the whole class.

> **Answers**
> 2 We don't have to pay.
> 3 She doesn't have to wear a uniform.
> 4 They mustn't use mobile phones in the classroom.
> 5 They don't have to work.
> 6 You mustn't read that letter.

2 should/shouldn't

Work it out for yourself

- Look at the pictures and ask: *What's the problem?* (*Tom's hurt his thumb badly.*) Students read the words spoken by Tom's mother and his friend and match them with sentences a and b.
- Ask them to answer questions 2 and 3 to explain the difference between *must* and *should*.

> **Answers**
> 1 a Picture 2 (Harry, Tom's friend)
>   b Picture 1 (Tom's mother)
> 2 Tom's friend
> 3 Tom's mother

- Students complete the sentences to give good advice.

> **Answers**
> 2 should   3 shouldn't   4 shouldn't, should
> 5 shouldn't   6 should

3 The passive

Work it out for yourself

A

- Students look at sentences 1 and 2 and then match them with statements a–c.
- Emphasise that in sentence 1 the subject is *Kim* and she does the cleaning. In 2 the subject is *the car*, which is the 'receiver' of the cleaning. We don't know who cleans it.

> **Answers**   1 a   2 b, c

B

- Students match sentences 1 and 2 with the explanations.
- You could remind them that if we do want to mention who does the action, we can use *by*. (For example, *The Prime Minister's car is cleaned by his driver every week.*)

> **Answers**   1 b   2 a

3.1 • Look at the example. Point out that here we use the present form of the passive (not the past) because coffee-growing in Kenya happens now, in the present time.
- Before students write, you could look at all the verbs in the exercise and elicit the participle forms.
- Students write the sentences with the passive form of the verbs. They could work on this in pairs.

> **Answers**
> 2 The first helicopter was built in 1939.
> 3 English is spoken all over the world.
> 4 The aeroplane wasn't invented in Britain.
> 5 When were the Pyramids built?
> 6 When was email invented?

3.2 • Look at the example. Ask students to identify the subject of the second sentence (*it = Kelly's bike*). Point out that the bike didn't do the stealing – it <u>was stolen</u> by an unknown person. Contrast this with sentence 2. Elicit the subject (*he = Rick*) and make it clear that he did the action – he <u>sold</u> his guitar.
- Ask students to complete the other sentences with active or passive verbs.

> **Answers**
> 2 sold it   3 was sold   4 was killed
> 5 won, weren't beaten   6 was performed

4 The passive + *by*

Work it out for yourself

- Students read the sentences and answer the question.

> **Answer** by

- Explain that the information in each sentence is wrong. Ask students to correct it using a passive sentence.
- They could compare answers in pairs before you check with the whole class.

> **Answers**
> 2 No, he didn't. It was invented by Alexander Bell.
> 3 No, they didn't. They were built by the Egyptians.
> 4 No, he didn't. It was painted by Picasso.
> 5 No, he didn't. It was written by Bob Dylan.

Study skills 5 Speaking

- Read through the sentences and make sure that students understand the meaning of *join in, aloud, pairwork, pretend* and *copy*.
- Set the time limit. Students re-read the questions and give themselves a score of one point each time they answer *yes*. They then add up their score and read the comment in the key.
- Point out that all the actions described in the list are worthwhile and helpful. Discuss how each one can help with the skill of speaking.
- Ask students to choose one action that they intend to do and tell the class, using *going to*.

How's it going?

Your rating

- Students look back at the exercises in the Grammar check and make their own assessment of how well they understand and remember the different language points.

Vocabulary

- Students write five new words which are difficult to pronounce.
- Ask them to identify the difficulty for each word. Invite suggestions about how they can mark the word in their notebook to help with the pronunciation. If they know the phonetic alphabet, ask them to write the word in this form.
- With the whole class, practise some of the words that students have chosen.

Test a friend

- Look at the example questions and elicit the correct answers.
- Students refer back to the texts in Units 9 and 10 and write several questions to test their partner. They then ask and answer in pairs.

> **Answers**
> [Student's own answer.]
> *Snow White and the Seven Dwarfs.*

Correcting mistakes

- The sentences listed here contain some common errors. Ask students to rewrite them correctly.
- Some sentences contain more than one error. Make sure students are aware of this, and that they find both errors in questions 1 and 5.
- Emphasise the importance of going back over their work to check for errors when they finish a piece of writing.

> **Answers**
> 1 You mustn't run in the corridor. You must walk.
> 2 Listen to her advice. You should go to the dentist.
> 3 You shouldn't eat too much. You'll feel sick.
> 4 Edam cheese is made in Holland.
> 5 The *Mona Lisa* was painted by Leonardo da Vinci.

Your Workbook

- Students should complete the Learning diary when they come to the end of each unit.

Coursework 5

My guidebook

Mini phrase book

- Ask students to look at the pictures of people on Ana's guidebook page and ask: *Where are they? What are they doing/talking about?*
- Give students time to read through the text on their own.
- Read out the English phrases and ask students to repeat them. Remind them that *How do you do?* is a very formal greeting, only used when we meet someone for the first time, and that *See you* is very informal. Point out that the expression *Bon appetit* is taken from French. Draw attention to the adverbs *awfully* and *terribly*, which make an apology stronger, and elicit some replies (*That's all right / OK, Don't worry [about it], No problem*).
- Ask some questions to check comprehension and to get students thinking about their own language, for example:
  - *When do you say 'See you soon'? What else can you say? What do we say in this country?*

Module 5 Review

- *When do you say 'Good night'? What's our word for 'Good evening'?*
- *What do you say in English if you want to find the post office? What do we say?*
- *In a shop, it isn't very polite to say 'I want' – so what do you say? What do we say?*

- You could elicit some ideas for other useful expressions, for example, words for *How are you?, Thanks (very much), You're welcome, That's great!* Encourage them to think about whether there are different ways to say the same thing in their language, and whether the use is formal or informal.

- Ask students to write down expressions in their language. Ask them to group together expressions that are similar and to think about what order to put them in.
- Students make short explanations in English for their expressions, following the situations and examples in the Student's Book, saying when/where they are used. Encourage them to illustrate their text as they wish.
- Set a time limit, allowing one to two weeks for work on the project. Some work may be done in class and some at home.
- Ask students to check their text before they write a final version and design their page.

Module 6

The way we live

See page 7 of the Introduction for ideas on how to use the Module opening pages.

Answers

1 e 2 a 3 d 4 b 5 c

11 Talking

STEP 1

Grammar: Reported speech
Vocabulary: Relationships
Communicative tasks:
  Talking about relationships
  Reporting what other people say

1 Key vocabulary *Relationships*

a
- Read out the sentences. Set the time limit and ask students to match the sentences with the illustrations.
- Play the recording. Students listen and check.
- Focus on the words and phrases in bold type and check comprehension. You could explain that *have a row (with someone)* is another expression for *have an argument (with someone)*. Provide or elicit some other sentences showing the use of *each other*, for example:
  – We (don't) like each other.
  – They see each other every day.
  – We've known each other for years.
- Play the recording again and ask students to repeat.

Tapescript/Answers

1 c My brother really annoys me.
2 g I get on well with my parents.
3 e Don't argue! Turn that music off now!
4 a They're having a row.
5 b Kelly is Tara's closest friend.
6 f I love my dog and my dog loves me. We love each other.
7 d I spend a lot of time with my friends.

b
- Ask students to say their own sentences using expressions from 1a.

2 Presentation

They said they weren't rebels

a
- Introduce the word *rebel* (used as a noun: /ˈrebl/).
- Play the recording while students listen and read. Ask them if the speakers are like teenagers in their country.

- Ask a few questions to check comprehension, for example: *Who doesn't get on very well with her parents? (Donna.) Does she argue with them? (No.) Who's a hard-working student? (Dave.) Do Gemma and her mum often have rows? (No.)*

b
- Ask students to read the article and listen to it. Ensure that students recognise the relationship between the article and the teenagers' opinions in 2a.
- Discuss the question with the class.

c
- Focus on the use of reported speech. Look at the sentences reporting Gemma's opinions and ask: *What did Gemma actually say?* Draw attention to the change from the present to the past tense when we report what someone said. Point out the use of *that* and the change of pronoun from *I/me* to *she/her*.
- Do the same with sentences reporting Dave's and Donna's words. Keep comparing the reported speech with the actual words the speakers used. Point out the past form of *have got* (*had*) and *can't* (*couldn't*).
- Draw attention to the difference between *said* (no object) and *told me*.
- Ask students to look back at the text and match the sentence parts.

Answers 1 e 2 a 3 d 4 c 5 b

3 Key grammar *Reported speech*

- Ask students to complete the examples. Point out that the word *that* is in brackets because we can leave it out.

Answers
didn't argue
were
had
couldn't

4 Practice

- Students write sentences using reported speech. They can either include the word *that* or leave it out. Point out the pronoun *my* in question 6 and ask students what it will change to (*her*).

Talking 95

> **Answers**
> 2 They said (that) they were going away.
> 3 He said (that) he didn't know.
> 4 She said (that) she had a new car.
> 5 He said (that) he could speak Chinese.
> 6 She said (that) she looked like her sister.
> 7 He said (that) he didn't often go out.
> 8 They said (that) they loved each other.

- Pattern drill: TRP page 16 (Unit 11, Step 1)

> **OPTION**
> You could practise reported speech with a 'chain' activity. The first student makes a sentence about his/her daily life, using the present simple. The next student reports what the previous person said, then adds a sentence, and so on:
> A: I'm in the school hockey team.
> B: Jorge said he was in the school hockey team. I like writing poems.
> C: Elena said she liked writing poems. I ...

5 Key grammar *say* and *tell*

- Ask students to look at the examples and complete the explanations.

> **Answers** say, tell, tell

6 Practice

- Students complete the sentences. They can do this orally or in writing.
- As you check answers for sentences 2, 4 and 5, you could ask students to say the words that the people actually used. (*There's a party on Sunday. I think it's at Pete's. I'm not having a party.*)
- Note that there is further work on comprehension and practice of reported speech and on *say* and *tell* in the Module 6 Review at the end of Unit 12.

> **Answers**
> 1 say 2 told 3 tell 4 said 5 told

7 Listening *Don't be so rude!*

a
- Ask students to look at the photo and ask: *What's happening?* (*Charlie and his dad are arguing/having a row.*) Ask them to guess why Mr Grant is angry.
- Play the recording. Students listen and check their predictions.

> **Answers**
> Because Charlie forgot to clean the car and because he was rude to his father.

Tapescript

MR GRANT: Charlie! At last! You're late! Where have you been?
CHARLIE: What do you mean?
MR GRANT: You promised to clean the car this afternoon. Remember?
CHARLIE: Oh, yeah. Sorry. I was playing football.
MR GRANT: And you forgot about the car.
CHARLIE: But I always play football on Sunday afternoon. Er ... I'll clean it now if you like.
MR GRANT: It's too late now, isn't it? I've done it.
CHARLIE: So what's the problem, then?
MR GRANT: The problem is, Charlie, that you never do anything to help.
MRS GRANT: Hi there! Are you two having another row?
CHARLIE: Dad thinks I'm selfish and lazy.
MR GRANT: Oh, don't be so stupid, Charlie.
CHARLIE: You're the stupid one, if you can't clean the car on your own.
MRS GRANT: Charlie, stop it! You're so rude!
MR GRANT: Listen, young man. Next week you're going to stay at home – every evening.
CHARLIE: You mean I can't go out for a week!
MR GRANT: That's right, Charlie. I mean you can't go out for a week.
CHARLIE: Oh, that isn't fair!

b
- Play the recording again. Pause after key speeches in the present tense and ask students to report what Charlie and his parents said. Prompt them with sentence openings, for example:
  - Charlie said he always ...
  - Charlie offered to ...
  - Mr Grant said that Charlie never ...
  - Charlie told his father that he was ...
  - Mrs Grant said that Charlie was ...
  - Mr Grant told Charlie that he ...
- Ask students to work out the meaning of *That isn't fair!* Ask them if they think Mr Grant's decision is fair or not.

> **Example answers**
> Charlie said he always played football on Saturday.
> Charlie offered to clean the car now.
> Mr Grant said that Charlie never did anything to help.
> Charlie told his father that he was stupid (if he couldn't clean the car on his own).
> Mrs Grant said that Charlie was rude.
> Mr Grant told Charlie that he couldn't go out for a week.

Unit 11

8 Writing and speaking
What did they say?

- Ask students to think of some questions for an article about teenage life in their country. You could elicit a few ideas before they begin, for example:
  - *Do you get on well with your parents?*
  - *Do you work hard at school?*
  - *Have you got a weekend job?*
- Divide the class into groups of four or five. Students interview each other and make brief notes of the answers they receive.
- Ask different students to report back about the people in their group.

STEP 2

Grammar: Question tags

Expressions: Asking for clarification

Communicative tasks:
  Asking if something is true, asking for agreement
  Asking for clarification

---

1 Share your ideas

- Ask students to look at the photo and explain the expression *in a bad mood* in the speech bubble. Briefly revise the conversation in Step 1 and ask students to guess why Charlie is in a bad mood.

Example answers
Charlie is arguing with his mother.
He isn't happy because he can't go out.
He was rude to his father.

2 Presentation
He isn't in a good mood, is he?

a • Read the introduction to the conversation. Ask the question, then play the recording while students listen and read. Ask them to answer the question.

Answer
He's annoyed/fed up because he has to stay at home/he can't go out. (He usually goes to karate on Tuesday.)

b • Play the recording again. Ask students to explain the meaning of *grounded* and *hang out with someone*. Make it clear that these are colloquial expressions.
- Focus on some of the sentences with question tags in the text. Point out that these can be used to ask for information or to ask for agreement.
- Drill some of the questions, for example:
  - *You're going out, aren't you?* ↑
  - *You didn't clean the car, did you?* ↓
  - *You weren't polite, were you?* ↓
  - *He isn't in a very good mood, is he?* ↓

- Explain to students that some question tags ask for information, for example, *You're going out, aren't you?* (↑), and others just ask for agreement; the speaker knows the answer, e.g. *You weren't very polite, were you?* (↓)
- Read out the sentences. Students look back at the text to work out whether they are true or false.

Answers
1 False. He's staying at home.
2 False. He's grounded.
3 True.
4 False. He was rude to his father.
5 True.
6 False. He wants to go out.
7 False. Charlie's in a bad mood.
8 True.
9 True.

3 Key grammar *Question tags*

a • Write the first two examples on the board. Show how the subject of the sentence and all or part of the main verb are repeated in the question tag.
- Emphasise that if the sentence is affirmative, the question tag is negative, and vice versa.
- Ask students to complete the other examples.
- Draw attention to the use of *don't* and *didn't* when the main verb is in the present or past simple.

Answers
were
won't
can't
did

b • Ask students to give a translation and discuss the differences between this and the English question tags.

4 Practice

a • Students match the sentences with the question tags. They can do this orally and/or in writing.
- They check with their partners; one student giving the sentence and the other adding the question tag.

Answers
1 c 2 d 3 a 4 g 5 b 6 i 7 h 8 f 9 e

- Pattern drill: TRP page 17 (Unit 11, Step 2)

b • Ask two students to read out the example dialogue. Point out the pattern: *Charlie's* (= *has*) *had ... hasn't he? Yes, he has.*
- In pairs, students take it in turns to ask one of the questions and to give the short answer with *Yes.* Walk round the class, giving help where necessary.

Talking 97

c
- Students write their own gapped sentence for their partner to complete.
- Note that there is further work on comprehension and practice of question tags in the Module 6 Review at the end of Unit 12.

Try this!
Answer: Ana's in the kitchen, isn't she?
They want to watch TV, don't they?

5 Key expressions *Asking for clarification*

a
- Discuss the translations with the class, and discuss when we say these expressions.

b
- Ask students to put the sentences in order.
- Explain that *stressed out* means 'extremely anxious and unable to relax'. It is a fashionable expression at present.
- Ask students to practise the dialogue in pairs.

Answers
– I'm feeling a bit stressed out today.
– Pardon?
– I said I was feeling a bit stressed out.
– What does 'stressed out' mean?
– It's difficult to explain. Have you got a dictionary?

6 Key pronunciation
Intonation in question tags

a
- Ask students to listen to the intonation at the end of the questions. Play the recording.
- Read through the explanations and play the questions again. Ask students to repeat.

b
- Play the recording. Pause after each question. Ask students to repeat and say whether the question goes up or down at the end. Ask: *Is he/she sure of the answer?* Then play the question and answer.

Answers
1 ↑   2 ↓   3 ↑   4 ↓   5 ↓

Tapescript
1 You're fourteen, aren't you?
   No, I'm not! I'm fifteen.
2 You like sport, don't you?
   Yes, you know I do.
3 You live in New York, don't you?
   Yes, that's right.
4 You haven't done your homework, have you?
   No, I haven't. Sorry.
5 This is really difficult, isn't it?
   Yes, it is!

7 Speaking *Finding out about a friend*

- Take the part of speaker A yourself and read out the conversation with a student. Change *Celine* to the student's name and add the name of your town. Point up or down with your finger to show the rising or falling intonation.
- Ask two students to read out the dialogue again, changing *Celine* to student B's name.
- In pairs, students practise the dialogue. Encourage them to ask more questions, using the appropriate intonation.

STEP 3

Reading skills: Skimming
Word work: Verbs for speaking
Communicative task:
  Writing a conversation using the correct punctuation

1 Share your ideas *Telephone talk*
- Discuss the questions with the class.

2 Reading

a **Reading skills** *Skimming*
- Focus on the picture and ask students for some ideas about what this conversation is about. You may want to introduce the expression *wrong number* before they read the text.
- Set the time limit (one minute only!) and ask students to read the text very quickly. Make it clear that they're looking for quite general information here – they shouldn't stop to puzzle over details.
- Ask students to answer the questions. Point out that we can pick up a lot of information by reading through a text quickly, without taking in every detail.

Answers
1 b   2 b   3 a   4 b   5 upset, angry

b **Comprehension check**
- Play the recording of the text while students listen and read. Pause to help with new vocabulary (for example, *at the other end, silence, definitely, exploded, be upset*).
- Draw attention to the telephone expressions: *Can I speak to ...? Sorry, he's not in. Is that ...? Do you know what time he'll be back? Can I take a message? Tell him to call me.* You could read these aloud and ask students to repeat.
- Look at the sentences and explain the meaning of *pretend*.
- Students look back at the text to find the answers. Ask them to correct the false sentences.
- As you check the answers, you could add some other questions, for example:
  1 Where does it say this in the text? ('Tell him that Alice called.')
  3 Who do you think Steve is? (Perhaps he's Ben's brother or flatmate.)

Unit 11

4 Does she know she's got the wrong number? (No, she doesn't.)

Answers
1 T
2 F There's no one in the house called Ben. We don't know his name.
3 F She wants to speak to a boy called Ben.
4 T
5 T
6 F She doesn't know who Karen is.
7 ?
8 F She's serious, but he's joking.

c
- Tell students that the answers to most of these questions aren't directly stated in the text. They will need to look carefully and sometimes 'read between the lines' to find the answers.
- Ask students what they think of the boy's behaviour.

Answers
1 In the evening, before ten o'clock.
2 Because he was bored and wanted to have some fun.
3 He's her boyfriend.
4 Three (Karen, Jennifer, Becky).
5 Because she thought that Ben was going out with lots of other girls.
6 He was having fun.

OPTION
You could ask students to practise the conversation in pairs, leaving out the narrative. Encourage them to read as expressively as possible, taking note of details like the 'long silence' and the different shades of feeling in Alice's voice: 'irritated' – 'shocked' – 'really angry' – 'exploded'. Ask one or two pairs to perform their conversation for the class.

3 Word work *Verbs for 'speaking'*

a
- Read out the words in the box and ask students to use them in the sentences.

Answers
2 asked   3 told   4 reply
5 shouted   6 say   7 talk

b
- Look at the example and elicit the answer (*tell*).
- Students write their own gapped sentence for their partner to complete.

4 Writing and speaking *A conversation*

- Look at the Writing guide with the class. Go through the examples, concentrating on the use of punctuation within inverted commas for written conversations. Point out in particular that if the speaker makes a statement and this is followed by 'he/she said', the punctuation at the end of the quotation is a comma.
- Look at the list of punctuation marks in the Writing guide and establish what they are used for. Note that it's possible to use double inverted commas (" ") for direct speech, but single ones are also commonly used.
- Discuss any differences in punctuation between English and the students' language.
- Ask students to write out the conversation using the correct punctuation. Remind them to start a new line for each speaker. Tell them to use the text in Exercise 2 as a model.
- Students count up the number of capital letters and punctuation marks and compare results with a partner.

Answer
The phone rang and Maria answered it.
'Hello,' she said.
'Hello. Is that Hannah?' a boy asked.
'No, it isn't,' Maria replied. 'I think you've got the wrong number.'
'Oh, sorry,' the voice at the other end said.
'That's OK. No problem,' Maria told him. 'Goodbye.'

Extra exercises

1
- Do the first sentence with the class. Ask students to say the full form of *Jodie's* (*Jodie has* – not *Jodie is*) and then to choose the correct question tag. Remind them that an affirmative sentence is followed by a negative tag, and vice versa.
- Students complete the exercise.

Answers
1 c   2 b   3 b   4 b   5 a

2
- Remind students that *tell* is followed by a noun or pronoun. Ask them to complete the conversation with the correct verbs.
- You could ask students to practise the conversation in pairs.

Answers
1 tell   2 told   3 say   4 told
5 said   6 says   7 tell   8 say

Talking 99

3
- Students complete the text. You can ask them to cover the alternatives below and to predict what the missing words will be as they read. They then look at the alternatives and choose the correct answers.

Answers
1 b   2 c   3 c   4 a   5 a   6 c

4
- Look at the example, drawing attention to the change of tense and pronoun. You may want to go through all the sentences before asking students to complete the exercise. Check that they know which pronoun (*he* or *she*) to use.

Answers
2 Veronica told Gary that she worked as a waitress three days a week.
3 Mum told my brother and me that we couldn't watch TV tonight.
4 Charles told his wife that there was nothing to eat in the fridge.
5 Mark told Jane that he wasn't playing tennis tonight.
6 They told their teacher that they weren't confident about the exam.

5
- Students change the reported speech to direct speech. Remind them to think carefully about the use of pronouns and to use punctuation correctly.
- You could ask them to compare answers with a partner before you check with the whole class.

Answers
2 'I'm having a party on Saturday night,' Tina said.
3 'I don't feel very well,' I said.
4 'We get on well with each other,' they said.
5 'I love adventure films,' Brian said.
6 'I can't go out with you,' Helen told Frank.

6
- Explain the meaning of *error message* (on a computer screen).
- Students read the dialogue and choose the correct replies.
- You could ask students to practise the dialogue in pairs.

Answers   1 b   2 e   3 a   4 g   5 d

7
- Ask students to work on the translations in pairs or small groups, and then discuss with the whole class.

Extra reading

Life and culture Central Park

Lead in
- Ask the question. Brainstorm with the class and write students' suggestions in note form on the board. Ask: *Do you ever visit a park? How often? What do you do there?*

Task
- Look at the photos and tell students that they show Central Park in Manhattan, New York. Ask them to say what the people are doing.
- Give students time to read through the text themselves. Ask them to pick out any other activities mentioned in the text, to add to the ones on the board. You might want to tell students that 1 mile = 1.6 km and 1 acre = 0.4 hectares.
- Read the text aloud and help with new vocabulary (for example, *relax, escape, have a rest, sunbathe, dirty, took control, playground, attractions, skating rink*). Elicit or explain the meaning of *it's worth it* at the end of the text.
- Ask students to read the sentences and look back at the text to find the answers. They could do this individually or in pairs.
- As you go through the answers, you could ask other questions, for example:
  2 Can you take rollerblades? (Yes, you can.)
  4 Where are the animals? (In a zoo.)
  5 How many people use it? (25 million.)
  7 Why didn't poor people go there? (Because it was too expensive to get there.)
  What happened to make it more popular? (Transport became cheaper.)
  9 What were some things that they spent the money on? (Trees, playgrounds, a skating rink.)

Answers
1 ?
2 F   You can go cycling in the park.
3 T
4 T
5 ?
6 F   There are nearly 60 miles of paths in the park.
7 F   Only rich people used it when it first opened.
8 F   It's more popular today.
9 T
10 T

100   Unit 11

12 New beginnings

STEP 1

Grammar: *used to*
Vocabulary: words from American English
Communicative tasks:
  Talking about differences between life in Britain and the USA
  Describing past habits

1 Key vocabulary *American English*

- Read out the American English words under the pictures.
- Set the time limit. Students match the two sets of words. They can do this individually or in pairs.
- 🔊 Play the recording. Students listen and check.
- You may want to explain that *pants* is used in British English, but it refers to underclothes. In both countries *gas* is used for substances like air or oxygen, but in the USA it also refers to the petrol that we put in our cars. You could point out that in the USA people fill up their cars at a *gas station* – compare the British terms *service station*, *petrol station* or simply *garage*. You may want to mention the American use of *store* in words like *bookstore*, *drugstore* (= chemist's), *shoe store* etc.
- 🔊 Play the recording again and ask students to repeat the words.
- Draw attention to American pronunciation of /r/ in *elevator*, *store* and *sneakers*.

Tapescript/Answers

1 vacation — holiday
2 sidewalk — pavement
3 cookies — biscuits
4 pants — trousers
5 elevator — lift
6 gas — petrol
7 closet — wardrobe
8 sneakers — trainers
9 store — shop

2 Presentation *They used to live in Cardiff*

a
- Read out the introduction to the text. Use the text to elicit the information that Cardiff is the capital of Wales and that Los Angeles is in California on the east coast of the USA.
- 🔊 Ask students to look for differences between the family's life in Britain and their new life in the USA. Play the recording while they listen and read.

Answer
There are six differences.
(In the USA: they go everywhere by car; they don't have to wear a school uniform; the weather's better; rollerblading is really popular; everyone watches baseball, not football; some words are different.)

b
- 🔊 Play the recording again. Pause after each person's statement and ask students to say some of the things that the people do now which they didn't do in the past.
- Make it clear that when Mr Richmond says that everyone's *crazy about* baseball, he means that they love it.
- Focus on *used to/didn't use to*. Make it clear that the speakers use these forms to describe their normal activities in the past. However, their life has changed and they do things differently now.
- Drill sentences with *used to*, for example:
  – *They used to walk to school.*
  – *I used to be a football fan.*
  – *I didn't use to be interested in baseball.*
  – *I didn't use to swim much.*
  – *I never used to go rollerblading.*
- Choose students to read out the questions. Draw attention to the question form: *Did ... use to* + verb, and help with the pronunciation of *use to*: /ˈjuːs tə/ (not /ˈjuːz tə/).
- Ask students to answer the questions. As you check the answers, you can follow up with other questions, for example:
  1 *How does Mrs Richmond travel now?* (By car.)
  2 *How did Holly and Seb use to get to school?* (They used to walk.)
  4 *Is Mr Richmond a football fan now?* (No, he isn't.)
  5 *Is there a uniform at Holly's American school?* (No, there isn't.)
  6 *Why does Holly swim more now?* (Because the weather's better in Los Angeles.)

Answers
1 By bus.
2 No, they didn't.
3 No, he didn't.
4 Football.
5 A uniform.
6 No, she didn't.
7 'I'd like a packet of crisps, please.' / 'Could I have a packet of crisps, please?'

3 Key grammar *used to*

- Ask students to complete the examples and then read through the explanations with them.

New beginnings 101

- You may want to point out that it would be possible to use the past simple in the examples. However, *used to* is better because it conveys the idea of habitual activity that no longer happens.
- Emphasise that *used to* (+ verb) is quite different from the verb *use*. Point out the difference in pronunciation: /ˈjuːs tə/ as distinct from /juːz/.

Answers
didn't
Did, use

4 Practice

a
- Look at the example with the class. Then ask students to look back at the list in Exercise 1 to make similar sentences for *wear*. Students can complete the exercise orally and/or in writing.

Answers
2 In Britain, we used to wear trainers/trousers. In the USA, we wear sneakers/pants.
3 In Britain, we used to put our clothes in a wardrobe. In the USA, we put our clothes in a closet.
4 In Britain, we used to walk along the pavement. In the USA, we walk along the sidewalk.
5 In Britain, we used to buy petrol for the car. In the USA, we buy gas (for the car).
6 In Britain, we used to get the lift to the seventh floor. In the USA, we get the elevator (to the seventh floor).
7 In Britain, we used to buy our food at the local shop. In the USA, we buy our food at the local store.

b
- Explain to the students that all the sentences are making a contrast between the past and the present. Point out that they need to look carefully at the second half of the sentence to decide whether to write *used to* or *didn't use to*.
- Students can do the exercise orally and/or in writing.
- Note that there is further work on comprehension and practice of *used to* in the Module 6 Review at the end of Unit 12.

Answers
1 used to have 2 used to live
3 used to go out with 4 didn't use to like
5 used to play 6 didn't use to drive

- 🔊 Pattern drill: TRP page 17 (Unit 12, Step 1)

OPTION
Give students cues for questions about when they were younger, for example:
What hobbies / have?
What games / play?
What school / go to?
What TV programmes / watch?
In pairs, students ask and answer the questions, for example:
A: When you were younger, what hobbies did you use to have?
B: I used to collect toy cars.

5 Listening *Song*

BACKGROUND

The song *This used to be my playground* was recorded by Madonna as the soundtrack for the 1992 film *A League of Their Own* and appeared on her album *Something to Remember* in 1995.

a
- 🔊 Read out the three topics and then play the recording. Students listen to get a general idea of what the song is about. Ask if any of them know the song and who sang it.

Answer c It's about memories.

b
- Read through the sentences and alternative answers with the class. Elicit the meaning of *I wish ...*
- 🔊 Play the recording again. You may also like to ask students to turn to the song words on page 144 and read them as they listen. You could pause at the start of the second and fourth verses to make it clear that the singer is in disagreement with other people ('they') who say 'Don't look back', 'Don't hold on to the past' and 'No regrets.'
- Ask students to choose the correct answers for the sentences.
- Look at the song words with the class and elicit or explain the meaning of some of the expressions.
- 🔊 Play the recording again and encourage students to sing along.

Answers 1 b 2 a 3 c 4 b

6 Writing and speaking *I'm different now!*

- Look at the examples and ask students for some suggestions to complete the unfinished sentences. You could start by telling them one or two things about yourself.
- Students write sentences and then read them out in pairs. Encourage them to ask their partner questions and to describe their own memories in more detail.

Unit 12

- Invite different students to tell the class about the way they used to be compared with the way they are now.

Example answers

I used to wear shorts all the time, but now I usually wear jeans or trousers.

I used to believe in ghosts, but now I don't think they exist.

I didn't use to like history, but now I'm really interested in it.

I used to put ketchup all over my food, but now I never eat it.

My brother and I used to argue a lot, but now we get on quite well.

STEP 2

Grammar: Second conditional
Expressions: Saying goodbye
Communicative tasks:
 Saying goodbye and thanking people after a visit
 Talking about imaginary situations

1 Share your ideas

- Read out the question, explaining the meaning of *destination*.
- Look at the example and elicit the full form of *I'd* (*I would*). You could give another example by telling the class a place you would choose and giving a reason.
- Invite different students to answer with *I'd like to …* Encourage them to give reasons for their choice of place.

2 Presentation
If I had a ticket, I'd go with you now!

a
- Look at the photos with the class. Ask: *Where are they?* (*At the airport.*) *Who's going away?* (*Ana.*) *Where do you think she's going?* (*She's going home to Mexico.*)
- 📷 Read the introduction. Ask the question, then play the recording. With books closed, students listen for the answer.

Answer Jay

b
- 📷 Play the recording again while students listen and read.
- Pause to explain or elicit the meaning of *kiss* and the key expressions *Thanks for having me, I've had a great time, I'll miss you, Keep in touch, Have a good journey*.
- Focus on the use of the second conditional. Take the first example: *If I had a ticket, I'd go with you now*. Elicit the full form of *I'd* (*I would*). Ask: *Would Penny like to go to Mexico with Ana?* (*Yes.*) *Has she got a ticket?* (*No.*) *Is she going to go?* (*No.*) Make it clear that she's imagining a situation that isn't really possible.

- Explain that when Ana asks Charlie about a goodbye kiss, she thinks it's a possibility but doesn't really expect him to say *yes*. Similarly, when Charlie talks about his father being easy-going, he's suggesting that this is very unlikely to happen.
- Students read the sentences and look back at the text to decide if they're true or false.

Answers

1 False. She's had a great time.
2 False. She'll miss her.
3 True.
4 True.
5 True.
6 True.
7 True.
8 True.
9 False. He hasn't come but he's called her on the phone.

OPTION You can ask students to practise the conversation in groups of four.

3 Key grammar *Second conditional*

- Look at the examples and the explanations. Make sure students recognise that the speakers are imagining situations which are either improbable or impossible.
- Point out the use of the past simple for the *if* clause and *would* for the result clause.
- You may want to contrast the first and second conditionals. Write on the board these two examples:
  If she had a ticket, she'd go.
  If she's got a ticket, she'll go.
  Point out that the 'if' situation and its result seem much closer to reality in the second example – they're more likely to happen.
- Ask students to complete the explanation about the form of the second conditional. Make it clear that we use the contracted form *'d* with pronouns and point out that the form of *would/'d* remains the same for all subjects. Draw attention to the comma at the end of the *if* clause.
- You could explain that, as with the first conditional, it's possible to put the two clauses in the opposite order (*We wouldn't argue if Dad was more easy-going. I'd go with you if I had a ticket.*). In this case we don't use a comma.
- Note that when the verb *be* appears in the *if* clause, you will sometimes see *were* used instead of *was* with a singular subject (*If Dad were more easy-going, …*). However, this usage is becoming less common and there is no need to complicate the explanation by mentioning it to students here. It remains commonly used in the expression *If I were you, I'd …*

New beginnings

Answers past, 'd

4 Practice

a
- Read out the introduction to the exercise and ask students to match the sentence parts.

Answers 1 c 2 e 3 d 4 a 5 b

b
- Look at the first two lines of the conversation and elicit the ending of B's sentence.
- In pairs, students work out the rest of the conversation and then practise it together. Ask them to swap roles and repeat if they have time.
- Invite one pair to read out the conversation for the class.

Answers
A: Does Holly know the boy's number?
B: No, she doesn't. If she knew his number, she'd phone him.
A: Has she got his address?
B: No, she hasn't. If she had his address, she'd write to him.
A: Has the boy got Holly's number?
B: No, he hasn't. If he had her number, perhaps he'd call her.
A: Does the boy go to Holly's school?
B: No, he doesn't. If he went to her school, she'd see him every day.

c
- Students complete the sentences with the correct verb forms. They can do this orally and/or in writing.

Answers
2 lived, 'd go   3 helped, 'd get on
4 were, wouldn't lose   5 had, 'd buy
6 didn't go, wouldn't be   7 went, 'd visit
8 didn't exist, would be

- Pattern drill: TRP page 17 (Unit 12, Step 2)

d
- Choose two students to read out the conversation. Then elicit some different ideas for the underlined replies.
- In pairs, students practise the conversation and then replace the underlined words with their own replies.
- Ask different students to ask and answer across the class.
- Note that there is further work on comprehension and practice of the second conditional in the Module 6 Review at the end of Unit 12.

OPTION

You could use the situation in 4d for a 'chain' activity. Start off with the *if* clause: *If I won a lot of money, ...* Invite a student to supply an ending and to say the whole sentence. The next student makes the ending into an *if* clause and completes the new sentence. Continue the chain for as long as possible. For example:
A: If I won a lot of money, I'd buy a plane.
B: If I bought a plane, I'd fly to the USA.
C: If I flew to the USA, I'd stay in Hollywood.
D: If I stayed in Hollywood, I'd meet ...
If it starts to become difficult to answer, start another chain, beginning either with the original *if* clause or with a different one (for example, *If I left school tomorrow, If I could choose any job in the world* etc.).

Try this!
Answers: book, watch, biscuits, poster, mirror, tea

5 Key expressions *Saying goodbye*

a
- Read out the expressions (1–5) and ask students to repeat.
- Explain the meaning of *host*. Ask students to decide who says each of the expressions.

Answers 1 a 2 a 3 c 4 c 5 b

b
- Students match the expressions with the meanings.
- Remind them that we can say *Thanks for ...ing* or *Thanks for* + noun.
- Point out that we use the present perfect in the sentence *I've had a great time*, as we're talking about an experience that's only just coming to an end now. You could mention similar expressions for saying thanks at the end of a social occasion, for example:
I've had a fabulous time/a lot of fun.
It's been great/a great evening/a lovely afternoon/a fantastic party.

Answers 1 c 2 e 3 d 4 a 5 b

6 Key pronunciation /θ/ /ð/

a
- Play the recording while students listen and read the words.
- Play the recording again and ask students to repeat. Demonstrate the placement of the tongue between the teeth for both sounds.

Unit 12

- Point out that the /θ/ sound in list 1 is unvoiced – that is, there is no movement of the vocal cords. Ask students to place their fingers on each side of their throat and to say the sound in isolation. There should be no vibration in their throat. Contrast this with the voiced /ð/ sound in list 2, where the vocal cords vibrate and there is a louder sound.

b
- Play the recording. Students repeat the words and identify the sounds.

Tapescript/Answers

that (2)   thing (1)   those (2)
throw (1)   their (2)   these (2)

> **OPTION**
> If you have time, you could write up one or two sentences with a mixture of the two consonant sounds, for example:
> *This is the third Thursday of the month.*
> *Put both those toothbrushes together in the bathroom.*
> Ask students to identify the /θ/ and /ð/ sounds and to repeat the sentences.

7 Speaking *Imagine ...*

- Ask different students to read out the questions and elicit some answers from the class.
- Give students time to consider their own answers to the questions. Encourage them to think of reasons for their answers.
- In pairs, students ask and answer. If possible, they should add one or two questions of their own to ask their partner.

STEP 3

Reading skills: Scanning
Word work: Synonyms
Communicative task: Writing an essay

---

1 Share your ideas *Finding information*

- Ask the question and elicit a range of replies.

> **Example answers**
> – going to a town library
> – consulting references books, newspapers or magazines
> – looking at Internet websites
> – visiting museums, galleries or local government offices
> – watching television documentaries
> – emailing or telephoning information services attached to institutions
> – consulting friends or family members who have relevant experience

2 Reading

a Reading skills *Scanning*

- Look at the photos with the class and ask students to say what they think each paragraph is about. Use the photos to introduce the words *koala*, *pouch* and *cell*.
- Point out to the students that the aim here is to find particular information in the text. They aren't expected to understand the whole of the text. Instead, they should look for the part which contains each piece of information and then read to extract it.
- Read through the questions with the class. Ask students to identify key words that they will need to look for in the text. Also ask them to look carefully at the question words to identify the sort of information they will be looking for (1: a certain number of hours, 2: a quantity in kilograms or tons, 3: a total number of cars, 4: a period of time, 5: the name of something/things that the body is made of).
- Set the time limit. Students read and make a very brief note in answer to each question.

> **Answers**
> 1 2 hours.   2 Over 600 million tons.
> 3 Over 15 million.   4 16 days.   5 Cells.

b Comprehension check

- Play the recording of the text while students listen and read. Pause after each paragraph to help with new vocabulary (for example, *marsupial, collect, six times bigger, mass-produced, eight-lane, jumbo jet, away* [= distant from here], *approximately, millimetres [mm], stretch*).
- Ask some questions, for example:
  - Why is a marsupial different from other mammals? (Because it carries its babies in a pouch.)
  - Do you know any other marsupials? (Kangaroo, wallaby, possum, wombat.)
  - Is rice our main food? Where is most of the world's rice eaten? (In Asia.)
  - Was the Model T the world's first car? (No.) What was special about it? (It was the first mass-produced car.)
  - Would you really be able to get to the moon or the sun in a jumbo jet? (No.)
  - Have scientists put all the cells in the human body in one line? (No.)
- Ask students to read the sentences and to look carefully at the text to find the answers. You could ask them to correct the false sentences.
- Ask students to say which piece of information they found the most surprising or interesting.

New beginnings   105

> **Answers**
> 1 T
> 2 F A koala is a marsupial, but a bear isn't.
> 3 ?
> 4 ?
> 5 F Henry Ford started producing Model T cars in 1908.
> 6 T
> 7 F This is true of 'most cells', but not all.
> 8 F The number given is for the average adult body, not everyone's body.

c
- Ask students to find all the examples of the second conditional in the text.
- Point out that the writer is asking us to imagine situations which are actually impossible so that we can get a picture of these huge numbers and quantities.

> **Answers**
> If you were a koala, you would need 22 hours of sleep.
> If you collected all the rice ..., you would have a mountain ...
> If they all went out ..., they would make an eight-lane traffic jam ...
> If you travelled to the moon by jumbo jet, it would take 16 days.
> If you wanted to go to the Sun, it would take 20 years.
> If all the cells ... were put in a line, they would stretch 1,000 km.

3 Word work *Synonyms*

a
- Students match the synonyms in the two lists.

> **Answers**
> over – more than, main – most important, almost – nearly, made – produced, approximately – about

b
- Students match the words to make seven more pairs of synonyms.

> **Answers**
> annoyed – irritated, big – large, fantastic – wonderful, certainly – definitely, unusual – strange, start – begin, expensive – dear

c
- Ask students to test each other in pairs.

4 Writing *My country*

- This exercise can be started in class and completed for homework.
- Introduce the topic and read through the questions.

- Read through the Writing guide with the class. Remind students of the work they have done during the course which may be useful for their essay. Use the notes on planning to show how to group ideas together in paragraphs. Also draw their attention to the expressions for stating personal opinions.
- Ask students to make notes in answer to the questions in the exercise. They may want to check information at home or in a library. Tell them that they don't have to include all the answers in their essay and point out that there may be other topics that they want to cover instead of these (for example, history, geography, climate, famous people, festivals etc.).
- Students expand their notes into an essay of three or four paragraphs, using the Writing guide for help with language and organisation.
- Ask them to check their work. Encourage pairs to read each other's essays and to suggest corrections or improvements to their partner.
- Collect the finished essays to mark and choose two or three to read out in the next lesson. You may want to make a display of the work in the classroom, allowing students to walk around and read each other's essays.

> **Example answer**
> Greece is in southeast Europe. The population is over 11 million and the capital is Athens. The main language is Greek but Macedonian is also spoken and most students learn English at school.
> Greece has got more than 2,000 islands, and tourists come from all over the world to enjoy the sun and the blue sea. They also come because the history of the country is very interesting. The most famous temple from ancient Greece is on the Acropolis in Athens, but there are also amazing old buildings in places like Olympia, Delphi, Mycenae, Crete and Delos.
> Greeks eat a lot of lamb, fish and seafood. We also enjoy salads with tomatoes, olives and feta cheese. Sweet cakes are made with honey and nuts. Olives are grown everywhere in Greece and the local olive oil is used in a lot of dishes.
> In my opinion, Greece is a lovely country and I love living here. People are friendly and easy-going and life is very relaxed. I don't want to live anywhere else.

Extra exercises

1
- Students read the sentences and choose the correct replies. Ask them to say which speaker is leaving in conversations 1–4.
- Ask different students to say the conversations across the class.

> **Answers** 1 c 2 b 3 a 4 b 5 b

2
- Ask students to choose the correct form of *used to* to complete each sentence.

> **Answers** 1 c 2 b 3 b 4 a 5 b

3
- Point out that the mixed-up words 1–8 are American English. Ask students to write the words and match them with the British words a–h underneath.
- Check their understanding by asking questions, for example: *Which two words mean things you wear on your feet? Which ones mean something you can use to go upstairs in a tall building?*

> **Answers**
> 2 cookies – a biscuits
> 3 sidewalk – h pavement
> 4 pants – c trousers
> 5 elevator – d lift
> 6 closet – e wardrobe
> 7 sneakers – g trainers
> 8 store – b shop

4
- Remind students of the form of the second conditional.
- Ask them to choose the correct words for the conditional sentences.
- After checking the answers, you may like to ask students to change the sentences to the first conditional. Point out the difference in meaning.

> **Answers** 1 b 2 a 3 c 4 a 5 a

5
- Students use their own ideas to complete the conversation. Explain that there are lots of possible answers here.

> **Example answers**
> I'd take it to the police station.
> What would you do?
> I'd give it to my father for his birthday.

6
- Ask students to work on the translations in pairs or small groups, and then discuss with the whole class.

Extra reading

Life and culture Living in the past

Lead in
- Ask the question and elicit a range of answers, encouraging the students to use *used to*. Write up ideas in note form on the board as students suggest them.
- If you can find any photographs of the town 100 years ago, especially ones showing the fashions and lifestyle of ordinary people, show them to the class as part of the discussion.

Task
- Look at the photos and ask where and when they were taken. Point out that only one of them is really from over 100 years ago and ask students to identify which one. (*The black and white one.*) Establish that the objects and clothing in the other photos all belong to the 1880s in the USA – but the photos were taken only a few years ago for a TV programme. You could tell the class that the name of the programme was *Frontier House* and explain the meaning of *frontier*.
- Ask students to say what they can see in the photos and use them to introduce the words *Wild West* and *wagon*.
- Give students time to read through the text themselves.
- Read the text aloud and help with new vocabulary (for example, *applicants, land, ancestors, tools, skills, oil lamps, the Bible, heat, supplies*). Make it clear that *sorry* in the last sentence is used to mean 'sad'.
- Ask some questions to check comprehension, for example:
  - *Were the people in the programme actors?* (No.)
  - *Did they want to be in the programme?* (Yes.)
  - *Were there thousands of people in the programme?* (No – only three families.)
  - *Did they know how to do all the things their ancestors did?* (No. They learnt a lot of new skills.)
- Look at the table and elicit an example for the *didn't use to* column.
- Students copy the table and complete it with information from the text.
- Ask students: *Would you like to try this life? What do you think would be most difficult thing to learn? What would you miss most?*

> **Example answers**
>
> | used to | didn't use to |
> | --- | --- |
> | look after farm animals | buy all their food in shops |
> | grow food to eat | have electric lights |
> | make butter | watch television |
> | catch fish | listen to the radio |
> | use oil lamps | have gas or electric cookers |
> | read the Bible and talk in the evening | have washing machines |
> | collect wood for cooking and heating | drive cars |
> | wash their clothes by hand | have lots of shops near them |
> | travel by horse and wagon | have mobile phones |
> | take hours to get to the store | have computers |
> | write letters | write emails |

New beginnings 107

Module 6 Review

Grammar check

1 Reported speech

Work it out for yourself

A
- Students compare the verbs in the direct and reported speech and complete the explanation.

Answer past

B
- Ask students to comment on the difference between *say* and *tell* and the use of *that*.

Answers
Tell is followed by an object (a person) but we use *say* on its own.
We can use *that* to introduce reported speech, but we often leave it out.

1.1 • Look at the example. Remind students that as well as changing the verb from the present to the past, we often need to use a different pronoun for reported speech.

Answers
2 They said (that) they all got on well with each other.
3 He said (that) his dog was his closest friend.
4 She said (that) she always had a row with her boyfriend at parties.
5 He said (that) he didn't listen to other people's advice.
6 They said (that) they didn't spend much time with their children.

1.2 • Students use the correct form of *say* or *tell*.

Answers
1 told 2 tell, said 3 say, told 4 told, tell, say

2 Question tags

Work it out for yourself

A
- Students match the sentences with the explanations. Ask student to say the two sentences, with falling intonation for 1 and rising intonation for 2.

Answers 1 b 2 a

B
- Students answer the questions.

Answers 1 affirmative 2 negative

C
- Ask students to study the sentences and then complete the explanations.

Answers 1 will 2 does, don't 3 did

- You may want to go through the whole exercise before asking students to write.
- Students supply the correct tags. Ask them to do this first without referring back to the examples in 2C and then to look back and check.

Answers
2 do you   3 did you   4 have you   5 didn't you
6 isn't she   7 wasn't it   8 doesn't it
9 were they   10 can't we

3 used to

Work it out for yourself

- Students complete the matching task to compare the past simple with *used to*.

Answers
1 a, c
2 a, b, d

3.1 • Ask students to put the words in the right order.

Answers
2 Where did you use to live?
3 I used to read comics.
4 I never used to drink coffee.
5 Did you use to be scared of dogs?
6 I didn't use to wear glasses.

3.2 • Students use the verbs in brackets with *used to*.

Answers
2 used to have   3 didn't use to like
4 used to be   5 Did you use to live

4 The second conditional

Work it out for yourself

- Students match the sentences with the explanations.

> **Answers** 1 B 2 A

- Look at the example with the class. You might want to go through the other sentences orally before students write.

> **Answers**
> 2 If I had €50, I'd buy a ticket.
> 3 If I didn't have a lot of homework, I'd go out.
> 4 If I saw a ghost, I wouldn't be scared.
> 5 If I didn't use a dictionary, I wouldn't be able to do my English homework.

Study skills 6 Checking your work

- Emphasise the importance of checking written work for errors.
- Students complete the matching task, and correct the mistakes in the sentences.
- Ask pairs to exchange some written work, preferably from Module 6. Ask them to mark any mistakes they find and to offer explanations and correction to their partner.
- You could ask students to make a note of errors that they often make at the back of their vocabulary notebook, with the corrected error underlined or highlighted in a colour.

> **Answers**
> 1 b 2 e 3 d 4 a 5 c

How's it going?

Your rating

- Students look back at the exercises in the Grammar check and make their own assessment of how well they understand and remember the different language points.

Vocabulary

- Students write sentences with five of the new words and then check for errors.

Test a friend

- Look at the example questions and elicit the correct answers.
- Students refer back to the texts in Units 11 and 12 and write several questions to test their partner. They then ask and answer in pairs.

> **Answers**
> No, he doesn't.
> No, she isn't.

Correcting mistakes

- The sentences listed here contain some common errors. Ask students to rewrite them correctly.
- Some sentences contain more than one error. Make sure students are aware of this, and that they find both errors in question 2.
- Emphasise the importance of going back over their work to check for errors when they finish a piece of writing.

> **Answers**
> 1 Dave told me he wasn't lazy. / Dave said that he wasn't lazy.
> 2 She told me she was sorry. / She said she was sorry.
> 3 You go to karate, don't you?
> 4 They didn't use to go to my school.
> 5 What would you do if you had a million dollars?

Your Workbook

- Students should complete the Learning diary when they come to the end of each unit.

Coursework 6

My guidebook

Entertainment

- Ask students to look at the pictures and photos on Ana's guidebook page and to say what the people are doing. Use the photos to introduce the words *dodgems* and *music festival*. Explain what a *radio station* is.
- Give students time to read through the text on their own.
- Ask some questions to check comprehension, for example:
  - *What's Time Out?* (A magazine.) *Why do people buy it?* (To find out what's happening in London.)
  - *Where's the Trocadero?* (At Piccadilly Circus.)
  - *What's Romeo and Juliet?* (A play.) *Who wrote it?* (Shakespeare.)
  - *What's Coronation Street?* (A soap opera.)
  - *What are the names of two radio stations?* (BBC Radio 1 and Radio 4.)
  - *When's the Glastonbury Festival?* (At the end of June.)
- Ask students for some ideas about entertainment in their country. Choose one or two of their examples and elicit some information that a visitor would find useful to know.
- Ask students to plan their text. They should write at least four paragraphs and illustrate their text as they wish.
- Set a time limit, allowing one to two weeks for work on the project. Some work may be done in class and some at home.
- Ask students to check their text before they write a final version and design their page.

Module 6 Review

Games

Twenty questions

Choose a particular category (for example, countries, places in town, outdoor activities, sports clothes, types of food). One student thinks of something in this category and the others have to guess what it is. They can only ask *yes/no* questions and they have a maximum of 20 questions that they can ask to guess the answer.

Team quiz

A team quiz can draw on students' general knowledge (with teams devising questions in the past simple or the passive, for example) but it can also be used to practise vocabulary (with teams providing definitions) or to test spelling or the recognition of numbers. Divide the class into teams of four or five students. Each team thinks of four questions using the target language to ask the other teams. In turn, each team reads out its questions, announcing the number of each one clearly. The other teams have a time limit of one minute to confer and write down their answer for each question. When all the questions have been asked, each team passes their answer sheet on to another team to mark. In turn, they read out the answers to the questions and the 'asking' team confirms correct answers or provides the correct answer where necessary. Teams score a point for each correct answer, and the winning team is the one with the highest total at the end. If there is any dispute about the correct answers, you will need to adjudicate. If a team gives an incorrect answer for one of their own questions, they lose two points.

Information memory game

When students give information about themselves or report back on their partner after a speaking activity, you can use the information as the basis for a memory game. Ask a number of students to give their information and tell everyone to listen carefully. Then divide the class into teams. Team A and B students take it in turns to say a true sentence reporting a piece of information they heard. The student who gave the information can say whether the sentence is correct or not. If it is correct, the team scores a point. If it is incorrect or repeats a previous answer, the team gets nothing.

Use the verbs

This team game is for revision of irregular verbs in the past simple or irregular past participles. Divide the class into two or three teams. Asking each team in turn, you say an irregular verb in the infinitive form. The team scores one point if a team member can say the verb in the target form (past simple or past participle) and two more points if they can make a correct sentence using this form. One member of the team answers each time, but can consult briefly with a neighbour. Keep the scores on the board. The team with the most points at the end is the winner.

Adverbs

Divide the class into two teams, A and B. Members of each team work together to think of six instructions using an action and an adverb (for example, *Dance sadly. Play tennis lazily. Write an email slowly.*). Ask them to write their instructions on separate slips of paper and fold them. A volunteer from Team A takes one of Team B's instructions and performs the action in the manner of the adverb. The others in Team A have to try to guess what he/she is doing (both the action and the adverb) in less than one minute. Then it is Team B's turn to pick one of Team A's instructions, and so the game continues. You can keep time. Record the times that the teams take to guess the answers in two lists on the board, and call 'Time's up!' if they can't guess within a minute. The team with the smallest time total at the end is the winner.

Workbook key and tapescripts

1 Connections

STEP 1

1
2 What's your name?
3 Do you live in Spain?
4 Where do you come from?
5 What are you doing in Spain?
6 Are you staying at the hostel?
7 What do you think of Barcelona?

2
2 Has / No, she hasn't.
3 Are / Yes, there are.
4 Does / Yes, she does.
5 Is / No, she isn't.
6 Are / Yes, they are.
7 Do / Yes, they do.
8 Have / No, they haven't.

3 Check individual answers.

4a
1 How are you?
2 I'm fine, thanks.
3 Jack, this is my friend Tina.
4 Nice to meet you, Tina.

4b
1 Mum, this is my science teacher, Mr Gray.
2 How do you, do, Mr Gray?
3 How do you do?

5 2 No 3 Yes 4 Yes 5 No 6 Yes 7 Yes

TAPESCRIPT

KELLY: Natalie, who's that guy over there?
NATALIE: Oh, he's my cousin. Come and meet him … Adam, this is my friend Kelly. Kelly, this is Adam.
ADAM: Hello, Kelly. Nice to meet you.
KELLY: Hi, Adam. You're Natalie's cousin, right?
ADAM: Yes, that's right.
KELLY: Do you live round here?
ADAM: No, I don't. I live in Bristol.
KELLY: Oh. So what are you doing in London?
ADAM: Well, I've got a holiday job here, so I'm staying with my uncle and aunt at the moment.
KELLY: Oh, right.
ADAM: What about you? Do you live here in London?
KELLY: Yes, I do. I was born in Ireland but my family moved here four years ago.
ADAM: And do you know Natalie well?
KELLY: Oh yeah. We're in the same class at school and we're really good friends …

6 Check individual answers.

STEP 2

1
2 Japan 3 French 4 Australian 5 Poland
6 American 7 Italian 8 Canada 9 Spanish
10 Argentina

2

	lives in Paris	walks to school	has lunch at home	likes art
Alice	✓	✗	✗	✗
Louise	✓	✓	✓	✓
Christine	✓	✓	✗	✓

Name of the girl in the photo: Louise

3 2 lives 3 work 4 isn't, go 5 doesn't play/ loves (or) likes

4 Answers may be in any order.
In picture A Peter and Helen are playing chess, but in picture B they're playing cards.
In picture A Helen's wearing glasses, but in picture B she isn't wearing glasses.
In picture A Rebecca's reading a magazine, but in picture B she's looking at photos.
In picture A it's raining, but in picture B it isn't raining.
In picture A the dog's eating, but in picture B it's drinking.

5 2 are playing 3 beats 4 isn't winning 5 's feeling
6 isn't watching 7 doesn't like 8 wants 9 's looking

6 Check individual answers.

STEP 3

1 technology, Earth

2 2 each other 3 French-speaking 4 over 5 Earth
6 technology 7 connect 8 communicate
9 worldwide 10 like

3 Check individual answers.

2 Past events

STEP 1

1
Across
4 argued
6 bought
8 ran
9 went
10 left
12 saw
14 sold
15 broke

Down
1 caught
2 began
3 wrote
5 stopped
7 tried
9 was
11 took
13 were

2 2 didn't sell 3 didn't take 4 didn't go / wasn't
5 didn't see / didn't catch 6 didn't buy / weren't

Workbook key and tapescripts 111

3
2 Where did she meet Jill?
3 Where did they go?
4 How did they get to the park?
5 When (or) What time did they arrive?
6 What did Sonia do at the park?
7 Did Jill go rollerblading too?

4
2 A 3 C 4 B 5 A

TAPESCRIPT

1 BOY A: So how was Saturday, Sam? What did you do in the afternoon?
  BOY B: I went to the cinema with Martina. She went swimming in the morning, so we met at that café next to the swimming pool.

2 GIRL: Tim, how did you get to the stadium yesterday?
  BOY: I got the 88 bus from the station. It doesn't stop at the stadium, so I got off at the church and walked across the park.

3 MOTHER: You're late home, Julie. It's ten to seven.
  JULIE: Yes, I know. We had a long band practice after school. We started at twenty to four and finished at half past five. And after that I went to Emma's.

4 CARLA: Sophie!
  SOPHIE: Hi, Carla.
  CARLA: You were on the phone for hours last night. I tried to phone you five times. Were you talking to Paul?
  SOPHIE: Oh yeah, probably. He rang about eight o'clock. I got a phone call from Robert too. And I called Lisa, but she wasn't at home.

5 BOY A: I saw Tony yesterday.
  BOY B: Oh, did he have a good holiday in Greece?
  BOY A: He didn't go to Greece. He travelled through France and got a train to Rome. He stayed there for a week and then he came home.

5
2 all right 3 Don't worry 4 doesn't matter
5 your fault

6
Check individual answers.

STEP 2

1
2 land   landed
3 fall   fell
4 crash   crashed
5 jump   jumped
6 sink   sank
7 hit   hit
8 fly   flew

2
3 were riding 4 wasn't going 5 fell 6 arrived
7 was coming 8 found 9 were flying 10 were trying
11 saw 12 was dancing 13 was laughing

3
2 Was / wasn't
3 Were / Yes/were
4 were / ran
5 fall / Yes/did
6 was / was coming
7 were / were trying
8 Was / No/wasn't/was laughing

4
1 Southampton 2 passengers 3 a few 4 sailor
5 survived 6 ocean

5
Check individual answers.

TAPESCRIPT

ALAN: Hi, how are you?
GIRL: Fine, thanks.
ALAN: I tried to find you at lunchtime yesterday. Where were you?
GIRL: I was in the school canteen.
ALAN: Oh, right. So what did you have for lunch?
GIRL: I had soup and pasta.
ALAN: Were you on your own?
GIRL: No, Beth and Joanne were sitting at my table.
ALAN: And what did you do after lunch?
GIRL: I had a maths class in Room 10.
ALAN: Yes, I see. Well, I must go. I'll see you later, OK?
GIRL: Yes, OK. Bye.

STEP 3

1
survive, fall asleep, shake, cut

2
2 knife 3 fall asleep 4 heart attack 5 below
6 survive 7 grass 8 shake 9 noise 10 cut
11 surface 12 passenger 13 branch 14 over

3
Check individual answers.

3 People

STEP 1

1
2 tall 3 young 4 friendly 5 curly 6 old 7 fast
8 short

2
3 younger than 4 the most popular 5 bigger than
6 heavier than 7 the most expensive 8 the busiest

3
2 more 3 than 4 worst 5 better 6 worse
7 most 8 best

4
2 T 3 F 4 T 5 ? 6 ? 7 F 8 T

112 Workbook key and tapescripts

5

2 Don't be stupid!
3 When ice starts to melt, it forms water.
4 Our friends from Oslo were staying here.
5 Is your uncle a nervous man?
6 Carol destroyed her brother's computer game.
7 Ring me tomorrow or send an email.
8 If you're tired, have a siesta.

Comparative	Superlative
slower	best
cleaner	nicest
worse	oldest
	easiest

STEP 2

1a
2 generous   3 clever   4 moody   5 shy   6 hard-working
7 adventurous   8 confident   9 easy-going   10 lazy

1b
2 confident   3 hard-working   4 generous   5 moody

2
2 isn't as hard-working as
3 'm as tall as
4 aren't as long as
5 'm as good as
6 is as dark as
7 is as good as
8 wasn't as bad as

3
2 i   3 a   4 g   5 f   6 c   7 j   8 d

4a
Harry – B   Erica – E   Simon – D

4b
1 b   2 b   3 c   4 a

TAPESCRIPT

MOTHER: Who's your best friend at school, Leo?
LEO: Well, Harry's a good mate – I really like him.
MOTHER: Harry? Do I know him? What does he look like?
LEO: Oh, he's about as tall as me and he's got fair curly hair. I think he's the cleverest person in our class.
MOTHER: Oh, really?
LEO: His sister's nice too – her name's Erica. She's two years younger than Harry, but she looks just like him.
MOTHER: And is she as intelligent as Harry?
LEO: Yes, she is, but she isn't very confident. People think she's moody but she isn't moody. She's just shy.
MOTHER: And who else is in your group?
LEO: Well, there's Simon. All the girls like him because he's tall and dark and good-looking.
MOTHER: What do you think of him?
LEO: Well, he makes me laugh. But his jokes are sometimes a bit cruel. He isn't as generous as Harry and Erica.

5
Check individual answers.

STEP 3

1
2 Click   3 takes   4 nearby   5 contact   6 untidy
7 embarrassing   8 jokes   9 captain   10 annoyed
11 tidy   12 fun

2
Check individual answers.

4 Places

STEP 1

1
2 department store   3 mosque   4 theme park
5 art gallery   6 castle   7 temple

2
2 h   3 e   4 g   5 c   6 a   7 b   8 d

3
2 take a boat trip
3 we have lunch
4 going to the art gallery
5 look round
6 don't we visit (or) go to the castle

4
2 (I think) That's a good
3 shall we go
4 don't mind
5 rather go to the castle
6 That's fine
7 we go to the swimming pool
8 don't really want to
9 don't we go to the beach
10 right then
11 go on the bus (or) go by bus (or) catch the bus

5
2 Square   3 free   4 10 o'clock   5 6 o'clock
6 Palace   7 Oxford   8 12.30

TAPESCRIPT

ROSA: Hello.
LUKE: Hi, Rosa. It's Luke.
ROSA: Oh hi, Luke. How are you?
LUKE: I'm fine. Listen, let's do something together tomorrow. How about going to the cinema?
ROSA: Ah … well, I need to look at some paintings for my art project. Why don't we go to the National Gallery?
LUKE: Where?
ROSA: The National Gallery – in Trafalgar Square.
LUKE: Oh, right. Yeah, that's fine with me. Does it cost much to get in?
ROSA: No, it's free.
LUKE: Oh, that's good. But are you sure it's open on Sunday?
ROSA: Yes, it opens at ten o'clock and closes at six in the evening.
LUKE: Right. Well, let's have lunch first.
ROSA: Yeah, that's a good idea. Shall we meet at the gallery café?
LUKE: Um, I think I'd rather have a pizza. Let's meet at the Pizza Palace in Oxford Street.
ROSA: OK, that's fine. About 12.30?
LUKE: Fine. See you at 12.30 tomorrow at the Pizza Palace.

6
Check individual answers.

Workbook key and tapescripts   113

STEP 2

1 2 many 3 a lot of 4 many 5 much
6 many 7 a lot of 8 much

2 1 too much 2 too many / enough 3 too much / enough 4 enough / too many 5 enough / too much 6 too many / enough

3 1 c 2 a 3 c 4 a 5 b

4 Check individual answers.

TAPESCRIPT

EMMA: How about going out somewhere on Saturday?
BOY: Yes, that's a good idea.
EMMA: Where shall we go? Have you got any suggestions?
BOY: Let's go to the museum.
EMMA: Oh, well … no, I don't really want to do that. I'd rather go shopping.
BOY: OK, that's fine with me.
EMMA: Great. So, where shall we meet?
BOY: Let's meet outside the post office.
EMMA: All right, then. What time?
BOY: How about 2.30?
EMMA: Fine. See you then.

STEP 3

1 midnight, g and h

2 1 all the time 2 as well 3 classmate 4 extra
5 get to 6 midnight 7 normal 8 packed lunch
9 still 10 pay

3 Check individual answers.

5 Goals

STEP 1

1 2 are meeting 3 is leaving 4 isn't going
5 'm not taking 6 're having 7 is starting
8 is bringing 9 're arriving

2 2 She's going to play basketball.
3 we're going to buy some tickets.
4 She's going to clean her teeth.
5 He's going to visit his wife.
6 They're going to catch the 7.30 train.

3 2 g 3 a 4 f 5 b 6 h 7 c 8 d

4 1 F 2 F 3 ? 4 T 5 T 6 F 7 T 8 ?

5 Check individual answers.

STEP 2

1 1 shorts 2 boots 3 tracksuit 4 trunks / swimsuit
5 wetsuit 6 goggles 7 socks

2a 2 a 3 f 4 e 5 b 6 c

2b 2 I'll make some sandwiches.
3 I'll pay for your ticket.
4 I'll wash the floor.
5 I'll show you.
6 I'll ring her.

3 Check individual answers.

4 1 C 2 C 3 A 4 B 5 B

TAPESCRIPT

1 BOY: Mum, where's my tracksuit? I want to go for a run before lunch.
MOTHER: Your tracksuit? It's in the washing machine.
BOY: Oh. OK, I'll wear my shorts.

2 BOY: Are you going to play volleyball this afternoon?
GIRL: I don't think so. I think I'll stay at home and watch the tennis.

3 FATHER: What are you going to do this morning?
BOY: I think I'll go to the beach. I'll take my surfboard with me.
FATHER: Are you sure? It's very cold!
BOY: That's OK. I'll wear my wetsuit.

4 GIRL A: Hey, Sue! I'm going to ride down to the river. Do you want to come?
GIRL B: Mmm, that's a good idea. Wait there and I'll get my bike. I won't be long.

5 BOY: Do you want to play cards?
GIRL: You're joking! You always beat me at cards. Anyway, the sports centre's open now. I think I'll go and have a swim.

5 2 How much is it?
3 the right size
4 size do you take
5 Can I try it on?

6 Check individual answers.

STEP 3

1 lazy, ambitious, forgetful, afraid, irritating, honest, successful, well-paid

2 2 ambitious 3 afraid 4 lazy 5 well-paid 6 forgetful
7 successful 8 honest

3 Check individual answers.

6 Choices

STEP 1

1
Across	Down
3 pepper	1 spoon
5 salt	2 glass
6 knife	4 plate
9 serviette	7 fork
	8 menu

2 2 a 3 h 4 g 5 f 6 b 7 e 8 c

3 2 a 3 c 4 b 5 a 6 c 7 c 8 b 9 a

4 2 Could you open the door, please?
3 I'd like a beefburger, please.
4 Could I use your phone, please?
5 I'd like an apple, please.
6 Could you pass me the water, please?

Workbook key and tapescripts

5 1 j, k 2 b, g, h 3 a, e, i

TAPESCRIPT

DAD: OK. Here's the waitress. Are we ready to order?
ADAM: Yes! I'm starving.
WAITRESS: Would you like to order?
DAD: Yes, please. Becky, what are you going to have?
BECKY: Could I have some pâté as a starter, please? And then for my main course, I'd like lasagne with green salad.
WAITRESS: I'm sorry; we haven't got any pâté at the moment.
BECKY: Oh. Oh, well … I won't have a starter. I'll have some ice cream for dessert.
WAITRESS: So that's lasagne with salad …
DAD: What about you, Adam?
ADAM: I'd like some soup. What soup have you got today?
WAITRESS: Vegetable or chicken.
ADAM: Um … chicken, please. And then I'd like steak.
WAITRESS: With chips?
ADAM: Yes, please.
WAITRESS: And for you, sir?
DAD: Could I have the vegetable soup, please … and then the fish.
WAITRESS: Would you like your fish with chips or new potatoes?
DAD: Potatoes, please.
WAITRESS: Fine. Anything else?
DAD: No, that's all, thanks.

6 2 serviette 3 plate 4 carrot 5 soup 6 vegetarians
7 tart 8 rice

STEP 2

1 2 won't be late
3 'll visit you again
4 'll send you an email
5 won't hurt
6 'll come in a minute

2 2 might snow 3 might not have 4 might not go
5 might belong 6 might not agree

3 2 won't go 3 might not have 4 'll be (very) good
5 might get

4 1 Nick 2 Gemma 3 Gemma 4 Gemma 5 Nick
6 Gemma 7 Nick 8 Gemma / Nick

5 Check individual answers.

TAPESCRIPT

PATRICK: I think I'll start with tomato salad. Are you going to have a starter?
GIRL: Yes, I think I'll have melon with ham.
PATRICK: What about the main course?
GIRL: I'll have chicken with mushroom sauce.
PATRICK: Yes, that'll be nice. And I might have some chocolate ice cream for dessert. What about you?
GIRL: I might have some coffee ice cream.
PATRICK: The waiter's coming now. Are you ready?
GIRL: Yes, I am.
WAITER: Would you like to order?
GIRL: Yes, please. Could I have melon with ham, and then chicken with mushroom sauce?

STEP 3

1 washing machine, coffee maker, computer chip

2 2 g 3 f 4 j 5 a 6 h 7 i 8 b 9 d 10 e

3 Check individual answers.

7 Achievements

STEP 1

1a 2 arrived 3 dropped 4 buy 5 did 6 done
7 break 8 broken 9 took 10 taken 11 forget
12 forgotten

1b 2 He's broken the window.
3 You've dropped your scarf.
4 She's forgotten her keys.
5 They've done the shopping.
6 I've invented a new machine.

2 2 hasn't finished 3 haven't met 4 hasn't done
5 haven't made 6 haven't taken 7 hasn't come back

3 1 T 2 F 3 F 4 T 5 ? 6 T 7 ? 8 F 9 F

4 2 What have they bought?
3 How many people have joined Park Rescue?
4 How much (money) have they raised?
5 Have they made a skateboarding area?
6 Has the café opened yet?
7 Has the (or) Selwood Park improved?

5 Check individual answers.

STEP 2

1 2 in 3 put 4 on 5 out 6 unplug

2 2 've bought / did you get 3 took / 's lost
4 haven't taken / put 5 dropped / 's promised
6 hasn't come / disappeared

3 2 Have you finished / explained / 've forgotten
3 's broken / did that happen / hit
4 Has Steve watched / did he think / hated

4 1 c 2 b 3 c 4 a 5 a

TAPESCRIPT

A fire has destroyed two shops and a factory in Bridge Street. Police are trying to discover what started the fire at about five o'clock this morning. They have closed the street and are asking people to stay out of the area.

Workbook key and tapescripts **115**

A Bristol teenager has saved the life of her young brother. Thirteen-year-old Karen Jones swam 100 metres to help her brother Greg, who fell into the river at a family picnic. The parents say that both children are well.

The Tate Modern in London has paid £14,000 for two paintings by local artist William Spencer. Mr Spencer has lived all his life in southwest England. He has painted more than 200 pictures of the landscape round his home.

The rock group *Wild Roses* met doctors at the Farnby town hospital this afternoon. The band has raised over £15,000 for a new heart machine at the hospital.

And finally, in sport: Bristol City football star Graham McShann will move from Bristol to Middlesbrough next year. McShann has played in 65 matches for Bristol City and has scored 34 goals.

5
2 I think so. But you need to turn it on.
3 I think so. She's getting better now.
4 I don't think so. They aren't great sports fans.
5 I think so. I saw them together a few days ago.
6 I don't think so. She's still in the kitchen.

6
2 travelled 3 taken 4 landed 5 learnt 6 built
7 studied

TAPESCRIPT

I've sailed along the Amazon,
I've travelled by balloon,
I've taken flights to outer space,
I've landed on the moon,
But still somehow I find
I can't leave you behind.

I've learnt eleven languages,
I've built a bridge or two,
I've studied Chinese writing and
The history of Peru,
But still somehow I find
You're always on my mind.

STEP 3

1 2 plant 3 endangered, determined 4 injured, channels 5 campaign, protect

2 2 volunteers 3 protect its babies 4 is endangered
5 's injured 6 determined person (or) girl
7 a campaign 8 channels

3 Check individual answers.

8 Experiences

STEP 1

1 1 surfing 2 bungee-jump 3 canoeing
4 snowboarding 5 scuba-diving 6 skateboarding
7 climbing 8 sailing

2
2 Have you ever ridden
  I haven't / 've never learnt
3 Has Fiona ever made
  she hasn't / 's never cooked

3
2 've just seen a ghost.
3 has just fallen asleep.
4 've just been to China.
5 has just learnt to walk.
6 've just swum 400 metres.

4 2 e 3 a 4 b 5 d

TAPESCRIPT
ROSA: Hi, Gary.
GARY: Hi, Rosa. How are you?
ROSA: Great. I've just been canoeing. I went about eight kilometres down the river this morning. Have you ever tried canoeing?
GARY: No, I haven't.
ROSA: I really love it.
GARY: Mmm. Everyone's doing something exciting.
ROSA: What do you mean?
GARY: Well, you know Megan? She's just played in the basketball final.
ROSA: Oh yes, I know. Megan was brilliant.
GARY: Yeah. I think she'll get into the national team one day.
ROSA: Yeah, maybe she will.
GARY: And then there's Jay. He's bought a wetsuit and goggles. He's going to take scuba-diving lessons.
ROSA: Oh, really? Great.
GARY: And I've just seen Tom. He's just done a bungee-jump. He said it was an amazing experience.
ROSA: Wow!
GARY: I've never done a bungee-jump! I've never done anything interesting.
ROSA: Gary, that's rubbish. Your paintings are really good. I think you might win the art prize at school this year.
GARY: Hmm, well, maybe …

5
2 Yes, I have. I tried it once when I was in France.
3 When did you go to France?
4 I went there a year ago with my uncle. Have you ever been to France?
5 No, I haven't, but I'd like to go there one day. Do you travel a lot with your family?
6 No, I don't, but I've been abroad twice.
7 You're lucky. I've never travelled outside England and I've never been on a plane.

6 1 bus driver 2 shop assistant 3 doctor 4 trainer
5 actress

STEP 2

1 1 the day before yesterday 2 a couple of days
3 the Saturday before last 4 ages 5 a few weeks
6 several months 7 last weekend

116 Workbook key and tapescripts

2a 2 since 3 for 4 for 5 since 6 Since 7 for

2b 1 c 2 b 3 b 4 a 5 c 6 c

3
2 Have your friends ever tried skateboarding? e
3 Has Dad bought a new coffee maker? f
4 How long have you known Sandra? a
5 Has Helen lived in London for a long time? d
6 How many times have you been camping? b

4
2 lived in London since [year] (or) for 30 years.
3 been in her room for two hours (or) since [time].
4 just finished his lunch.
5 had this watch since January (or) for [number] months.
6 been interested in Africa for nine years (or) since she was eight.
7 just started his exam.

5 Check individual answers.

TAPESCRIPT

SARA: Have you lived here all your life?
BOY: No, I haven't. I came here with my family nine years ago.
SARA: Oh, right. Have you ever travelled abroad?
BOY: Yes, I've been to Greece twice to stay with my grandparents.
SARA: How long have you been at your school?
BOY: For three years.
SARA: Have you enjoyed studying English?
BOY: Yes, it's been good.
SARA: What's your favourite sport?
BOY: Basketball.
SARA: Have you ever played in a school competition?
BOY: No, I haven't.

STEP 3

1 huge

2 1 fight 2 AIDS 3 perform 4 success 5 biography
6 album 7 field 8 awards 9 including 10 huge

3 Check individual answers.

9 Getting it right

STEP 1

1 2 don't have to 3 have to 4 has to 5 have to
6 doesn't have to 7 have to 8 have to
9 doesn't have to 10 don't have to

2
2 ~~have to~~ mustn't
3 ~~has to~~ doesn't have to
4 ~~have to~~ don't have to
5 ~~have to~~ don't have to
6 ~~have to~~ mustn't
7 ~~have to~~ mustn't
8 ~~has to~~ doesn't have to

3
2 have to = d   3 don't have to = a
4 have to / mustn't = c

4a 1 C 2 A 3 D 4 B

4b 1 T 2 F 3 ? 4 T 5 T 6 T 7 F 8 F 9 ?

5 Check individual answers.

STEP 2

1 1 fainted 2 sick 3 broken 4 sore 5 hurt
6 backache 7 injection 8 headache

2 2 shouldn't worry 3 should feel 4 should / do
5 shouldn't work 6 should get 7 should go

3 Example answers
1 You should buy her a present now.
2 They should put an advert in the newspaper.
3 He should go to the doctor.
4 You should buy a dictionary.

4a 1 f 2 b 3 a 4 g 5 d

4b 1 Emma 2 Claire 3 Tom 4 Sally's 5 Adam

TAPESCRIPT

1 MAN: Ow! It hurts.
  WOMAN: Adam, you really should go to the dentist.
  MAN: Yes, you're right. I'll ring him. Perhaps he'll be able to see me this afternoon.

2 GIRL A: Hi, Claire! How are you feeling?
  CLAIRE: Awful.
  GIRL A: But we've got the concert tonight.
  CLAIRE: I know, but I don't think I'll be able to sing. I'm losing my voice.

3 BOY: I've just been to see Emma.
  GIRL: Oh, how is she?
  BOY: Well, it was a bad accident. She'll be in hospital for two or three days and she won't be able to walk for a week.
  GIRL: Oh, poor Emma.

4 BOY: Oh, I'm not feeling very well.
  FATHER: Well, that's your fault, Tom. You've just had three beefburgers. And you shouldn't eat so fast.
  BOY: Oh! All right. I know.

5 BOY: Sally! Are you OK?
  SALLY: Yes, I think so. But I feel a bit strange.
  BOY: Phew! I was worried when you fell. And you didn't open your eyes for ages.
  SALLY: Can we go outside? I need some fresh air.

5 1 c 2 e 3 h 4 a 5 g 6 b

6
2 fainted   (The others are adjectives.)
3 earache   (The others are parts of the body.)
4 ambulance   (The others are jobs.)
5 first-aid   (The others are illnesses.)
6 move   (The others are past participles.)
7 mobile   (The others are verbs.)

Workbook key and tapescripts 117

STEP 3

1 accidentally, noisily

2
2 ~~birthday~~ funeral   3 ~~intelligently~~ accidentally
4 ~~sing~~ apologise   5 ~~crocodile~~ custom   6 ~~leg~~ thumb
7 ~~wash~~ lick   8 ~~come here~~ go away   9 ~~bathroom~~ wedding   10 ~~quietly~~ noisily

3 Check individual answers.

10 Where is it made?

STEP 1

1 1 glass   2 leather   3 cotton   4 silver   5 metal
6 wood   7 gold   8 plastic

2a 1 Picture F   2 Picture H   3 Picture C   4 Picture A
5 Picture E

2b Picture A cotton   Picture C glass   Picture E metal
Picture H gold

TAPESCRIPT

1 Now come on, ladies! Come and have a look at these bags. All made of real leather from Brazil. And all at special cheap prices today. What about you, madam? Would you like to …

2 CUSTOMER: How much is this necklace?
   STALLHOLDER: Let's see. That one is … £215.
   CUSTOMER: Oh, that's expensive!
   STALLHOLDER: Well, it's gold, of course, and it's over a hundred years old …

3 CUSTOMER: Can I see that bowl at the back?
   STALLHOLDER: Yes, of course … It's a nice little bowl, that. Lovely colour.
   CUSTOMER: Yes, it is nice.
   STALLHOLDER: It's Italian glass. Comes from Venice.
   CUSTOMER: Oh, I see …

4 STALLHOLDER: Can I help you, or are you just having a look?
   CUSTOMER: Um … I'm thinking about one of these skirts. Is it OK to put them in the washing machine?
   STALLHOLDER: Oh yeah, that's fine. They're all made of cotton so you can wash them in the machine. No problem at all …

5 CUSTOMER: Oh! That's a lamp, is it?
   STALLHOLDER: That's right. In the shape of a bird. It's clever, isn't it? Kids love these.
   CUSTOMER: What's it made of? Plastic?
   STALLHOLDER: No, it's all metal. And it's only £8.99 …

3 1 are played   2 isn't used   3 is imported
4 aren't made   5 are spoken   6 isn't usually eaten
7 is grown   8 aren't found

4 Example answers
The Golden Gate Bridge isn't made of gold.
Fiat cars are made in Italy.
Fiat cars are sold in Italy (or) all over the world.
English is spoken all over the world.
Rice isn't grown in very cold countries.
Rice is sold in Italy (or) all over the world.

5 Example answers
2 That's incredible! That's amazing!
3 That's crazy! That's strange!
4 That's awful! That's terrible!
5 That's interesting! That's strange!

6 born, broken, done, eaten, known, learnt, lost, read, said, seen, sold, spoken, stolen, taken, won, written

STEP 2

1
2 were / built
3 weren't eaten
4 was stolen / wasn't found
5 was (or) were sold
6 was held / weren't watched

2
2 Curry is eaten with rice.
3 This leather was produced in South America.
4 Some DVD players were stolen.
5 These magazines aren't sold in Spain.
6 French is spoken by a lot of Canadians.
7 *Lord of the Rings* wasn't written by Shakespeare.
8 Computers weren't invented by the Americans.

3
2 Where was it made?
3 Is it made of leather?
4 Where did you buy it?
5 How much was it?
6 Is it open on Saturday afternoon?

4 1 b   2 c   3 b   4 a   5 c   6 b

5 Check individual answers.

TAPESCRIPT

FRANK: What's your favourite film?
GIRL: *Titanic*.
FRANK: Oh yeah? I haven't seen that. What's it like?
GIRL: It's quite sad, but it's very exciting.
FRANK: How many times have you seen it?
GIRL: Only once. I saw it on TV in August.
FRANK: What's it about?
GIRL: It's about a ship called the *Titanic*. It sank in the Atlantic and a lot of people died.
FRANK: Who are the main characters?
GIRL: Rose and Jack. They're passengers on the ship and they fall in love.
FRANK: Was it made in America?
GIRL: Yes, it was.
FRANK: Have you got it on DVD?
GIRL: No, I haven't.

Workbook key and tapescripts

1 Job: engineer Part of the body: muscle

2 Picture 1 emotion Picture 2 software
Picture 3 muscle Picture 4 script Picture 5 realistic
Picture 6 engineer Picture 7 introduce
Picture 8 computer-animated

3 Check individual answers.

11 Talking

1 A good relationship   A bad relationship
2 3 5 6   4 7

2 2 everything was free
3 it stayed open until eleven o'clock
4 we could have a game of tennis
5 there was an Olympic-size swimming pool
6 we could get something to eat at the café

3 3 He said (that) he had two tickets.
4 Kathy said (that) he could take someone else.
5 He told her (that) he wanted to go with her.
6 She said (that) she didn't want to go.
7 Pete said (that) he knew Ms Dynamite and that they could meet her after the concert.
8 Kathy told him (that) she didn't believe him.

4 2 F 3 F 4 ? 5 T 6 T 7 F 8 T

5 Check individual answers.

1 2 g 3 h 4 i 5 d 6 b

2 3 doesn't it? 4 Yes, it does. 5 can they?
6 No, they can't. 7 are you? 8 No, I'm not.
9 aren't you? 10 Yes, I am.

3 2 isn't it?
   China.
3 wasn't he?
   American presidents.
4 do they?
   Penguins.
5 haven't you
   The key.
6 didn't you?
   A match.

4 1 It's cold, isn't it?
2 You don't like it, do you?
3 They're too short, aren't they?
4 We haven't got enough paint, have we?

5 1 c 2 b 3 c 4 a 5 c 6 b
TAPESCRIPT
ASSISTANT: Could you give me your surname, please?
CLAIRE: It's Simmonds.
ASSISTANT: Pardon?
CLAIRE: Simmonds. S - I - double M - O - N - D - S.
ASSISTANT: And your address?

CLAIRE: 3 Church Street, Brighton.
ASSISTANT: And what's the postcode?
CLAIRE: BN7 8FL.
ASSISTANT: Could you say that again?
CLAIRE: BN7 8FL.
ASSISTANT: And you're going to pay by credit card, aren't you?
CLAIRE: Yes, that's right.
ASSISTANT: Can I have the number of the card?
CLAIRE: Yes, it's 883 765 9324.
ASSISTANT: OK, Mrs Simmonds. We'll send your CD ROM in a few days, and certainly before the end of the week.
CLAIRE: Thanks very much. Goodbye.

6 Check individual answers.

1 shocked, upset

2 1 reply 2 ring 3 definitely 4 upset 5 be back
6 shocked 7 phone call 8 be in 9 wrong number

3 Check individual answers.

12 New beginnings

1 2 sneakers 3 sidewalk 4 wardrobe 5 shop
6 elevator 7 cookies 8 pants 9 gas

2 2 I didn't use to like
3 I didn't use to stay
4 My brother and I used to watch
5 We never used to read
6 My mum used to read

3 2 Did she use to stay in bed late?
3 What did they use to watch?
4 Did they use to read magazines?
5 What did her mum use to read to her?
6 Did she use to like dogs?

4a 1 c 2 b 3 b 4 a 5 a 6 a 7 c 8 c 9 c 10 b
11 c 12 b

4b 2 He used to watch American movies. / From American movies.
3 He was feeling nervous.
4 He couldn't speak English.
5 His brothers and sisters in Guinea.
6 Because he wants to look like an American teenager.

5 Check individual answers.

1 2 I could / I'd choose
3 my parents weren't / we wouldn't argue
4 my hair was shorter / would I look
5 I went / I'd go
6 you had / would you do
7 I didn't have / I wouldn't be able to

Workbook key and tapescripts 119

2

2 If her boyfriend was at the party, she wouldn't feel sad.
3 If my suitcase was bigger, I could take a lot of holiday souvenirs home.
4 If I didn't feel sick, I'd go surfing this afternoon.
5 If I got on well with my sister, I'd spend more time with her.
6 If my brother didn't drink eight cups of coffee a day, he wouldn't get bad headaches.
7 If there were enough buses and trains, people wouldn't go everywhere by car.
8 If I had enough time, I'd have piano lessons.

3

2 Thanks for the fabulous meal.
3 Have a good journey.
4 I've had a great time.
5 I'll miss you.
6 Keep in touch.

4

1 b   2 c   3 b   4 b   5 a   6 b

TAPESCRIPT

MOLLY: Goodbye, Duncan. Thanks for having me. I've had a great time.
DUNCAN: Goodbye, Molly. We'll miss you.
MOLLY: I'll miss you too. If I could choose, I'd stay for another month.
DUNCAN: Well, you must come back one day. Thanks for your English lessons. The children said you were a very good teacher.
MOLLY: And they were fantastic students.
DUNCAN: What time's your flight?
MOLLY: Three o'clock.
DUNCAN: How long is the flight to London?
MOLLY: It's about eight hours.
DUNCAN: Well, if you leave now, you'll be at the airport at half past one.
MOLLY: That's fine. I'll have time to buy some souvenirs for my family.
DUNCAN: Have a good journey. And keep in touch.
MOLLY: Yes, of course. I'll send you lots of emails. You can translate them for the children.
DUNCAN: OK. Let's say goodbye in Swahili. Kwa heri, Molly.
MOLLY: Kwa heri!

5

Check individual answers.

TAPESCRIPT

SALLY: Have you got any plans for the holidays?
BOY: Yes, I'm going to stay with my grandparents for a week.
SALLY: What else will you do?
BOY: I'll probably go surfing and I might join a tennis club.
SALLY: What would you do if you could choose?
BOY: Oh, I'd go to California. Surfing's brilliant there.
SALLY: Are you going to get a holiday job?
BOY: Yes. I might work in my dad's shop.
SALLY: Right. We must keep in touch. What's your email address?
BOY: paul@netlink.co.uk.

STEP 3

1

Verbs: grow, stretch, contain
Nouns: traffic jam, cell
Adjectives: main, awake
Adverb: almost

2

1 grow   2 traffic jam   3 contain   4 stretch   5 cell
6 awake   7 main   8 almost

3

Check individual answers.

Acknowledgements

The publishers are grateful to the following contributor:

pentacor**big**: text design and layouts